Uncertain Judgment

The War/Peace Bibliography Series

RICHARD DEAN BURNS, EDITOR

This Series has been developed in cooperation with the Center for the Study of Armament and Disarmament, California State University, Los Angeles.

Uncertain Judgment

A Bibliography of War Crimes Trials

Compiled by

JOHN R. LEWIS

ABC-Clio, Inc.

Santa Barbara, California
Oxford, England

Library of Congress Cataloging in Publication Data
Lewis, John Rodney, 1949-
  Uncertain judgment.
  (The War/peace bibliography series; 8
  Includes index.
  1. War crime trials—Bibliography. I. Title.
Z6464.W33L48   JX5433   016.3416'9   78-27904
ISBN 0-87436-288-1

American Bibliographical Center—Clio Press
2040 Alameda Padre Serra
Santa Barbara, California 93103

Clio Press, Ltd.
Woodside House, Hinksey Hill
Oxford, OX1 5BE, England

Manufactured in the United States of America

Pour Wendy
encore et toujours

About the War/Peace Bibliography Series

With this bibliographical series, the Center for the Study of Armament and Disarmament, California State University, Los Angeles, seeks to promote a wider understanding of martial violence and the alternatives to its employment. The Center, which was formed by concerned faculty and students in 1962–63, has as its primary objective the stimulation of intelligent discussion of war/peace issues. More precisely, the Center has undertaken two essential functions: (1) to collect and catalogue materials bearing on war/peace issues; and (2) to aid faculty, students, and the public in their individual and collective probing of the historical, political, economic, philosophical, technical, and psychological facts of these fundamental problems.

This bibliographical series is, obviously, one tool with which we may more effectively approach our task. Each issue in this series is intended to provide a comprehensive "working," rather than definitive, bibliography on a relatively narrow theme within the spectrum of war/peace studies. While we hope this series will prove to be a useful tool, we also solicit your comments regarding its format, contents, and topics.

RICHARD DEAN BURNS
SERIES EDITOR

Contents

Acknowledgments

In compiling a reference work having as many varied elements as this, one garners to himself a significant number of debts. I was fortunate in being able to share the onerous task of proofreading the typescript with Mr. Alessio Capra (Italian entries), Professor Seymour Chapin (French entries), Professor Jay Harris (Japanese entries), Dr. Lawrence Palkovic (Spanish entries), Mrs. Jutta Smith (German entries), and Professor John Zimmerman (Russian entries), each of whom graciously contributed his expertise and many hours; to each I am extremely grateful.

I owe a special debt to Professor Hans Adolf Jacobsen, Director of the Seminar for Political Science (Bonn University) and one of the most eminent historians of modern Germany, who reviewed and commented in detail upon the whole of the bibliography. I am likewise indebted to Professor Telford Taylor of the Harvard Law School—previously chief prosecutor at the U.S Military Tribunals, Nuremberg, Germany (1946–1949)—who read the completed manuscript and gave me the benefit of his unique knowledge and experience.

I have received an abundance of moral and tangible encouragement from three of my former teachers, Professor Arthur L. Smith, Jr., Professor Richard D. Burns, and Professor Earl H. Phillips, each of whom has shown extraordinary interest in my academic career. I gladly take this opportunity to publicly express my gratitude for their numerous kindnesses to me.

Portions of the manuscript were typed, with accuracy and dispatch, by Marge Gilbert and Josie Del Valle—often on very short notice. Christine J. Caldwell, Inter-Library Loan Secretary, John F. Kennedy Memorial Library, California State University, Los Angeles, obtained literally dozens of books and articles from all parts of the country for my perusal, with speed and efficiency. Richard Dean Burns III performed the burdensome job of compiling the index.

My wife good naturedly allowed our home to be invaded by thousands of bibliographic entry cards, often in boxes, sometimes in piles of varying heights, but always in profusion! Without her support and indulgence this volume could not have appeared.

While I have been assisted by many, I alone bear responsibility for the contents and structure of this bibliography.

Chronology

2d Millenium B.C.	Development by the Egyptians and Sumerians of rules on the initiation of war (*jus ad bellum*)
7th Century B.C.	Babylonians establish rules for the treatment of prisoners of war, and the distinction between "voluntary" and "obligatory" wars
5th Century B.C.	431–404, Peloponnesian War (origin of the concept of punishment for crimes committed in war)
427–347 B.C.	Plato's *Republic* (introduction to the idea of war as a means of "friendly correction" rather than destruction and enslavement)
4th Century B.C.	Development by the Hittites of rules for conduct in war; appearance of Sun Tzu's *The Art of War,* and the Hindu *Book of Manu,* both of which set forth regulations on the conduct of land warfare
220 A.D.	*Canon of Hippolytus* (nos. 74 and 75 outline rules of conduct in war)
354–430	St. Augustine elaborates and gives authority to the concept of the "just war" in his letters to Faustus the Manichaean and to Boniface

Prohibition on War by the Church of Rome

989	First "Peace of God" (declared in Charroux)
1035	"Truce of God" (proclaimed by the Archbishop of Arles)
1122	First Lateran Council
1139	Second Lateran Council
1215	Fourth Lateran Council
1245	First Council at Lyon
1274	Second Council at Lyon
	St. Thomas Aquinas' *Summa Theologica* (outline of conditions under which a just war must be fought)
1474	The Trial of Peter von Hagenbach, Breisach (considered the first trial for crimes in war)
1532	Francisco de Vitoria, *De Indis et de iure belli relectiones* [On the Indies and the Laws of War]
1582	Balthazar Ayala, *De iure et officiis bellicis et disciplina militari libri III* [Three Books on the Law of War and on the Duties Connected with War]
1598	Alberico Gentili, *De jure belli*
1625	Hugo Grotius, *De jure belli ac pacis libri tres*
1758	Emerich de Vattel, *Les Droit des gens*
1832	Karl von Clausewitz, *Vom Kriege*
1856 (16 April)	Declaration of Paris Respecting Maritime Law in Time of War
1863	Francis Lieber, U.S. Army General Order 100: *Instructions for the Government of Armies in the Field*

1864 (22 August)	First Geneva Convention on the Amelioration of the Condition of the Sick and Wounded in the Field (Red Cross Convention)
1865	The trial of Captain Henry Wirtz, Confederate States Army (Andersonville Trial), Washington, D.C.
1868 (11 December)	St. Petersburg Declaration on the use of inhumane weapons
1874 (27 August)	Brussels Conference on the Laws and Customs of War
1899	First Hague Peace Conference
1903	Trials of United States officers accused of cruelty in the Philippine Insurrection
1906	Second Geneva Convention on the Amelioration of the Condition of the Sick and Wounded in the Field
1907	Second Hague Peace Conference
1909 (26 February)	Declaration of London of the International Naval Conference
1919	Paris Peace Conference
1919 (28 April)	Covenant of the League of Nations
1921	Trials of the German war criminals before the Supreme Court, Leipzig
1921 (12 November)– 1922 (6 February)	Washington Naval Conference
1922 (4 February)	Conference Establishing a Commission of Jurists to Consider Laws of War

1922 (6 February)   Treaty in Relation to the Use of Submarines and Noxious Gases in Warfare

1923 (February)   Hague Rules of Air Warfare

1925 (17 June)   Geneva Protocol for the Prohibition of Chemical and Bacteriological Methods of Warfare

1925 (25 September)   League of Nations (Sixth Assembly) Resolution Declaring Wars of Aggression to be International Crimes

1925 (October)   Locarno Treaties

1927 (June-August)   Geneva Conference for the Limitation of Naval Armaments

1928 (20 February)   Resolutions of the Sixth International Conference of American States (Havana), declaring wars of aggression to be international crimes and condemning war in general as an instrument of national policy in their mutual affairs

1928 (27 August)   General Pact for the Renunciation of War (Kellogg-Briand Pact)

1929 (27 July)   Convention Relative to the Treatment of Prisoners of War

1929 (27 July)   Third Geneva Convention on the Treatment of Wounded and Sick of Armies in the Field (Red Cross Convention)

1930   First London Conference on Naval Armaments

1932 (3 August)   Chaco Declaration of the American States

1933 (10 October)   Anti-War Treaty of Non-Aggression and Conciliation, Rio de Janeiro

1935	Second London Conference on Naval Armaments
1936 (23 December)	Inter-American Conference for the Maintenance of Peace, Buenos Aires
World War II	
1942 (13 January)	Inter-Allied Declaration on the Punishment for War Crimes (St. James Conference)
1943 (5 January)	Inter-Allied Declaration against Acts of Dispossession
1943 (1 November)	Inter-Allied Declaration on Atrocities (Moscow Declaration)
1945 (26 June)	United Nations Charter
1945 (8 August)	Inter-Allied Charter and Agreement on the Prosecution of the Major War Criminals of the European Axis (London Charter)
1945 (August)	Potsdam Conference
1945 (14 November)– 1946 (1 October)	International Military Tribunal (Trials of the Major War Criminals)
1946–1949	U.S. Military Tribunals, Nuremberg, Germany (Control Council Trials)
1946 (May 3)–1948 (16 April)	International Military Tribunal, Far East, Tokyo, Japan
1948	United Nations Convention on Genocide
1949 (12 August)	Geneva Conventions I–IV Relative to the Treatment of Prisoners of War and Victims of War
1954–1962	Algerian Civil War

1961–1962	Apprehension, Trial, and Execution of Adolf Eichmann
1967	Stockholm ("Bertrand Russell") Tribunal, on United States war crimes in Vietnam
1969 (20 November)	United Nations Report on Human Rights in Armed Conflict
1969	Extension of West German statute of limitations on World War II crimes
1970 (18 September)	United Nations Report on Human Rights in Armed Conflicts
1970–1971	Trial of Lieutenant William Calley
1970 (9 December)	United Nations Resolution on the Protection of Civilians in Armed Conflicts
1971 (May–June)	International Commission of the Red Cross Draft Protocol on Protection of the Wounded and Sick in War
1971	Trial of Captain Ernest Medina
1972 (10 April)	Convention on the Prohibition of Development, Production and Stockpiling of Bacteriological and Toxic Weapons
1972–1973	Pakistan Civil War
1974 (April)	United Nations Definition of Aggression by Consensus
1976	Mozambique Mercenaries Trial, Luanda

Introduction

The person who creates a guide to sources of information that others may use with profit does not proceed haphazardly. Although not definitive, this volume is the first comprehensive bibliography of war crimes trials, their history, and their extremely varied ramifications.* The bibliography that follows is not merely a listing of sources but is specifically organized to provide the widest range of historical interpretation, factual presentation, and breadth of chronology. It is intended for use by scholars of law and history, and for graduate and undergraduate students as well. The bibliography is designed primarily to be used in an *integrated* manner; however, each of the major sections may also stand alone as specialized bibliographic entries.

Because of the deep and enduring impact of the International Military Tribunal held at Nuremberg, Germany, between November 1945 and October 1946, it seems appropriate to use the tribunal to briefly illustrate the use of this bibliography. Section III lists books and articles delineating every facet and point of view of the proceedings of the Nuremberg Trial, as well as entries on the Allied Powers war crimes policy and trial planning; United States and European printed and archival documentation; works by and about the defendants, prosecutors, and judges; and postwar literature on the efficacy of the trial and its precedents. Section II includes a broad selection of the historical and interpretive literature on the law of war and on the theory and philosophy of war crimes upon which the trial was founded. Here too are listed the texts, histories, and analyses of the most prominent conferences and treaties which comprised the corpus of international law that formed the basis for prosecution. Section IV in-

---

*Only two other bibliographies have been devoted in any large measure to war crimes trials; both were conceptually limited and both are now dated. See Helen F. Conover, comp., *The Nazi State, War Crimes, and War Criminals* (Washington, D.C.: Library of Congress, 1945), which was compiled for the use of the Nuremberg prosecution team; and Inge S. Neumann et al., *European War Crimes Trials: A Bibliography* (New York: Carnegie Endowment for International Peace, 1951).

cludes subsections delimiting works on broader legal issues relating to or emanating from the trial (i.e., superior orders, ex post facto prosecution, group criminality); also, other subsidiary topics relating to the trial will be found in this section (i.e., Allied Occupation, the extradition of war criminals).

The bibliography has four major subject divisions. Section I— "General Reference"—is divided into three parts. Part one, "Basic Reference Guides," is intended largely for students hitherto unfamiliar with doing research in the fields of law, history, and political science. For the student new to these areas the works of John Brown Mason, *Research Resources: Annotated Guide to the Social Sciences,* 2 vols. (1968–1971), Miles O. Price and Harry Bitner, *Effective Legal Research* (1962), and Frederick Holler, *The Information Sources of Political Science,* 5 vols. (1971), will be particularly helpful. A highly diverse and well-organized source on these topics for the twentieth century is Karl Dietrich Bracher et al., *Bibliographie zur Politik in Theorie und Praxis* (1976); approximately half of its 7,901 entries are in English.

Part two—"Bibliographies"—includes bibliographies of a general nature. The user should note that more specialized bibliographies and compendiums may be found preceding the subsections to which they pertain. Also, since this is a bibliography of war crimes trials and *not* war crimes per se, the user seeking a more detailed listing on the latter should consult Y. Van Garse, *A Bibliography of Genocide, Crimes against Humanity, and War Crimes* (1970): Wiener Library, *Books on Prosecution* (1949); and, under selected headings, Janet Ziegler, comp., *World War II: Books in English, 1945–1965* (1971).

Part three, Section I—"Guides and Indexes"—lists thirty-one of the most important sources from which information on the periodical articles and books (American and foreign) listed in this bibliography were obtained: abstracts, guides, indexes to books and book reviews, general and legal periodicals, newspapers, and official documents. Anyone wishing to supplement the references to specific subtopics—especially in Sections II and IV—will profit from consulting these guides and indexes. Further, the reader should consult the indispensable *National Union Catalog (Pre-1956 Imprints),* and the Library of Congress, *National Union Catalog: Author List,* and *Subject Catalog.*

Section II—"Background Issues"—deals with the philosophical concepts and international law of war crimes upon which twentieth-century war crimes prosecutions have been conducted. Part one lists a wide variety of works on the laws of war, their history, formulation, and application. A good general introduction to these areas may be found in J. L. Brierly, *The Law of Nations: An Introduction to the International Law of Peace* (1963); Percy Edward Corbett, *Morals, Law, and Power in International Relations* (1956); Richard Falk, *Law, Morality and War in the Contem-*

porary World (1963); and Morris Greenspan, *The Modern Law of Land Warfare* (1959). Part one also cites official government compilations of military law for the use of military authorities, as well as British, French, German, Italian, and American field manuals printed between 1863 and 1956. These important sources contain the rules and regulations under which these particular nations governed the conduct of their own soldiers during wartime.

Part two of Section II—"Conferences and Treaties"—lists the texts (as well as the general, historical, and interpretive literature) of the most important treaties and conventions which have attempted over the past century to regulate the conduct of war, the breaches of which were explicitly cited in various war crimes trials as prosecutable offenses. The user is directed to Vaclov Mostecky, *Index to Multilateral Treaties* (1965), Adolf Sprudzs, *Treaty Sources in Legal and Political Research* (1971), and the United States Air Force, *Treaties Governing Land Warfare* (1958), which are good starting points. Sources for bilateral and multilateral agreements of less historical importance may also be found in these compilations, or in the works cited under the subheadings "Treaties: Guides and Indexes" and "Treaties: Textual Compilations."

"Theory and Philosophy of War Crimes"—part three—contains a series of entries relating to war crimes and their punishment in the most sweeping legal and philosophical context. Users wishing a convenient introduction should consult G. Brand's 1949 article in the *British Yearbook of International Law,* "War Crimes Trials and the Laws of War"; Richard Falk, Gabriel Kolko, and Jay Lifton, *Crimes of War* (1971); Robert H. Jackson et al., "The Legal Basis for the Trial of War Criminals—A Symposium," which appeared in *Temple Law Review* (1946); and Lord Wright's introduction to the *History of the United Nations War Crimes Commission* (1948).

Section III—"Historical Works"—is the central core of the bibliography and presents nearly two thousand entries on war crimes trials, commencing with the Trial of Peter von Hagenbach (1474), generally conceded to be the first war crimes trial widely chronicled, and concluding with the events of the Luanda Trial (1976). The most significant subheadings (other than those dealing with World War II) are the "United States Civil War, 1861–1865" and "World War I, 1914–1918." The Civil War entries highlight the role of Francis Lieber in the formation of the modern rules for battlefield conduct (the so-called Lieber Code), and the Andersonville Trial of 1865, likely the most important pre–twentieth-century war crimes trial precedent. The World War I entries focus on the fiasco of the war crimes trials held primarily in Leipzig, Germany, following World War I; for these the user should see Gordon Bailey's doctoral dissertation, "Dry Run for the Hangman" (1971), and Claude Mullins's *The Leipzig Trials* (1921).

Not surprisingly, most of the cited works deal with the trials of World War II. All aspects of these trials are covered; included are works on the Allied government's planning, guides to sources for printed and manuscript materials on the proceedings, books and articles by and about the major defendants, prosecutors, and judges, and numerous narratives on the trials. By far the largest of the subsections are devoted to the International Military Tribunal, Nuremberg (1945–1946), the United States Military Tribunals (1946–1949), also conducted at Nuremberg and the most important of the many subsidiary trials (on which literature exists) held in Germany between 1945 and 1951. These German proceedings are comprehensively surveyed. Also included is representative literature on the post–World War II trials, conducted by and within sixteen western nations (including Germany), not under the auspices of the Allied Occupation authorities.

The literature on Nuremberg is vast. The documentary sources are listed in detail under the heading "Primary Evidentiary Documents"; on their use the following will be helpful: Wiener Library, *Catalogue of Nuremberg Documents* (1961); United Nations, Archives Section, *Guide to Records of the War Crimes Trials Held in Nürnberg, Germany, 1945–1949* (1949); and the two 1949 articles by Fred Niebergall. (Guides are presently in preparation at the National Archives for the microfilm publication of all the evidentiary documents of the Nuremberg Trial.) The following are good general accounts of the trial: Victor H. Bernstein, *Final Judgement: The Story of Nuremberg* (1947); Eugene Davidson, *The Trial of the Germans* (1966); Sheldon Glueck, *The Nuremberg Trial and Aggressive War* (1946); Whitney R. Harris, *Tyranny on Trial* (1954); Joe J. Heydecker and Johannes Leeb, *The Nuremberg Trial* (1962); Bradley Smith, *Reaching Judgment at Nuremberg* (1976); John H. Morgan, *The Great Assize* (1948); and, finally, Telford Taylor's excellent standard work, *Nuremberg Trials, War Crimes and International Law* (1949). Generally, on the United States Military Tribunal proceedings (1946–1949) see Paul M. Herbert, "Nürnberg Subsequent Trials," *Insurance Counsel Journal* (July 1949), and William A. Zeck, "Nuremberg: Proceedings Subsequent to Goering, et al.," *North Carolina Law Review* (June 1948).

Scholars and others have shown far greater interest in the European trials than in those in Japan and elsewhere in the Far East. Although there are fewer works devoted to the Far East trials noted in this volume, a comprehensive survey of the available materials is included. The most significant subsidiary trials (i.e., those of Generals Yamashita and Homma) are also represented. For a broad view of the Tokyo and other Far East trials the reader should consult George F. Blewett's article "Victor's Injustice: The Tokyo War Crimes Trials," *American Perspective* (Summer 1950); F. E. Meek's "War Crimes' Trials in the Pacific," *Idaho State Bar Proceedings* (1947); Frederick Mignone's "After Nuremberg,

Tokyo," *Texas Law Review* (May 1947); and Richard H. Minear's recent and somewhat polemical *Victor's Justice: The Tokyo War Crimes Trials* (1971). The best single source remains Solis Horowitz's November 1950 article, "The Tokyo Trial," which filled a whole volume (465) of *International Conciliation.* For those wishing an introduction to secondary materials applicable to the Tokyo Trial, Delmer M. Brown's "Instruction and Research: Recent Japanese Political and Historical Materials," *American Political Science Review* (October 1949), deserves special attention. Sung Yoon Cho's "The Tokyo War Crimes Trial" in the *Quarterly Journal of the Library of Congress* (October 1967) is a fine primer on the sources of the trial proceedings. Numerous excellent new Japanese-language sources are cited in transliteration.

The subsections of Section III entitled "Establishment of the 'Law of Nuremberg': Contemporary Review Articles, 1945–1951," and "World War II Trials: Retrospective Literature, 1951–," cover far-ranging entries analyzing the political, legal, social, and historical ramifications of the World War II trials, written during the course of the postwar Allied-conducted trials (1945–1951) and in the more than two and a half decades since their conclusion. Some of the most interesting entries in these sections are Montgomery Belgion, *Victor's Justice* (1949); Karl Jaspers, "The Significance of the Nürnberg Trials for Germany and the World," *Notre Dame Lawyer* (January 1947); Quincy Wright, "The Law of the Nuremberg Trial," *American Journal of International Law* (January 1947); Jay W. Baird's compilation *From Nuremberg to My Lai* (1972); W. E. Benton and G. Grimm, eds., *Nuremberg: German Views of the War Crimes Trials* (1955); Eugene Davidson, *The Nuremberg Fallacy: Wars and War Crimes since World War II* (1973); Richard Falk, "Nuremberg: Past, Present and Future," *Yale Law Journal* (June 1971); Frank Hirschbach's very interesting "Black Milk: The Treatment of Guilt in German Post War Literature," *Minnesota Review* (Winter 1963); and Bernard V. A. Röling, "The Tokyo Trial in Retrospect" in *Buddhism and Culture,* edited by Yamaguchi Susumu (1960).

The final subsection of Section III—"Post–World War II Era"— covers the four primary instances of war crimes trials since the conclusion of the Allied trials in 1951. Much has been written on the legal aspects of the United States involvements in Vietnam, especially on the trials of Calley and Medina—the My Lai Trials. The reader is urged to review Richard Falk, *The Six Legal Dimensions of the Vietnam War* (1968); Tom Farer, R. G. Gard, and Telford Taylor, "Vietnam and the Nuremberg Principles: A Colloquy on War Crimes," *Rutgers Camden Law Journal* (Fall 1973); Telford Taylor, *Nuremberg and Vietnam: An American Tragedy* (1970); Richard Hammer, *The Court-Martial of Lt. Calley* (1971); and Mary McCarthy, *Medina* (1972). On the unique, and unofficial, Stockholm ("Bertrand Russell") Tribunal of 1967, consult H. A. De

Weerd, *Lord Russell's War Crimes Tribunal* (1967). Those seeking information beyond the entries in this volume should see the excellent bibliography by Milton Leitenberg and Richard Dean Burns, *The Vietnam Conflict* (1973). On the Algerian Civil War see Pierre Leulliette's compelling *St. Michael and the Dragon: Memoirs of a Paratrooper* (1964).

Without doubt, the trial of Adolf Eichmann in Jerusalem for war crimes has been the most important to take place in the postwar decades. The subsection on Eichmann, therefore, not only contains works relating to his 1962 trial but to his apprehension and execution as well. An illustrative group of official and unofficial documents collections is included. The beginning researcher will benefit by reading Hannah Arendt, *Eichmann in Jerusalem* (1963); Victor Gollancz, *The Case of Adolf Eichmann* (1961); Lord Russell of Liverpool, *The Record: The Trial of Adolf Eichmann . . .* (1963); Telford Taylor, "Large Questions in the Eichmann Case," *Revue de Droit International* (1961); and the memoir of the chief Israeli prosecutor Gideon Hausner, *Justice in Jerusalem* (1966).

Section IV—"Subsidiary Issues"—is divided into subsections which cite works on the central legal issues emanating from or relating to war crimes trials since the promulgation of the Lieber Code. Certainly of fundamental concern must be the legal basis and mode of conduct for any war crimes trial. The reader will find a number of good basic sources noted under the headings "Trial Procedures" and "Ex Post Facto": Benjamin B. Ferencz, "Nürnberg Trial Procedure and the Rights of the Accused," *Journal of Criminal Law and Criminology* (July-August 1948); Robert H. Jackson, "The Nuremberg Trial: An Example of Procedural Machinery . . ." in *David Dudley Field,* edited by Alison Reppy; John Mendelsohn, "Trial by Document," *Prologue* (Winter 1975); Eli E. Nobleman, "Procedure and Evidence . . . ," *Federal Bar Journal* (January 1947); Paul C. Tsai, "Judicial Administration of the Laws of War" (1957); Gordon Ireland, "*Ex Post Facto* from Rome to Tokyo," *Temple Law Quarterly* (1947); and Milton Konvitz, "*Ex Post Facto* at Nuremberg," *Commentary* (July 1946). The user will also find the related subsections "Occupation Government," "Allied Administration of Justice," and "Extradition of War Criminals" very useful, and in Section III, "Wartime Dialogue Regarding War Crimes Trials."

Three of the subsections may be conveniently grouped as defense arguments: "Superior Orders, Command Responsibility, and Military Necessity"; "'Acts of State,' Sovereign Immunity of Rulers"; "'Just War' and 'Preventive War' Concepts." Of the three, the defense of superior orders remains perhaps the hardest to deal with; the user is directed to Aubrey M. Daniel, "The Defense of Superior Orders," *University of Richmond Law Review* (1973); the four articles of N. C. H. Dunbar (1951–1957); L. C. Green, "Superior Orders and the Reasonable Soldier," *Canadian Yearbook of International Law* (1970); Guenter Lewy, "Superior Orders,

Nuclear Warfare, and the Dictates of Conscience," *American Political Science Review* (March 1961); David Paston, *Superior Orders as Affecting Responsibility for War Crimes* (1946); and the three articles, in French, by Stefan Glaser. Likewise, three other subsections may be practically combined as comprising reasons for prosecution: "Treatment of Prisoners of War, Noncombatants, and Irregulars"; "Forced and Slave Labor"; and "Collaboration." In every war, prisoners are taken, and the issue of their treatment, starting with the Geneva Convention of 1864, has been one of the most comprehensively considered aspects of the laws of war—see William Flory, *Prisoners of War* (1942); and W. Wynne Mason, *Prisoners of War* (1954). A sound and comprehensive survey of the legal aspects of the treatment of noncombatants and irregulars (such as guerrillas and partisans), may be found in Bernard Brungs's doctoral dissertation, "Hostages, Prisoner Reprisals, and Collective Penalties," 3 vols. (1968). Slave and forced labor, as well as collaboration with the enemy, were issues of the greatest importance during and following World War II; the dimensions and magnitude of each during the period were unprecedented. Edward L. Homze's work *Foreign Labor in Nazi Germany* (1967) is a first-rate starting point on the subject of forced and slave labor. The general literature on collaboration is noted, and the trials of four notable collaborators are taken as representative: Marshal Graziani, Pierre Laval, Henri Philippe Pétain, and Vidkun Quisling.

The issues of organizational and group criminality, aggressive war as a war crime, and militarism also grew in importance during World War II. The highly structured nature of the various groups participating in the crimes of that war, such as the SS and the Gestapo, engendered a fresh concept in war crimes theory: that a group, including all of its members, may be prosecuted for the crimes of war—see Richard Arens, "Nuremberg and Group Prosecution," *Washington University Law Quarterly* (June 1951); and Robert H. Jackson, "Law under Which Nazi Organizations Are Accused of Being Criminal," *Temple Law Quarterly* (April 1946). The charge of conspiring to wage aggressive war was first brought at Nuremberg; it was a departure from all precedent—see Leo Gross, "Criminality of Aggressive War," *American Political Science Review* (April 1947); Philip C. Jessup, "The Crime of Aggression and the Future of International Law," *Political Science Quarterly* (March 1947); and the two articles by Quincy Wright (1935, 1946).

Because of the nature of the accusations against the German and Japanese officer corps and because of the special place of the military in those societies prior to 1945, a large subsection—"The Problem of the Military"—has been included; it contains entries in the fields of civil-military relations and militarism in general, with more specific and extended subsections relating to Germany and Japan. Basic information on German militarism and civil-military relations may be found in the works of Gerhard Ritter, Gordon Craig, Harold Deutsch, Walter Görlitz, Harold Gordon, Robert O'Neill, Gaines Post, Telford Taylor, and Sir John Wheeler-Bennett; and on Japan, in the works of Ruth Benedict, Dorothy Borg, Kenneth Colegrove, F. H. Conroy, John Maki, Richard Smethurst, and Takehiko Yoshihashi. Readers interested generally in the areas of militarism and civil-military relations should see Alfred Vagts, *A History of Militarism* (1959); Arthur Larson, *Civil-Military Relations and Militarism: A Bibliography* (1971); and Social Science Research Council, *Civil-Military Relations: An Annotated Bibliography 1940–1952* (1954).

The founding of the United Nations in 1945 necessarily interjected a new element into the processes of definition of and prosecution under the international laws of war. The crucial role of the United Nations War Crimes Commission (1942–1947) is outlined in Franz Schick, "War Criminals and the Law of the United Nations," *University of Toronto Law Journal* (Lent term 1947); Egon Schwelb, "The United Nations War Crimes Commission," *British Yearbook of International Law* (1946); and the official history, *History of the United Nations War Crimes Commission and the Development of the Laws of War* (1948). On the broad role of the United Nations check Robert H. Jackson, "The United Nations Organization and War Crimes," *American Society of International Law Proceedings* (1952), and Lord Maugham's *U.N.O. and War Crimes* (1951).

The last two subsections of Section IV deal with the related issues of clemency for convicted war criminals, and the concept of statute of limitations on war crimes. The entries listed under "Clemency Issues" are concerned solely with the release of war criminals convicted following World War II. The "Statutory Limitations on War Crimes" subsection deals with the question generally and in specific cases, including the debate within West Germany in the mid-1960s on the extension of the Federal Republic's statute of limitations law—see J. E. S. Fawcett, "Time Limit for Punishment of War Crimes?" *International and Comparative Law Quarterly* (April 1965), and Nathan Lerner, "Convention on the Non-Applicability of Statutory Limitations to War Crimes," *Israel Law Review* (October 1969).

NOTE: In some cases entries have necessarily been placed *under the most appropriate heading.* The user will, therefore, find it useful to seek references under a combination of subheadings within a given section.

Abbreviations

GPO	United States Government Printing Office
HMSO	His/Her Majesty's Stationery Office
IMT	International Military Tribunal (Nuremberg)
IMTFE	International Military Tribunal, Far East (Tokyo)
IPS	International Prosecution Section (IMTFE)
SCAP	Supreme Commander for the Allied Powers (Tokyo)
UNWCC	United Nations War Crimes Commission

Uncertain Judgment is title #8 in The War/Peace Bibliography Series, Richard Dean Burns, series editor. For the publisher: editorial, Paulette Wamego; proofing, Jean Hozinger; typography, Shelly Lowenkopf; cover art, Graphics Two, Los Angeles, Calif. Composition: Westview Press, Boulder, Colo. Printing and binding: the Crawfordsville, Ind. manufacturing division of R. R. Donnelley and Sons Co., Inc.

I. General Reference

I. General Reference

Basic Reference Guides

1 Bracher, Karl Dietrich; Hans-Adolf Jacobsen; and Manfred Funke; eds. *Bibliographie zur Politik in Theorie und Praxis.* Düsseldorf: Droste Verlag, 1976.

2 Burns, Richard Dean, comp. *Arms Control and Disarmament: A Bibliography.* Santa Barbara: ABC-Clio, 1977.

3 Holler, Frederick, comp. *The Information Sources of Political Science.* 5 vols. Santa Barbara: ABC-Clio, 1971.

4 Mason, John Brown, comp. *Research Resources: Annotated Guide to the Social Sciences.* 2 vols. Santa Barbara: ABC-Clio, 1968, 1971.

5 Poulton, Helen J. *The Historian's Handbook: A Descriptive Guide to Reference Works.* Norman: University of Oklahoma Press, 1972.

6 Price, Miles O., and Harry Bitner. *Effective Legal Research.* Student rev. ed. Boston: Little, Brown, 1962.

7 Sheehy, Eugene, et al. *Guide to Reference Books.* 9th ed. Chicago: American Library Association, 1976.

8 Totok, Wilhelm, and Rolf Weitzel. *Handbuch der bibliographischen Nachschlagewerke.* Frankfurt am Main: Klostermann Verlag, 1974.

9 Walford, A. J., ed. *Guide to Reference Material.* 2 vols. 3d ed. Chicago: American Library Association, 1975.

10 Zawodny, J. K. *Guide to the Study of International Relations.* San Francisco: Chandler, 1966.

Bibliographies

INTERNATIONAL LAW

11 Carnegie Endowment for International Peace. *Bibliographies and Catalogues of International Law.* Miscellaneous Reading List, no. 36. Washington, D.C.: Carnegie Endowment for International Peace, Library, 1931.

12 ———. *Bibliography, 1915–1957: Quincy Wright.* New York: Carnegie Endowment for International Peace, 1957.

13 ———. *Bibliography of the Writings of James Brown Scott.* Washington, D.C.: Carnegie Endowment for International Peace, Library, 1928.

14 ———. *Bibliography of the Writings of James Brown Scott: Supplement.* Washington, D.C.: Carnegie Endowment for International Peace, Library, 1932.

15 De Schutter, Bart, comp., with the collaboration of Christian Eliaerts. *Bibliography on International Criminal Law.* Leiden: Sijthoff, 1972.

16 Erickson, Richard J. "Selected Bibliography Concerning the Laws of War Including the Law Applicable to Air Operations," *Air Force Law Review* 16 (Summer 1974):75–95.

17 Gendrel, M., and P. La Farge. *Eléments d'une bibliographie mondiale du droit pénal militaire, des crimes et délits contre la sûreté de l'état et du droit pénal international.* Paris: R. Pichon et R. Durand-Auzias, 1965.

18 Hannigan, Jane A., comp. *Publications of the Carnegie Endowment for International Peace, 1910–1967: Including International Conciliation, 1924–1967.* New York: Carnegie Endowment for International Peace, 1971.

19 Herre, Wybo P. *International Bibliography of Air Law, 1900–1971.* Dobbs Ferry, N.Y.: Oceana Publications, 1972.

20 Koppel, W. *Justiz im Zwielicht: Dokumentation, Gerichtsurteile, Personalaktenkatalog beschuldigter Juristen.* Karlsruhe: Selbstverlag, 1963.

21 "Literatuuropgave over oorlogsmisdadigers en hun berechtiging," *Tijdschrift voor Strafrecht* 56 (1947):61–62.

22 United Nations, Secretariat. *Bibliography on International Criminal Law and International Criminal Courts.* A/CN. 4/28. Lake Success, N.Y., 1950.

23 Van Garse, Y. *A Bibliography of Genocide, Crimes against Humanity, and War Crimes.* St. Niklaas: Studiecentrum voor Kriminologie en Gerechtelijke Geneeskunde, 1970.

WORLD WAR II

24 Bloomberg, Marty, and Hans H. Weber, comps. *World War II and Its Origins: A Select Annotated Bibliography of Books in English.* Littleton, Colo.: Libraries Unlimited, 1975.

25 De Voto, A. *Bibliografa dell'oppressione nazista fino al 1962.* Firenze: Olschki, 1964.

26 Funk, Arthur, et al., comps. *A Select Bibliography of Books on the Second World War, in English, Published in the United States, 1966–1975.* San Francisco: American Committee on the History of the Second World War, 1975.

27 Kosicki, Jerzy. *Bibliografiá piśmiennictwa polskiego za lata 1944–1953 o hitlerowskich zbrodniach wojennych.* Warsaw: Wydawn. Prawnicze, 1955.

28 Morton, Louis, comp. *Writings on World War II.* Service Center for Teachers of History, Publication no. 66. Washington, D.C.: American Historical Association, 1967.

29 Wiener Library. *Books on Persecution: Terror and Resistance in Nazi Germany.* Catalogue Series, no. 1. London: Wiener Library, 1949.

30 Ziegler, Janet, comp. *World War II: Books in English, 1945–1965.* Hoover Bibliographical Series, no. 45. Stanford: Stanford University, Hoover Institution Press, 1971.

HISTORICAL QUESTIONS

31 Alfoldi, Laszlo M., comp. *The Armies of Austria-Hungary and Germany, 1740–1914.* Special Bibliography no. 12, vol. 1. Carlisle Barracks, Penn.: U. S. Military History Research Collection, 1975.

32 Carnegie Endowment for International Peace. *Hugo Grotius.* Miscellaneous Reading List, no. 4. Washington, D.C.: Carnegie Endowment for International Peace, Library, 1922.

33 *International Bibliography of Historical Sciences.* New York: H. W. Wilson, 1926–.

Guides and Indexes

PERIODICAL LITERATURE

34 Boehm, Eric H., ed. *Historical Abstracts: Bibliography of the World's Periodical Literature.* Santa Barbara: ABC-Clio, 1955–.

35 *Index to Foreign Legal Periodicals and Collections of Essays.* Chicago: William D. Murphy, 1960–.

36 *Index to Legal Periodical Literature [1791–1932].* 6 vols. Boston: Boston Book Co., 1888–1919; Boston: Chipman, 1924; Indianapolis: Bobbs-Merrill, 1933; Los Angeles: Parker and Baird, 1939.

37 *Index to Legal Periodicals.* New York: H. W. Wilson, 1908–.

38   *Index to New Zealand Periodicals.* Wellington: National Library of New Zealand, 1940–.

39   *Index to Periodical Articles Related to Law.* New York: Glenville Publications, 1959–.

40   *International Index to Periodicals: A Guide to Periodical Literature in the Social Sciences and Humanities.* New York: H. W. Wilson, 1907–.

41   *Reader's Guide to Periodical Literature.* New York: H. W. Wilson, 1900–.

42   *Social Sciences and Humanities Index.* New York: H. W. Wilson, 1913–.

BOOK REVIEWS

43   *Book Review Digest.* New York: H. W. Wilson, 1905–.

44   *Book Review Index.* Detroit: Gale Research, 1965–.

45   *Das historisch-politische Buch: Ein Wegweiser durch das Schrifttum.* Göttingen: Musterschmidt-Verlag, 1953–.

46   *Wissenschaftlicher Literaturanzeiger.* Freiburg: Verlag Rombach, 1962–.

NEWSPAPERS

47   *Index to the [London] Times.* London: The Times, 1906–.

48   *The New York Times Index.* New York: The New York Times, 1913–.

NATIONAL BIBLIOGRAPHIES

49   *British National Bibliography.* London: British Museum, 1950–.

50   Conover, Helen F., comp. *Current National Bibliographies.* Washington, D.C.: Library of Congress, General Reference and Bibliography Division, 1955.

51   *Deutsche Bibliographie: Das deutsche Buch, Auswahl wichtiger Neuerscheinungen.* Frankfurt am Main: Buchhändler-Vereinigung, 1950–.

52   *Deutsche Nationalbibliographie und Bibliographie des im Ausland erschienenen deutschsprachigen Schrifttums.* Leipzig: VEB Verlag für Buch- und Bibliothekswesen, 1931–.

53   *Deutsches Bücherverzeichnis.* Leipzig: VEB Verlag für Buch- und Bibliothekswesen, 1911–.

ABSTRACTS

54   *Dissertation Abstracts: Abstracts of Dissertations and Monographs.* Ann Arbor: University Microfilms, 1952–.

55 *International Political Science Abstracts.* Oxford: Basil Blackwell, 1951–.

OFFICIAL PUBLICATIONS

56 *Cumulative Subject Index to the Monthly Catalog of United States Government Publications, 1900–1971.* 14 vols. Washington, D.C.: Carrollton Press, 1972.

57 Plischke, Elmer, comp. *American Foreign Relations: A Bibliography of Official Sources.* College Park: University of Maryland, College of Business and Public Affairs, Bureau of Government Research, 1955.

58 United Nations, Dag Hammarskjöld Library. *United Nations Documents Index.* New York: United Nations, 1950–.

59 United States, Department of State. *Publications of the Department of State: October 1, 1929 to January 1, 1953.* State Department Pub. no. 5059. Washington, D.C.: GPO, 1954.

COMPENDIUMS OF INTERNATIONAL LAW

60 Hachworth, Green Haywood, comp. *Digest of International Law.* 8 vols. Washington, D.C.: GPO, 1940–1944.

61 United States, Congress, House of Representatives. *A Digest of International Law,* by John Bassett Moore. 56th Cong., 2d sess. 8 vols. Washington, D.C.: GPO, 1906.

62 Whitman, Marjorie, comp. *Digest of International Law.* 15 vols. Washington, D.C.: GPO, 1963–1970.

DOCUMENTS COLLECTIONS

63 United States, Department of State. *Documents on German Foreign Policy, 1918–1945.* Series C. 5 vols. Washington, D.C.: GPO, 1957–1966.

64 _____. *Documents on German Foreign Policy, 1918–1945.* Series D. 13 vols. Washington, D.C.: GPO, 1949–1964.

65 _____. *Foreign Relations of the United States: Diplomatic Papers.* Washington, D.C.: GPO, 1862–.

66 Woodward, E. L., and Rohan Butler, eds. *Documents on British Foreign Policy, 1919–1939.* First Series. 8 vols. London: HMSO, 1947–1958.

II. Background Issues

Laws and Rules of War

OFFICIAL COMPILATIONS OF MILITARY LAW AND FIELD MANUALS

67 France, Ministry of War. *Les lois de la guerre continentale.* 4th ed. Paris, 1919.

68 Garner, James W. *The German War Code: A Comparison of the German Manual of the Law of War with Those of the United States, Great Britain and France. . . .* Urbana: University of Illinois, 1918.

69 Great Britain, War Office. *The King's Regulations for the Army and the Royal Army Reserve, 1940.* London: HMSO, 1940.

70 _____. *Land Warfare: An Exposition of the Laws and Usages of War on Land for the Guidance of Officers of His Majesty's Army.* London: HMSO, 1912.

71 _____. *Manual of Military Law.* Edited by Sir Frederick Liddell. London: HMSO, 1899.

72 _____. *Manual of Military Law.* London: HMSO, 1884.

73 _____. *Manual of Military Law.* London: HMSO, 1914.

74 _____. *Manual of Military Law, 1929.* London: HMSO, 1929.

75 _____. *Manual of Military Law, 1929: Amendments (No. 12), 1936.* London: HMSO, 1941.

76 Herz, Paul, and George Ernst, comps. *Militärstrafgesetzbuch für das Deutsche Reich.* Berlin: F. Whalan, 1908.

77 Hoche, Werner, comp. *Deutsches Kriegsrecht: Umfassende, systematisch geordnete Sammlung der seit Kriegsausbruch erlassenen Gesetze und Verordnungen.* 2 vols. Berlin: F. Vahlen, 1939.

78 Italy, Ministero della Guerra. *Codici Penali Militari Di Pace E Di Guerra.* Rome: Instituto Poligrafico della Stato Liberia, 1941.

79 _____. *Racolta delle Disposizioni per L'Amministrazione della Giustizia Militaire Complementari dei Codici Peu ali Militari.* Edited by Umberto Meranghihi. Rome: Instituto Poligrafico dello Stato Liberia, 1941.

80 *Manuel de Droit International à l'usage des officiers de l'armes de terre.* 3d ed. Paris, 1893.

81 *Militärstrafgesetzbuch in der Fassung vom 10. Oktober 1940-mit Einführungsgesetz und Kriegsstrafrechtsordnung.* Berlin: Walter de Gruyter Verlag, 1943.

82 Prussia, Kriegsministerium. *Kompendium über Militärrecht.* Berlin: Mittler, 1910.

83 _____. *Militärstrafgesetzbuch für das Deutsche Reich vom 20. Juni 1872.* Berlin: Mittler, 1883.

84 United States, Department of the Army. *Basic Field Manual FM 27-10: Rules of Land Warfare.* Washington, D.C.: GPO, 1940.

85 _____. *The Law of Land Warfare: Department of the Army Field Manual FM 27-10.* Washington, D.C.: GPO, 1956.

86 United States, Department of the Navy. *Law of Land Warfare.* NWIP 10-2. Washington, D.C.: GPO, 1955.

87 United States, Department of War. *Instructions for the Government of Armies of the United States in the Field* General Order 100, April 24, 1863 , by Francis Lieber. Washington, D.C.: Department of War, 1863.

88 _____. *Rules of Land Warfare.* Doc. no. 467. Washington, D.C.: GPO, 1917.

GENERAL WORKS

89 Amos, Sheldon. *Political and Legal Remedies for War.* London: Cassell, Petter Galpin, 1880.

90 Argúas, M., and I. Ruiz Moreno. "Efectos sobre el derecho internacional de las decisiones de los tribunales con respecto a los criminales de guerra," *Revista Peruana de Derecho Internacional* 7 (July-December 1947): 202-08.

91 Baily, Sydney Dawson. *Prohibitions and Restraints in War.* London: Oxford University Press for the Royal Institute of International Affairs, 1972.

92 Ballis, William. *The Legal Position of War: Changes in Its Practice and Theory from Plato to Vattel.* The Hague: Nijhoff, 1937.

93 Bassiouni, M. C. "War Power and the Law of War," *De Paul Law Review* 18 (1968):188-201.

94 Baty, T., and J. H. Morgan. *War: Its Conduct and Legal Results.* London: J. Murray, 1915.

95 Belli, Pierino. *De Re Militari et Bello Tractatus.* Translated by Herbert C. Nutting. 2 vols. Oxford: Clarendon Press, 1936.

96 Bindschedler, Robert D. *A Reconsideration of the Law of Armed Conflict.* New York: Carnegie Endowment for International Peace, 1971.

97 Blackstone, Sir William. *Commentaries on the Laws of England.* Edited by George Scharswood. 2 vols. Philadelphia: Lippincott, 1881.

98 Bluntschli, J. C. *Le droit international codifie.* Translated by M. C. Lardy. 4th ed. Paris: Librairie Guillaumin et Cie, 1886.

99 _____. *Das moderne Völkerrecht der civilisierten Staaten als Rechtsbuch dargestellt.* 3d ed. Nördlingen: Ebend, 1878.

100 Bordwell, Percy. *The Law of War between Belligerents: A History and Commentary.* Chicago: Callaghan, 1908.

101 Brand, G. "The Development of the International Law of War," *Tulane Law Review* 25 (February 1951):186–204.

102 Brierly, J. L. *The Law of Nations: An Introduction to the International Law of Peace.* 6th ed. New York: Oxford University Press, 1963.

103 Butler, Sir Geoffrey G., and Simon Maccoby. *The Development of International Law.* London: Longmans, Green, 1928.

104 Cadoux, Cecil John. *The Early Christian Attitude toward War: A Contribution to the History of Christian Ethics.* London: George Allen and Unwin, 1919.

105 Carnegie, A. R. "Jurisdiction over Violations of the Laws and Customs of War," *British Yearbook of International Law* 39 (1963): 402–24.

106 Castrén, Erik. *The Present Law of War and Neutrality.* Helsinki: Annales Academiae Scientiarum Fennicae, 1954.

107 Clausewitz, Carl von. *On War.* Edited and translated by Michael Howard and Peter Paret. Princeton: Princeton University Press, 1976.

108 _____. *On War.* Translated by J. J. Graham. 3 vols. Rev. ed. London: Routledge and Kegan Paul, 1956.

109 Cohen, Marshall. "Taylor's Conception of the Laws of War," *Yale Law Journal* 80 (June 1971):1492–1500.

110 Colby, Elbridge. "Laws of Aerial Warfare," *Minnesota Law Review* 10 (1926):123–48, 207–33.

111 Corbett, Percy E. *Law and Society in the Relations of States.* Princeton: Princeton University Press, 1951.

112 _____. *Morals, Law, and Power in International Relations.* Los Angeles: John Randolph Haynes and Dora Haynes Foundation, 1956.

113 Decker, Charles L. *Roman Military Law.* Austin: University of Texas Press, 1968.

114 Derathé, Robert. "Jean-Jacques Rousseau et le progrès des idées humanitaires du XVIe au XVIIIe siècle," *Revue Internationale de la Croix-Rouge* 40 (October 1958):523–43.

115 De Saussure, H. "Laws of Air Warfare: Are There Any?" *Air Force JAG Journal* 12 (1970):242.

116 Draper, G. I. A. D. "Ethical and Juridical Status of Constraints in War," *Military Law Review* 55 (1972):169.

117 Dumbauld, Edward. *The Life and Legal Writings of Hugo Grotius.* Norman: University of Oklahoma Press, 1969.

118 Durat-Lasalle, Louis. *Droit législation des armées de terre et de mer.* 10 vols. Paris: Chez l'Auteur, 1842–1857.

119 Edmunds, Sterling E. "The Laws of War: Their Rise in the Nineteenth Century and Their Collapse in the Twentieth," *Virginia Law Review* 15 (February 1929):321–49.

120 Edwards, Charles Schaar. "The Law of Nature, the Law of Nations and the Law of War in the Thought of Hugo Grotius." Ph.D. dissertation, Princeton University, 1969.

121 _____. "Law of War in the Thought of Hugo Grotius," *Journal of Public Law* 19 (1970):371–97.

122 Eichoff, Johann Andreas. "Wo halten wir bei den Arbeiten für die internationale Gewährleitung der Menschenrechte?" *Menschrecht* 6 (June 1950):1–2.

123 Engelson, M. "L'Etablissement d'une Paix Durable par l'Application d'un Nouveau Droit Pénal Internationale," *Revue de Droit International, de Sciences Diplomatiques et Politiques* 24 (April-September 1946):47–54.

124 _____. "Pour un droit pénal international," *Revue Internationale de Droit Pénal* 18 (1947):208–14.

125 Falk, Richard A. *Law, Morality and War in the Contemporary World.* New York: Praeger, 1963.

126 _____. *Legal Order in a Violent World.* Princeton: Princeton University Press, 1968.

127 Fenwick, Charles G. "War as an Instrument of Policy," *American Journal of International Law* 22 (October 1928):826–29.

128 Foch, Ferdinand. *The Principles of War*. Translated by Hillaire Belloc. New York: H. Holt, 1920.

129 Fratcher, William F. "The New Law of Land Warfare," *Missouri Law Review* 22 (April 1957):143–61.

130 Friedman, Leon. *The Law of War: A Documentary History*. 2 vols. New York: Random House, 1972.

131 Fuller, J. F. C. *The Conduct of War, 1789–1961*. New Brunswick: Rutgers University Press, 1961.

132 Garcia-Mora, M. R. "International Law and the Law of Hostile Military Expeditions," *Fordham Law Review* 27, no. 3 (August 1958): 309–31.

133 Garner, James W. "International Regulation of Air Warfare," *Air Law Review* 3 (1932):103.

134 _____. "Punishment of Offenders against the Laws and Customs of War," *American Journal of International Law* 14 (1920):70–94.

135 _____. *Recent Developments in International Law*. Calcutta: University of Calcutta, 1925.

136 Genet, Raoul. *Droit Maritime pour le temps de guerr, 1936–1938*. 2 vols. Paris: E. Muller, 1939, 1940.

137 Goldman, Harvey A. "Jurisdictional Problems Related to the Prosecution of Former Servicemen for Violation of the Law of War," *Virginia Law Review* 56 (June 1970):947–67.

138 Greenspan, Morris. *The Modern Law of Land Warfare*. Berkeley: University of California Press, 1959.

139 Grob, Fritz. *The Relativity of War and Peace: A Study in Law, History and Politics*. New Haven: Yale University Press, 1949.

140 Grotius, Hugo. *De Jure belli ac pacis libri Tres*. Translated by F. W. Kelsey. Indianapolis: Bobbs-Merrill, 1925.

141 Guggenheim, Paul. "Der Völkerrechtliche Schutz der Menschenrechte," *Friedens-Warte* 49 (1949):177–90.

142 Hall, J. A. *Law of Naval Warfare*. London: Chapman and Hall, 1914.

143 Hall, William Edward. *A Treatise on International Law*. 4th ed. Oxford: Clarendon Press, 1895.

144   Halleck, Henry W. *Elements of International Law and Laws of War*. Philadelphia: Lippincott, 1874.

145   Hart, H. L. A. *Punishment and Responsibility: Essays in the Philosophy of Law*. Oxford: Clarendon Press, 1968.

146   Heffter, A. W. *Das europäische Völkerrecht der Gegenwart auf den bisherigen Grundlagen*. 4th ed. Berlin: Schroeder, 1861.

147   Henrard, Paul Jean Joseph. *Les lois de la guerre sur terre*. Brussels, 1881.

148   Hershey, Amos S. "The History of International Relations during Antiquity and the Middle Ages," *American Journal of International Law* 5 (1911):901–32.

149   Hertz, W. G. *Das Problem des völkerrechtlichen Angriffs*. Leiden: Sijthoff, 1936.

150   Higgins, A. Pearce. "Submarine Warfare," *British Yearbook of International Law* 7 (1926):547–60.

151   _____, and C. John Colombos. *The International Law of the Sea*. 3d rev. ed. London: Longmans, Green, 1954.

152   Holland, Sir Thomas E. *The Laws of War on Land (Written and Unwritten)*. Oxford: Clarendon Press, 1908.

153   _____. *Studies in International Law*. Oxford: Clarendon Press, 1898.

154   Husserl, G. "The Conception of War as a Legal Remedy," *University of Chicago Law Review* 12 (February-April 1945):115–39, 258–75.

155   Jennings, W. Ivor. "Rule of Law in Total War," *Yale Law Journal* 50 (January 1941):365–86.

156   Jessup, Philip, et al. *Neutrality: Its History, Economics and Law*. 4 vols. New York: Columbia University Press, 1935–1963.

157   Jobst, U. "Is the Wearing of the Enemies' Uniform a Violation of the Laws of War?" *American Journal of International Law* 35 (July 1941): 435–42.

158   Josephus, Flavius. *Complete Works*. Translated by William Whiston. Grand Rapids: Kregel Publications, 1960.

159   Keen, Maurice H. *The Laws of War in the Late Middle Ages*. Toronto: University of Toronto Press, 1965.

160   Kelson, Hans. *General Theory of Law and State*. Cambridge: Harvard University Press, 1949.

161 _____. *Law and Peace in International Relations.* Cambridge: Harvard University Press, 1942.

162 _____. *Peace through Law.* Chapel Hill: University of North Carolina Press, 1944.

163 _____. *Principles of International Law.* New York: Rinehart, 1959.

164 Kerr, Alex A. "International Law and the Future of Submarine Warfare," *United States Naval Institute Proceedings* 81 (October 1955): 1105–10.

165 Kirchheimer, Otto. *Political Justice: The Use of Legal Procedure for Political Ends.* Princeton: Princeton University Press, 1961.

166 Korovin, Eugene A. "The Second World War and International Law," *American Journal of International Law* 40 (October 1946):742–55.

167 Kotzsch, Lothar. *The Concept of War in Contemporary History and International Law.* Geneva: Droz, 1956.

168 Kubicki, L. "Zbrodnie wojenne jako zagadnienie kodyfickacyjne w prawie karnym wewnatrz-krajowym," *Pantswo i Prawo* 8-9 (1961): 334–44.

169 Kunz, Josef L. "The Chaotic Status of the Laws of War and the Urgent Necessity of Their Revision," *American Journal of International Law* 45 (January 1951):37–61.

170 Lachs, Manfred. "The Unwritten Laws of Warfare," *Tulane Law Review* 20 (October 1945):120–28.

171 Laurentie, J. *Les Lois de la guerre.* Paris: Michal et Godde, 1917.

172 McNair, Sir Arnold Duncan. *Legal Effects of War.* 4th ed. Cambridge: Cambridge University Press, 1966.

173 Marvin, Miguel A. "The Evolution and Present Status of the Laws of War," *Hague Academy of International Law* 92 (1957):629–754.

174 Miller, Richard I. "Far Beyond Nuremberg: Steps toward International Criminal Jurisdiction," *Kentucky Law Journal* 61 (1972–1973): 925–30.

175 Moreno Quintana, Lucio M. "Régimen jurídico de las hostilidades," *Revista del Instituto de Derecho Internacional* 4 (July-December 1951): 159–72.

176 Mosler, Hermann. "Die Kriegshandlung in rechtswidrigen Kriege," *Jahrbuch für Internationales und Ausländisches Öffentliches Recht* 1 (1948):335–57.

177   Murray, John Courtney. "Remarks on the Moral Problems of War," *Theological Studies* 20 (1959):40–61.

178   Nussbaum, Arthur. *A Concise History of the Laws of Nations.* Rev. ed. New York: Macmillan, 1953.

179   Palmer, Benjamin W. "The Natural Law and Pragmatism," *Notre Dame Lawyer* 23 (March 1948):313–41.

180   Pella, Vespasian V. "Les illusions de la paix," *Revue de Droit International, de Sciences Diplomatiques et Politiques* 14 (1936):281–93.

181   ⸻. "Towards an International Criminal Court," *American Journal of International Law* 44 (January 1950):37–68.

182   Phillips, C. P. "Air Warfare and Law," *George Washington Law Review* 21 (January 1953):331–35; 21 (March 1953):395–422.

183   Phillipson, Coleman. *The International Law and Custom of Ancient Greece and Rome.* 2 vols. London: Macmillan, 1911.

184   Pillet, Antoine. *Le Droit de la guerre: Conférences faites aux officiers de la garrison de Grenoble pendant l'année 1891–1892.* Paris: Rousseau, 1892–1893.

185   ⸻. *La guerre et la droit: Leçons données à l'université de Louvain en 1921.* Louvain: A. Uystpruyst-Diendonne, 1922.

186   Proudhon, Pierre Joseph. *La guerre et la paix, recherches sur le principe et la constitution du droit des gens.* Paris: M. Rivière, 1927.

187   Pufendorf, Samuel. *De Jure Naturae et Gentium Libri Octo.* 2 vols. Oxford: Clarendon Press, 1934.

188   Puttkamer, E. von. *War and the Law.* Chicago: University of Chicago Press, 1944.

189   Quadri, R. "Sulla colpevolezza dei reati di guerra," *La Giurisprudenza Italiana* 4 (1947):170ff.

190   Raja Gabaglia, A. C. *Guerra e direito internacional.* São Paulo, Brazil: Saraiva, 1949.

191   Ralston, Jackson H. *International Arbitration from Athens to Locarno.* Stanford: Stanford University Press, 1929.

192   Robertson, Horace B., Jr. "Submarine Warfare," *JAG Journal* (November 1956):3–9.

193   Rolin, Alberic. *Le droit moderne de la guerre.* 3 vols. Brussels: Albert Dewitt, 1920–1921.

194 Röling, Bernard V. A. "The Laws of War and the National Jurisdiction since 1945," *Hague Academy of International Law* 100 (1952):323–456.

195 Royse, Morton W. *Aerial Bombardment and the International Regulation of Warfare.* New York: H. Vinal, 1928.

196 Schenk, Reinhold. *Seekrieg und Völkerrecht: Die Massnahmen der deutsche Seekriegsführung im 2. Weltkrieg in ihrer völkerrechtlichen Bedeutung.* Cologne: Heymann, 1958.

197 Schwarzenberger, Georg. "The Inductive Approach to International Law," *Harvard Law Review* 60 (April 1947):539–70.

198 Scott, James Brown. *The Spanish Origin of International Law.* Oxford: Clarendon Press, 1934.

199 Sloan, F. Blaine. "Comparative International and Municipal Law Sanctions," *Nebraska Law Review* 27 (November 1947):1–29.

200 Smith, Emory C. "Legal Aspects of Surface and Aerial Warfare," *JAG Journal* (September-October 1956):9–15.

201 Smith, H. A. *The Law and Custom of the Sea.* 2d ed. London: Stevens, 1950.

202 Sohler, Herbert. *U-Bootkrieg und Völkerrecht.* Frankfurt am Main: Mittler, 1956.

203 Spaight, J. M. *Air Power and War Rights.* 3d ed. London: Longmans, Green, 1947.

204 _____. *War Rights on Land.* London: Macmillan, 1911.

205 Taylor, Telford. "The Concept of Justice and the Laws of War," *Columbia Journal of Transnational Law* 13, no. 2 (1974):189–207.

206 Tucker, Robert W. *The Law of War and Neutrality at Sea.* Washington, D.C.: GPO, 1957.

207 Tunkin, G. I. *Theory of International Law.* Translated and edited by William E. Butler. Cambridge: Harvard University Press, 1974.

208 Vattell, Emmerich de. *The Law of Nations.* Translated by Joseph Chitty. Philadelphia: T. and J. W. Johnson, 1863.

209 Vitoria, Francisco de. *De Indis et de jure belli relectiones.* Edited by Ernest Nys. Translated by John Pawley Bate. Washington, D.C.: Carnegie Institution of Washington, 1917.

210 Wechsler, Herbert. *Principles, Politics, and Fundamental Law: Selected Essays.* Cambridge: Harvard University Press, 1961.

211   Wehberg, Hans. *Capture in War on Land and Sea.* Translated by John M. Robertson. London: P. S. King and Son, 1911.

212   Wheaton, Henry. *History of the Law of Nations in Europe and America from the Earliest Times to the Treaty of Washington.* New York: Gould, Banks, 1845.

213   Winthrop, William W. *Military Law and Precedents.* 2d ed. Washington, D.C.: GPO, 1920.

214   Wolff, Christian. *Jus Gentium Methodo Scientifica Pertractum.* 2 vols. Oxford: Clarendon Press, 1934.

215   Wright, Quincy. *The Enforcement of International Law through Municipal Law in the United States.* Urbana: University of Illinois, 1916.

216   _____. "The Outlawry of War and the Law of War," *American Journal of International Law* 47 (July 1953):365–76.

217   _____. *Problems of Stability and Progress in International Relations.* Berkeley: University of California Press, 1954.

218   _____. "Proposal for an International Criminal Court," *American Journal of International Law* 46 (January 1952):60–72.

219   _____. *The Role of International Law in the Elimination of War.* Manchester, Eng.: Manchester University Press, 1961.

220   _____. *A Study of War.* 2d ed. Chicago: University of Chicago Press, 1965.

Conferences and Treaties

TREATIES: GUIDES AND INDEXES

221   Mostecky, Vaclov, ed. *Index to Multilateral Treaties: A Chronological List of Multi-Party International Agreements from the Sixteenth Century through 1963, with Citations to Their Text.* Cambridge: Harvard University Press, Law School Library, 1965.

222   Parry, Clive, and Charity Hopkins, comps. *An Index of British Treaties, 1101–1968.* 3 vols. London: HMSO, 1970.

223   Phillimore, Sir W. G. F. *Three Centuries of Treaties of Peace and Their Teaching.* London: J. Murray, 1917.

224   Sprudzs, Adolf. *Treaty Sources in Legal and Political Research: Tools, Techniques, and Problems–The Conventional and the New.* International Studies no. 3. Tucson: University of Arizona, Institute of Government Research, 1971.

225 United States, Department of State. *Catalogue of Treaties, 1814–1918.* Washington, D.C.: GPO, 1919.

TREATIES: TEXTUAL COMPILATIONS

226 Bevan, Charles I., comp. *Treaties and Other International Agreements of the United States of America, 1776–1949.* 4 vols. to date. Washington, D.C.: GPO, 1968–.

227 Davenport, Frances Gardiner, ed. *European Treaties Bearing on the History of the United States and Its Dependencies.* 4 vols. Washington, D.C.: Carnegie Institution of Washington, 1917–1937.

228 Grenville, J. A. S., comp. *The Major International Treaties 1914–1973: A History and Guide with Texts.* New York: Stein and Day, 1974.

229 Hurst, Michael, ed. *Key Treaties of the Great Powers, 1814–1914.* 2 vols. New York: St. Martin's Press, 1972.

230 League of Nations. *Treaty Series.* 205 vols. Geneva: League of Nations, Publications Department, 1920–1946.

231 Martin, Lawrence, comp. *The Treaties of Peace, 1919–1923.* 2 vols. New York: Carnegie Endowment for International Peace, 1924.

232 Oakes, Sir Augustus, and R. B. Mowat. *The Great European Treaties of the Nineteenth Century.* Oxford: Clarendon Press, 1918.

233 United Nations. *United Nations Treaty Series.* 810 vols. to date. New York: United Nations, 1946–.

234 United States, Department of the Air Force. *Treaties Governing Land Warfare.* AFP 110–1–3. Washington, D.C.: GPO, 1958.

235 United States, War Department. *Treaties Governing Land Warfare: Technical Manual TM–27–251.* Washington, D.C.: War Department, 1944.

GENEVA CONVENTION, 1864

236 "The Geneva Convention for the Amelioration of the Condition of the Sick and Wounded of Armies in the Field, Concluded, August 22, 1864," *American Journal of International Law* 1 Supplement (1907): 90–95.

ST. PETERSBURG DECLARATION, 1868

237 Bruns, Paul. "Inhumane Kriegs-Geschosse," *Archiv für Klinische Chirugie* 57 (1898):602–07.

238 ———. *Über die Wirkung der Bleispitzengeschosse 'Dum Dum' Geschosse.* Tübingen: Laupp, 1898.

239 "Declaration of St. Petersberg, Dec. 11, 1868," *American Journal of Law* 1 [Supplement] (1907):95–96.

240 Meyrowitz, Henri. "Reflections on the Centenary of the Declaration of St. Petersberg," *International Review of the Red Cross* 93 (December 1968):611–25.

241 Spiers, Edward M. "The Use of the Dum Dum Bullet in Colonial Warfare," *Journal of Imperial and Commonwealth History* 4, no. 1 (October 1975):3–14.

BRUSSELS CONFERENCE, 1874

242 *Actes de la conférence de Bruxelles (1874).* Brussels: F. Hayez, 1874.

243 *Actes de la conférence de Bruxelles de 1874: Sur le projet d'une convention internationale concernant la guerre.* Paris: A. Wittersheim et Cie, Librairie des Publications Legislatives, 1874.

244 Cowles, Willard B. "The Dakin Index to the Proceedings of the Brussels Conference of 1874," *American Journal of International Law* 43 (July 1949):546–47.

245 Mechelynck, Albert, ed. *La convention de la Haye concernant les lois et coutumes de la guerre sur terre, d'après les actes et documents des conférences de Bruxelles de 1874 et de La Haye de 1899 et 1907.* Gent: A. Hoste, 1915.

246 "Project of an International Declaration Concerning the Laws and Customs of War, Adopted by the Conference of Brussels, August 27, 1874," *American Journal of International Law* 1 [Supplement] (1907): 96–103.

HAGUE CONVENTIONS, 1899, 1907

Documents

247 Carnegie Endowment for International Peace, Division of International Law. *The Proceedings of the Hague Peace Conferences: The Conferences of 1899 and 1907, Index Volume.* New York: Carnegie Endowment for International Peace, 1921.

248 ———. *The Proceedings of the Hague Peace Conferences: Translation of the Official Texts.* 5 vols. New York: Oxford University Press, 1920–1921.

General

249 Albertini, Luigi. *The Origins of the War of 1914.* Translated and edited by Isabella M. Massey. 3 vols. London: Oxford University Press, 1952.

250 Choate, Joseph H. *The Two Hague Conferences.* Princeton: Princeton University Press, 1913.

251 Davis, Calvin DeArmond. *The United States and the First Hague Peace Conference.* Ithaca: Cornell University Press, 1962.

252 _____. *The United States and the Second Hague Peace Conference.* Durham: Duke University Press, 1976.

253 Dickinson, G. Louis. *The International Anarchy, 1904–1914.* New York: Century, 1926.

254 Ford, Thomas K. "The Genesis of the First Hague Peace Conference," *Political Science Quarterly* 51, no. 3 (1936):354–82.

255 Higgins, A. Pearce. *The Hague Peace Conferences and Other International Conferences Concerning the Laws and Usages of War.* Cambridge: Cambridge University Press, 1909.

256 Holls, Frederick W. *The Peace Conference at the Hague and Its Bearings on International Law and Policy.* New York: Macmillan, 1909.

257 Hudson, Manley O. "Present Status of the Hague Conventions of 1899 and 1907," *American Journal of International Law* 25 (1931):114–17.

258 Hull, William Isaac. *The Two Hague Conferences and Their Contributions to International Law.* Boston: Ginn, 1907.

259 Mahan, Alfred Thayer. "The Peace Conference and the Moral Aspects of War," *North American Review* 149 (October 1899):433–47.

260 Matthews, Mary Alice, comp. *Third Hague Peace Conference.* Brief Reference no. 16. Washington, D.C.: Carnegie Endowment for International Peace, 1939.

261 Merignhac, Alexandre G. J. A. *La lois et coutumes de la guerre sur terre d'après le droit international moderne et la codification de la Conférence de la Haye de 1899.* Paris: A. Chevalier-Marescq, 1903.

262 Pillet, Antoine. *Le lois actuelles de la guerre.* 2d ed. Paris: Rousseau, 1901.

263 Robinson, Margaret. *Arbitration and the Hague Peace Conferences, 1899 and 1907.* Philadelphia, 1936.

264 Schücking, Walther. *The International Union of the Hague Conferences.* Translated by Charles G. Fenwick. Oxford: Clarendon Press, 1918.

265 Scott, James Brown, ed. *The Declaration of London, February 26, 1909.* New York: Oxford University Press, 1919.

266 _____. *The Hague Peace Conferences of 1899 and 1907.* 2 vols. Baltimore: Johns Hopkins Press, 1909.

267   Wehberg, Hans. *The Problem of an International Court of Justice.* Translated by Charles G. Fenwick. Oxford: Clarendon Press, 1918.

GENEVA CONVENTION, 1906

268   Carnegie Endowment for International Peace. *The Geneva Convention of 1906 for the Amelioration of the Condition of the Wounded in Armies in the Field.* Washington, D.C.: Carnegie Endowment for International Peace, 1916.

269   Great Britain, Parliament. *Sick and Wounded in War: Papers Relating to the Geneva Conveniton, 1906.* Cd. 3933. London: HMSO, 1908.

270   United States, Congress, Senate. *Amelioration of the Condition of Wounded in Armies: Message from the President of the United States, Transmitting an Authenticated Copy of Convention Signed at Geneva on July 6, 1906.* 59th Cong., 2d sess. Washington, D.C.: GPO, 1906.

PARIS PEACE CONFERENCE, 1919

Documents

271   De Lapradelle, Albert G., ed. *La Paix de Versailles.* 12 vols. Paris: Le Editions Internates, 1929–1939.

272   Mantoux, Paul, ed. *Les Délibérations de conseil de quatre (24 mars–28 juin 1919).* 2 vols. Paris: Centre national de la recherche Scientifique, 1955.

273   Miller, David Hunter. *My Diary at the Peace Conference.* 21 vols. New York: Appeal Printing Co., 1924.

274   Paris Peace Conference. *Report, Commission on Responsibility of the War and for Enforcement of Penalties.* Oxford, 1919.

275   United States, Department of State. *Papers Relating to the Foreign Relations of the United States: The Paris Peace Conference 1919.* 13 vols. Washington, D.C.: GPO, 1943.

General

276   Adams, William. "The American Peace Commission and the Punishment of Crimes Committed during the War," *Law Quarterly Review* 39 (1923):245–51.

277   Albrecht-Carrié, Rene. *Italy at the Paris Peace Conference.* New York: Columbia University Press, 1938.

278   Berber, Friedrich, ed. *Das Diktat von Versailles.* 2 vols. Essen: Deutsches Institut für Aussenpolitik, 1939.

279   Birdsall, Paul. *Versailles Twenty Years After.* New York: Reynal and Hitchcock, 1941.

280 Burnett, Philip M. *Reparation at the Paris Peace Conference from the Standpoint of the American Delegation.* 2 vols. New York: Columbia University Press, 1940.

281 Graux, Lucien. *Histoire des violations du traité de paix.* 4 vols. Paris: G. Crès, 1921–1927.

282 Hankey, Lord. *The Supreme Control of the Paris Peace Conference, 1919.* London: George Allen and Unwin, 1963.

283 House, Edward M., and Charles Seymour, eds. *What Really Happened in Paris: The Story of the Paris Peace Conference, 1918–1919.* New York: Scribner's, 1921.

284 Lansing, Robert L. *The Peace Negotiations: A Personal Narrative.* Boston: Houghton Mifflin, 1921.

285 Leers, Johann von. *Das ist Versailles!* Berlin: H. Hillger, 1933.

286 Lersner, Kurt Freiherr von. *Versailles! Volkskommentar des Friedensdiktats.* Berlin: Staatspolitischer Verlag, 1921.

287 Lloyd George, David. *The Truth about the Treaties.* 2 vols. London: V. Gollancz, 1938.

288 ———. *War Memoirs of David Lloyd George.* 6 vols. Boston: Little, Brown, 1933–1937.

289 Luckau, Alma M. *The German Delegation at the Paris Peace Conference.* New York: Columbia University Press, 1941.

290 Marston, Frank S. *The Peace Conference of 1919: Organization and Procedure.* New York: Oxford University Press, 1944.

291 Nelson, Harold I. *Land and Power: British and Allied Policy on Germany's Frontiers, 1916–1919.* London: Routledge and Kegan Paul, 1963.

292 Nicholson, Harold. *Peacemaking, 1919.* London: Constable, 1933.

293 Noble, George B. *Policies and Opinions at Paris, 1919.* New York: Macmillan, 1935.

294 Schiff, Victor, with contributions by Otto Landsberg, Hermann Müller, and Friedrich Stampfer. *The Germans at Versailles, 1919.* Translated by Geoffrey Dunlop. London: Williams and Norgate, 1930.

295 Schwendemann, Karl. *Versailles nach 15 Jahren, der Stand der Revision des Versailler Diktats.* Berlin: Zentralverlag, 1935.

296 Seymour, Charles, ed. *The Intimate Papers of Colonel House.* 4 vols. Boston: Houghton Mifflin, 1926–1928.

297   Tardieu, Andre. *The Truth about the Treaty.* Indianapolis, Bobbs-Merrill, 1921.

298   Temperly, H. W. V., ed. *A History of the Peace Conference of Paris.* 6 vols. London: Oxford University Press, 1920–1924.

299   Wegerer, Alfred von. *A Refutation of the Versailles War Guilt Thesis.* Translated by Edwin H. Zeydel. New York: Knopf, 1930.

WASHINGTON NAVAL CONFERENCE, 1921–1922

Documents

300   Great Britain, Foreign Office. *Conference on the Limitation of Armaments: Washington, 1921–1922.* Cmd. 1627. London: HMSO, 1922.

301   United States, Department of State. *Conference on the Limitation of Armament: Washington, November 12, 1921-February 6, 1922; Conférence de la limitation des armaments, 12 novembre 1921-6 Fevrier 1922.* Washington, D.C.: GPO, 1922.

General

302   Birn, Donald S. "Britain and France at the Washington Conference, 1921–1922." Ph.D. dissertation, Columbia University, 1964.

303   Braisted, William Reynolds. *The United States Navy in the Pacific, 1909–1922.* Austin: University of Texas Press, 1971.

304   Buckley, Thomas H. *The United States and the Washington Conference.* Knoxville: University of Tennessee Press, 1970.

305   Buell, Raymond Leslie. *The Washington Conference.* New York: D. Appleton, 1922.

306   Bywater, Hector C. "Japan's Sequel to the Washington Conference," *United States Naval Institute Proceedings* 49 (May 1923):811–27.

307   Hoag, Charles L. *Preface to Preparedness: The Washington Disarmament Conference and Public Opinion.* Washington, D.C.: American Council on Public Affairs, 1941.

308   Ichihashi, Yamato. *The Washington Conference and After: A Historical Survey.* Stanford: Stanford University Press, 1928.

309   Kawakami, Kiyoshi K. *Japan's Pacific Policy: Especially in Relation to China, the Far East, and the Washington Conference.* New York: E. P. Dutton, 1922.

310   Knox, Dudley W. *The Eclipse of American Sea Power.* New York: American Army and Navy Journal, 1922.

311 Socas, Roberto E. "France, Naval Armament and Naval Disarmament, 1918–1922." Ph.D. dissertation, Columbia University, 1965.

312 Sprout, Harold and Margaret Sprout. *Toward a New Order in Sea Power.* Princeton: Princeton University Press, 1943.

313 Vinson, John Chalmers. *The Parchment Peace: The United States Senate and the Washington Conference, 1921–1922.* Athens: University of Georgia Press, 1955.

GENEVA PROTOCOL, 1925

314 Buergenthal, T., and R. R. Baxter. "Legal Aspects of the Geneva Protocol of 1925," *American Journal of International Law* 64 (October 1970):853–79.

315 United States, Congress, Senate. Committee on Foreign Relations. *The Geneva Protocol of 1925.* 92d Cong., 1st sess. Washington, D.C., 1972.

LOCARNO PACT, 1925

316 Bretton, Henry L. *Stresemann and the Revision of Versailles: A Fight for Reason.* Stanford: Stanford University Press, 1953.

317 Grun, George A. "Locarno: Idea and Reality," *International Affairs* 31 (1955):477–85.

318 Jacobson, Jon. *Locarno Diplomacy: Germany and the West, 1925–1929.* Princeton: Princeton University Press, 1972.

319 Rossler, Hellmuth, ed. *Locarno und die Weltpolitik, 1924–1932.* Göttingen, 1969.

320 Thimme, Annelise. "Die Lokarnopolitik im Lichte des Stresemann-Nachlasses," *Zeitschrift für Politik* 3 (1956):42–63.

321 Zimmermann, Ludwig. "Die Locarnoverträge als Versuch einer Lösung der Sicherheitsfrage," in *Studien zur Geschichte der Weimarer Republik, Erlanger Forschungen.* Series A, no. 6. Erlangen: Universitätsbund Erlangen, 1956.

GENEVA NAVAL CONFERENCE, 1927

Documents

322 Great Britain, Foreign Office. *Geneva Conference for the Limitation of Naval Armaments, June-August, 1927: Speeches in Plenary Session by the Right Hon. W. C. Bridgeman, M.P., First Lord of the Admiralty.* Cmd. 2964. London: HMSO, 1927.

323   United States, Congress, Senate. *Records of the Conference for the Limitation of Naval Armaments Held at Geneva, Switzerland from June 20 to August 4, 1927.* 70th Cong., 1st sess. Washington, D.C.: GPO, 1927.

General

324   Custer, Ben Scott. "The Geneva Conference for the Limitation of Naval Armament—1927." Ph.D. dissertation, Georgetown University, 1948.

325   Dubbay, Robert W. "The Geneva Naval Conference of 1927: A Study of Battleship Diplomacy," *Southern Quarterly* 8 (January 1970): 177–99.

326   Hooker, Richard. "The Geneva Naval Conference," *Yale Review* 17 (January 1928):263–80.

327   Kawakami, K. K. "The Hidden Conflict at the Three-Power Naval Conference," *Current History* 27 (1927):106–11.

328   Noel-Baker, Phillip J. *Disarmament and the Coolidge Conference.* London: Hogarth Press, 1927.

KELLOGG-BRIAND PACT, 1928

Documents

329   United States, Congress, Senate. *Hearings before the Committee on Foreign Relations on the General Pact for the Renunciation of War.* 70th Cong., 2d sess. Washington, D.C.: GPO, 1928.

330   United States, Department of State. *Foreign Relations: Notes Exchanged between the United States of America and Other Powers on a Multilateral Treaty for the Renunciation of War, June 30, 1927 to July 20, 1928.* Washington, D.C.: GPO, 1928.

330a   _____. *Foreign Relations: The General Pact for the Renunciation of War.* Washington, D.C.: GPO, 1928.

331   _____. *Renunciation of War Treaty, Paris, August 27, 1928.* Washington, D.C.: GPO, 1933.

332   _____. *Treaty for the Renunciation of War: Text of the Treaty, Notes Exchanged, Instruments of the Ratification and of Adherence and Other Papers.* State Department Pub. no. 468. Washington, D.C.: GPO, 1933.

General

333   Berdahl, Clarence A. "Implications of the Kellogg Pact with Respect to American Foreign Policy," *New York University Law Quarterly Review* 15 (November 1937):82–106.

334 Borchard, Edwin M. "The Multilateral Treaty for the Renunciation of War," *American Journal of International Law* 23 (January 1929): 116–20.

335 Brown, Philip M. "Japanese Interpretation of the Kellogg Pact," *American Journal of International Law* 27 (January 1933):100–102.

336 Bryn-Jones, David. *Frank B. Kellogg: A Biography*. New York: Putnam, 1937.

337 Chamberlin, Waldo. "Origins of the Kellogg-Briand Pact," *Historian* 15 (November 1952):77–92.

338 Ellis, L. Ethan. *Frank B. Kellogg and American Foreign Relations, 1925–1929*. New Brunswick: Rutgers University Press, 1961.

339 Fenwick, Charles G. "The Implications of Consultation in the Pact of Paris," *American Journal of International Law* 26 (October 1932): 787–89.

340 Ferrell, Robert H. *Peace in Their Time: The Origins of the Kellogg-Briand Pact*. New York: Yale University Press, 1952.

341 Finch, George A. "Pact of Non-Aggression," *American Journal of International Law* 27 (October 1933):725–32.

342 Gerould, James Thayer, ed. *The Pact of Paris*. New York: H. W. Wilson, 1929.

343 Gonsiorowski, Miroslas. "Legal Meaning of the Pact for the Renunciation of War," *American Political Science Review* 30 (August 1936): 653-80.

344 Hassman, Heinz. *Der Kellogg-Pakt*. Munich: Thing-Verlag, 1930.

345 Kneeshaw, Stephen John. "The Kellogg-Briand Pact: American Reaction." Ph.D. dissertation. University of Colorado, 1971.

346 Lansing, Robert L. "The Fallacy of 'Outlaw War,'" *Independent* 113, (August 16, 1924):95–96.

347 Lodge, Henry Cabot. "The Meaning of the Kellogg Treaty," *Harper's Magazine* 158 (December 1, 1928):32–41.

348 Miller, David Hunter. *The Peace Pact of Paris: A Study of the Briand-Kellogg Treaty*. New York: Putnam, 1928.

349 Myers, D. P. *Origin and Conclusion of the Paris Pact*. Boston: World Peace Foundation, 1929.

350 Roosevelt, Franklin Delano. "Our Foreign Policy: A Democratic View," *Foreign Affairs* 6 (July 1928):573–86.

351   Shotwell, James T. *The Pact of Paris.* Worcester, Mass.: Carnegie Endowment for International Peace, 1928.

352   ———. "The Pact of Paris with Historical Commentary," *International Conciliation* 243 (October 1928):447–59.

353   ———. *War as an Instrument of National Policy and Its Renunciation at the Pact of Paris.* New York: Harcourt, Brace, 1929.

354   Stimson, Henry L. *The Pact of Paris: Three Years of Development.* State Department Pub. no. 357. Washington, D.C.: GPO, 1932.

355   Vinson, John Chalmers. *William G. Borah and the Outlawry of War.* Athens: University of Georgia Press, 1957.

356   Wehberg, Hans. *The Outlawry of War: A Series of Lectures. . . .* Translated by Edwin Hermann Zeydel. Carnegie Endowment for International Peace, Division of International Law, Pamphlet Series no. 52. Washington, D.C.: Carnegie Endowment for International Peace, 1931.

357   Wheeler-Bennett, John W. *Information on the Renunciation of War, 1927–1928.* London: George Allen and Unwin, 1928.

358   Wright, Quincy. "Meaning of the Pact of Paris," *American Journal of International Law* 27 (January 1933):39–61.

359   ———. "The Outlawry of War," *American Journal of International Law* 19 (January 1925):76–103.

GENEVA CONVENTION, 1929

360   Rasmussen, Gustav. *Code des prisonniers de guerre.* Copenhagen: Levin and Munksgaard, 1931.

LONDON NAVAL CONFERENCE, 1930

Documents

361   Australia, Delegation to the Naval Conference. *Limitation of Naval Armament: Report of the Australian Delegate.* Canberra: H. J. Green, Government Printer, 1930.

362   Great Britain, Foreign Office. *Documents of the London Naval Conference, 1930.* London: HMSO, 1930.

363   United States, Army, Far East Command, General Headquarters, Military Intelligence Section, General Staff. *Memoirs: Supplement: Prince Saionji and the London Disarmament Treaty.* Tokyo, 1946.

364   United States, Congress, Senate. *Hearings before the Committee on Foreign Relations on Treaty on the Limitation of Naval Armaments.* 71st Cong., 2d sess. Washington, D.C., 1930.

365 _____. *Hearings before the Committee on Naval Affairs on the London Naval Treaty of 1930.* Washington, D.C.: GPO, 1930.

366 United States Department of State. *London Naval Conference: Digest of the London Naval Treaty of 1930, with Fleet-Tonnage Tables.* State Department Conference Series no. 4. Washington D.C., 1930.

367 _____. *Proceedings of the London Naval Conference of 1930 and Supplementary Documents.* State Department Conference Series no. 6. Washington, D.C., 1931.

General

368 Arnold-Forster, William. *The Disarmament Conference.* London: National Peace Council, 1931.

369 Bellairs, Comdr. Carolyn W. *The Naval Conference and After.* London: Farber and Farber, 1930.

370 Bouy, Raymond. *Le désarmement naval: La Conférence de Londres.* Paris: Éditiòns des Presses universitaires de France, 1931.

371 Dewar, Alfred C. "The London Naval Treaty," *Brassy's Naval and Shipping Annual* (1931):69–84.

372 Engely, Giovanni. *The Politics of Naval Disarmament.* Translated by H. V. Rhodes. London: Williams and Norgate, 1932.

373 Estienny, Paul. *Le probleme de la limitation et de la déduction des armaments navals (1921–1931).* Toulouse: Imprimerie Andrau et Laporte, 1931.

374 Godfrey, James L. "Anglo-American Naval Conversations Preliminary to the London Naval Conference of 1930," *South Atlantic Quarterly* 49 (1950):303–16.

375 Hankey, Lord. *Diplomacy by Conference: Studies in Public Affairs, 1920–1946.* London: E. Benn, 1946.

376 Kawakami, K. K. "The London Naval Conference as Viewed from Japan," *Nineteenth Century and After* 106 (1929):731–42.

377 Lippmann, Walter. "The London Naval Conference: An American View," *Foreign Affairs* 8 (1930):499–518.

378 O'Connor, Raymond G. *Perilous Equilibrium: The United States and the London Naval Conference of 1930.* Lawrence: University of Kansas Press, 1958.

379 Read, Conyers. "Recent United States and British Government Publications on the London Naval Conference of 1930," *American Historical Review* 54 (1949):307–14.

380 Wallin, Homer N. "Permissible Building Programs under the London Naval Treaty," *United States Naval Institute Proceedings* 56 (1930):1074–79.

LONDON NAVAL CONFERENCE, 1935

Documents

381 Great Britain, Foreign Office. *Documents of the London Naval Conference, 1935.* London: HMSO, 1935.

382 United States, Department of State. *The London Naval Conference of 1935.* Washington, D.C.: GPO, 1936.

General

383 Berg, Meredith W. "The United States and the Breakdown of Naval Limitation, 1934–1939." Ph.D. dissertation. Tulane University, 1966.

384 Leuchtenberg, William E. *Franklin D. Roosevelt and the New Deal, 1932–1940.* New York: Harper and Row, 1963.

385 Levine, Robert H. "The Politics of Naval Rearmament, 1930–1938." Ph.D. dissertation, Harvard University, 1972.

386 Nomura, Adm. Kichisaburo. "Japan's Demands for Naval Equality," *Foreign Affairs* 13 (January 1935):196–203.

387 Pelz, Stephen E. *Race to Pearl Harbor: The Failure of the Second London Conference and the Onset of World War II.* Cambridge: Harvard University Press, 1974.

388 Richmond, Adm. Sir Hubert W. "Naval Problems of 1935," *Foreign Affairs* 13 (October 1934):45–54.

389 Wolf, William T. "London Naval Disarmament Conference, 1935–1936." Ph.D. dissertation, University of California, 1962.

ANGLO-GERMAN NAVAL AGREEMENT, 1935

Documents

390 Great Britain, Foreign Office. *British and Foreign State Papers.* London: Harrison, 1941–1948, vol. 139, 182–85.

General

391 Giraud, Andre. "France and the Anglo-German Naval Treaty," *Foreign Affairs* 14 (October 1935):51–61.

392 Haraszti, Eva. *Treaty-Breakers or Realpolitiker: The Anglo-German Naval Agreement of June 1935.* Boppard am Rhein: Harald Boldt Verlag, 1974.

393 Papp, Nicholas G. "The Anglo-German Naval Agreement of 1935." Ph.D. dissertation, University of Connecticut, 1969.

394 Watt, Donald C. "The Anglo-German Naval Agreement of 1935: An Interim Judgment," *Journal of Modern History* 28 (June 1956):155-75.

GENOCIDE CONVENTION, 1948

395 Brügel, J. W. "Die Konvention zur Verhütung und Bekämpfung des Gruppenmords," *Europa-Archiv* 4 (1949):2307-13.

396 Carlston, K. S. "The Genocide Convention: A Problem for the American Lawyer," *American Bar Association Journal* 36 (1950):206-09.

397 Claught, R. "The Crime of Genocide," *American Journal of Economics and Sociology* 8 (1949):351-65.

398 Finch, George A. "The Genocide Convention," *American Journal of International Law* 43 (1949):732-38.

399 Genchio, B. A. "La elaborazione internazionale di un nuoro crimine il genocidio," *Revista Penale* 74, pt. 1 (1949):603ff.

400 Jescheck, Hans Heinrich. "Die internationale Genocidium-Konvention vom 9. Dezember 1948 und die Lehre vom Völkerstrafrecht," *Zeitschrift für die Gesamte Strafrechtswissenschaft* 66 (1954):193-217.

401 Kuhn, A. "The Genocide Convention and States Rights," *American Journal of International Law* 43 (1949):498-501.

402 Kunz, J. L. "The United Nations Convention on Genocide," *American Journal of International Law* 43 (1949):738-46.

403 Landsberg, William H. "Gruppenmord als internationales Verbrechen: Das 'Genocide'-Abkommen der Vereinten Nationen," *Aussenpolitik* 4 (1953):310-21.

404 Lemkin, Raphael. *Le crime de génocide.* Paris: La documentation Française, 1946.

405 ———. "Le crime de génocide," *Revue de Droit International, de Sciences Diplomatiques et Politiques* 24 (October-December, 1946):213-22.

406 ———. "Le génocide," *Revue Internationale de Droit Pénal* 17 (1946):371-86.

407 _____. "Genocide as a Crime under International Law," *American Journal of International Law* 41 (January 1947):145–51.

408 Miaja de la Muela, Adolfo. "El genocidio, delito internacional," *Revista Española de Derecho Internacional* 4 (1951):363–408.

409 Mosheim, Berthold. "Die Arbeiten der Vereinten Nationen zur Frage der Rechte des Individuums und des Verbrechens der Genocide," *Archiv des Völkerrechts* 2 (1949-1950):180–93.

410 Phillips, O. L. "The Genocide Convention: Its Effects on Our Legal System," *American Bar Association Journal* 35 (1949):623–25.

411 Planzer, Antonio. *Le crime de génocide.* St. Gall: F. Schwald, 1956.

412 Stillschweig, Kurt. "Das Abkommen zur Bekämpfung von Genocide," *Friedens-Warte* 49 (1949):93–104.

GENEVA CONVENTIONS, 1949

Documents

413 United States, Department of State. *Geneva Conventions of August 12, 1949, for the Protection of War Victims.* State Department Pub. no. 3938. Washington, D.C.: GPO, 1950.

General

414 Albrecht, A. R. "War Reprisals in the War Crimes Trials and in the Geneva Conventions of 1949," *American Journal of International Law* 47 (October 1953):590–614.

415 Baxter, R. R. "The Geneva Conventions of 1949 before the U.S. Senate," *American Journal of International Law* 49 (October 1955): 550–55.

416 Brügel, J. W. "Die Konvention zur Verhütung und Bekämpfung des Gruppenmords," *Europa-Archiv* 4 (1949):2307–13.

417 Castro Ramirez, Manuel, Jr., et al. "La protection pénale des Conventions internationales humanitaires," *Revue International de Droit Pénal* 24 (1953):11–67, 661–95, 833–73.

418 De La Pradelle, Paul. *La Conférence diplomatique et les nouvelles Conventions de Genève du 12 août 1949.* Paris: Les Éditions internationales, 1951.

419 Dillon, J. V. "Genesis of the 1949 Convention Relative to the Treatment of Prisoners of War," *Miami Law Quarterly* 5 (December 1950): 40–63.

420   Downey, William G., Jr. "Revision of the Rules of Warfare," *American Society of International Law Proceedings* (1949):102–08.

421   Draper, G. I. A. D. *The Red Cross Conventions.* New York: Praeger, 1958.

422   Esgain, A. J., and W. A. Solf, "The 1949 Geneva Convention Relative to the Treatment of Prisoners of War: Its Principles, Innovations and Deficiencies," *North Carolina Law Review* 41 (1963): 537–96.

423   "Geneva Conventions for Protection of War Victims," *Department of State Bulletin* 33 (July 11, 1955):69–79.

424   "The Geneva Diplomatic Conference," *Revue Internationale de la Croix-Rouge* [English supplement, Geneva] 2 (June 1949):192–94.

425   Glaser, Stefan. "La Convention de Genève et les criminels de guerre," *Revue de Droit Pénal et de Criminologie* 32 (February 1952): 517–22.

426   Groh, Franz. *Das Recht der Kriegsgefangenen und Zivilpersonen nach den Genfer Konventionen vom 12. August 1949.* Hamburg: Forschungsstelle für Völkerrecht und ausländisches öffentliches Recht der Universität Hamburg, 1953.

427   Gutteridge, Joyce A. C. "The Geneva Convention of 1949," *British Yearbook of International Law* 26 (1949):249–326.

428   Honig, F. "Ratification of the Geneva Conventions 1949," *Law Journal* 107 (September 20, 1957):597–99.

429   Kunz, Josef L. "The Geneva Conventions of August 12, 1949," in *Law and Politics in the World Community,* edited by George A. Lipsky. Berkeley: University of California Press, 1953, pp. 279–316.

430   McCahon, William H. "Toward Revision of the Geneva Convention," *Department of State Bulletin* 19 (October 10, 1948):464–65.

431   McGinness, John R. "An International Bill of Rights for Prisoners of War," *Cleveland-Marshall Law Review* 2 (Winter 1953):158–65.

432   Orcasitas Llorente, Luís. "Los prisioneros de guerra en las Conferencia de Ginebra de 1949 (Convenio III)," *Revista Española de Derecho Internacional* 3 (1950):473–500.

433   Paquin, Jean. "Le problème des sanctions disciplinaires et pénales dans la IIIe Convention de Genève du 12 août 1949," *Revue de Droit International, de Sciences Diplomatiques et Politiques* 29 (January-March 1951):52–63.

434   Pictet, Jean S. "The New Geneva Conventions for the Protection of War Victims," *American Journal of International Law* 45 (July 1951): 462–75.

435   Schlögel, Anton. *Die Genfer Rotkreuz-Abkommen vom 12. August 1949.* 3d ed. Mainz: Verlagsanstalt Hüthig und Dreyer, 1955.

436   Siordet, Frédéric. *The Geneva Conventions of 1949: The Question of Security.* Geneva: International Committee of the Red Cross, 1953.

437   Strebel, Helmut. "Die Genfer Abkommen vom 12. August 1949— Fragen des Anwendungsbereichs," *Zeitschrift für Ausländisches Öffentliches Recht und Völkerrecht* 13 (February 1950):118–45.

438   Yingling, Raymond T., and Robert W. Ginnane. "The Geneva Convention of 1949," *American Journal of International Law* 46 (July 1952): 393–427.

Theory and Philosophy of War Crimes

439   Agus, Jacob B. "Mass Crime and the Judeo-Christian Tradition: I," *Minnesota Review* 3, no. 2 (Winter 1963):205–19.

440   Aronéanu, Eugène. *Le crime contre l'humanité. Nouvelle Revue de Droit International Privé* 13 (1946):369-418.

441   ———. *Le crime contre l'humanité.* Paris: Dalloz, 1961.

442   ———. "Le crime contre l'humanité et la juridiction pénale internationale," *Revue de Droit International, de Sciences Diplomatiques et Politiques* 28 (April-June 1950):229–46.

443   ———. "Les droits de l'homme et le crime contre l'humanité," *Revue de Droit International, de Sciences Diplomatiques et Politiques* 25 (July-September 1947):187–96.

444   ———. "Responsabilités pénales pour crime contre l'humanité," *Revue de Droit International, de Sciences Diplomatiques et Politiques* 26 (April-June 1948):144–81.

445   Baxter, Richard R. "The Municipal and International Law Basis of Jurisdiction over War Crimes," *British Yearbook of International Law* 28 (1951):382–93.

446   Bayle, François. *Croix gammée contre caducée: Les expériences humaines en Allemagne pendant la deuxième guerre mondiale.* Neustadt, 1950.

447   Boissarie, M. A. "Rapport sur la définition du crime contre l'humanité," *Revue International de Droit Pénal* 18 (1947):201–07.

448   Boissier, Pierre. "La répression des 'petits' crimes de guerre," *Revue Internationale de Droit Pénal* 19 (1948):293–309.

449 Brachmann, Botho. "Kriegsverbrechen und Verbrechen gegen die Menschlichkeit sind unverjährbar," *Archivmitteilungen* 19, no. 1 (1969): 6–8.

450 Brand, G. "War Crimes Trials and the Laws of War," *British Yearbook of International Law* 26 (1949):414–27.

451 Brierly, J. L. "The Nature of War Crimes Jurisdiction," *Norseman* 2 (1944):166–72.

452 Bulnes Galván, Carlos. *La guerra y el derecho castrense.* Mexico City, 1961.

453 Calderón Serrano, Ricardo. "Crímenes de guerra," *Boletín jurídico Militar* 15–17 (March-April 1949/January-February 1951):1–378. Appended to each issue with separate page numbers.

454 Cohn, K. "Crimes against Humanity," *German Foreign Policy* 6 (February 1967):160–69.

455 Colas, R. "La compétence des juridictions militaires dans la répression des crimes de guerre," *Revue de Science Criminelle et de Droit Pénal Comparé* 22 (1967):482–93.

456 Dahm, Georg. *Zur Problematik des Völkerstrafrechts.* Göttingen: Vandenhoeck und Rupprecht, 1956.

457 Daniel, J. *Le Problème du châtiment des crimes de guerre d'après les enseignements de la deuxième guerre mondiale.* Cairo: R. Schindler, 1946.

458 Dautricourt, J. Y. "Crime against Humanity—European Views on Its Conception and Its Future," *Journal of Criminal Law and Criminology* 40 (July-August 1949):170–75.

459 ———. "La définition du crime contre l'humanité," *Revue de Droit International, de Sciences Diplomatiques et Politiques* 25 (October-December 1947):294–313.

460 Del Rosal Fernández, Juan. *Acerca de los crímenes contra la humanidad.* Valencia, Spain, 1950.

461 Dickenson, Edwin D. "Jurisdiction with Respect to Crime," *American Journal of International Law* 29 [Supplement] (1935):437–651.

462 Eyben, William Edler von. *Thi kendes for ret: Retsopgøret efter besaettelsen.* Copenhagen: Juristforbundet, 1968.

463 Falk, Richard A.; Gabriel Kolko; and Robert Jay Lifton; comps. *Crimes of War: A Legal, Political Documentary and Psychological Inquiry into the Responsibility of Leaders, Citizens, and Soldiers for Criminal Acts of War.* New York: Random House, 1971.

464   Feldmann, H. *Das Verbrechen gegen die Menschlichkeit.* Essen: West. Verlag, 1948.

465   Garner, James W. "Punishment of Offenders against the Laws and Customs of War," *American Journal of International Law* 14 (1920): 70–94.

466   Gernet, Mikhail N. *Prestupleniia gitlerov tsev protiv Chelovechnosti.* Moscow, 1946.

467   Goldstein, Anatole. *Anti-Semitism and War Crimes.* New York: World Jewish Congress, Institute of Jewish Affairs, 1955.

468   _____. "Crimes against Humanity—Some Jewish Aspects," *Jewish Yearbook of International Law* 1 (1948):206–25.

469   Graven, Jean. "Les crimes contre l'humanité," *Recueil des Cours de l'Académie Droit International de la Haye* 76 (1950):427–607.

470   _____. "La définition et la répression des crimes contre l'humanité," *Revue de Droit International, de Sciences Diplomatiques et Politiques* 26 (January-March 1948):1–32.

471   _____. "Le nouveau droit pénal international," *Revue de Droit International, de Sciences Diplomatiques et Politiques* 37 (October-December 1959):362–79; 38 (January-March 1960):6–29; 38 (April-June 1960):126–36; 38 (July-September 1960):252–73; 39 (January-March 1961):14–25; 39 (April-June 1961):125–40; 39 (July-September 1961): 245–64.

472   Halprin, Lee S. "American Liberalism, Literature, and World War II," *Minnesota Review* 3, no. 2 (Winter 1963):179–91.

473   Hebrew University, Jerusalem. *Symposium on War Crimes, Crimes against Humanity, and Statutory Limitations, Jerusalem, May 28, 1968.* Publication of the Institute of Criminology no. 15. Jerusalem: Hebrew University, 1968.

474   Herzog, Jacques-Bernard. "Contribution à l'étude de la définition du crime contre l'humanité," *Revue Internationale de Droit Pénal* 18 (1947):155–70.

475   _____. "Les Principes juridiques de la répression des crimes de guerre," *Schweizerische Zeitschrift für Strafrecht* 61(1946):277–304.

476   Instituto Hispano-Luso-Americano-Filipino Penal y Penitenciario. *Delincuencia politica internacional (aula penal): Conferencias Pronunciadas en Madrid los dias 7, 8 y 10 de octubre de 1952. . . .* Madrid: Ediciones Cultura Hispanica, 1953.

477 Jackson, Robert H., et al. "The Legal Basis for the Trial of War Criminals—A Symposium," *Temple Law Quarterly* 19 (January 1946): 133–235.

478 Jacomet, Robert. *Les lois de la guerre continentale.* Paris: L. Fournier, 1913.

479 Jager, Herbert. *Verbrechen unter totalitärer Herrschaft.* Olten, 1967.

480 Jaszai, D. "On the Proscription of War Crimes and of Certain Punishments Inflicted for Them," *Hungarian Law Review* 5 (January-June 1965):5–11.

481 Johanny, Karl. *Der Tatbestand des Kriegsverbrechens und moderner Kleinkreig unter Berücksichtigung der Legitimität seiner Teilnehmer.* Würzburg, 1966.

482 Keegan, John. *The Face of Battle.* New York: Random House, 1976.

483 Kelson, Hans. *Peace through Law.* Chapel Hill: University of North Carolina Press, 1944.

484 Kuhn, Arthur K. "International Criminal Jurisdiction," *American Journal of International Law* 41 (April 1947):420–33.

485 ———. "International Law and National Legislation in the Trial of War Criminals—The Yamashita Cases," *American Journal of International Law* 44 (July 1950):559–62.

486 Lakshmanan, R. "Convention on the Non-Applicability of Statutory Limitations to War Crimes and Crimes against Humanity: A Critique," *Indian Journal of International Law* 9 (April 1969):22–230.

487 Leur, Salvatore S. I. *Crimini di guerra e delitti contro l'umanità.* Rome: Edizioni La Civita Cattolica, 1948.

488 Levasseur, G. "Les crimes contre l'humanité et le problème de leur prescription," *Journal de Droit International* 93 (April-May-June 1966): 259–84.

489 Leyrat, P. de. "Crime de la guerre et crimes de guerre," *Cahiers du Monde Nouveau* 2 (1945):557–606.

490 Lütem, Ilham. "Some Controversial Aspects of War Crimes," *Annals de la Faculté de Droit d'Istanbul* 2 (1952–1953):146–69.

491 McKinnon, Harold R. "Natural Law and Positive Law," *Notre Dame Lawyer* 23 (January 1948):125–39.

492 Mangoldt, Hermann von. "Das Kriegsverbrechen und seine Verfolgung in Vergangenheit und Gegenwart: Eine völkerrechtliche Studie," *Jahrbuch für Internationales und Ausländisches Öffentliches Recht* 1 (1948):283–334.

493 Marina, F. A. "La punizione dei crimini di guerra come reati internazionali da parte delle Potenze alleate," *La Giustizia Penale* 52, pt. 1 (1947):91–95.

494 Miller, Robert H. "The Convention of the Non-Applicability of Statutory Limitations to War Crimes and Crimes against Humanity," *American Journal of International Law* 65 (July 1971):476–501.

495 Mittermaier, Wolfgang. "Das Verbrechen gegen die Menschlichkeit," *Schweizerische Juristen-Zeitung* 45 (July 15, 1949):213–18.

496 Morton, Louis. "From Fort Sumter to Poland: The Question of War Guilt," *World Politics* 14 (January 1962):386–92.

497 Mouton, Martinus Willem. *Oorlogsmisdrijven en het internationale recht.* The Hague: A. A. M. Stols, 1947.

498 Pal, Radhabinod. *Crimes in International Relations.* Calcutta: University of Calcutta, 1955.

499 Paoli, Jules. "Contribution à l'etude des crimes de guerre et des crimes contre l'humanité en droit pénal international," *Revue générale de Droit International Public* 49 (1941–1945):129–65.

500 Parsons, George R., Jr. "International Law: Jurisdiction over Extraterritorial Crime: Universality Principle: War Crimes: Crimes against Humanity: Piracy: Israel's Nazi and Nazi Collaborators (Punishment) Law," *Cornell Law Quarterly* 46 (Winter 1961):326–36.

501 Pella, Vespasian V. *La Guerre-crime et les criminels de guerre, réflexions sur la justice pénale internationale.* Paris: Éditions A. Pedone, 1946.

502 Pius XII, Pope. "International Code for the Punishment of War Crimes," *St. John's Law Review* 28 (December 1953):1–18.

503 Quintano Ripollés, Antonio. "Problemática de jurisdicción en la repression de la criminalidad contra la humanidad," *Revista de Derecho Internacional* 54 (September 1948):17–40.

504 Radbruch, G. "Zur Diskussion über das Verbrechen gegen die Menschlichkeit," *Süddeutsch Juristenzeitung* 2 (1947):131–36.

505 Radin, Max. "International Crimes," *Iowa Law Review* 32 (November 1946):33–50.

506   Reik, Otto E. "War Crimes–A Refutation of Objection," *Kentucky Law Journal* 39 (March 1951):317–26.

507   Róheim, Géza. *War, Crime and the Covenant.* Monticello, N.Y.: Medical Journal Press, 1945.

508   Sandmel, Samuel. "Mass Crime and the Judeo-Christian Tradition II," *Minnesota Review* 3, no. 2 (Winter 1963): 220–27.

509   Sarker, L. "The Proper Law of Crime in International Law," *International and Comparative Law Quarterly* 11 (April 1962):446–70.

510   Schaefer, Marx. *Crimes against Peace.* Ambilly: Les Presses Savoie, 1952.

511   Schick, Franz B. "Crimes against Peace," *Journal of Criminal Law and Criminology* 38 (January-February 1948):445–65.

512   Schwelb, Egon. "Crimes against Humanity," *British Yearbook of International Law* 23 (1946):178–228.

513   Sibley, Mulford G. "War Crimes, Morals, and Civilization," *Minnesota Review* 3, no. 2 (Winter 1963):142–53.

514   Sobotker, H. Rodríguez von. "El castigo de los criminales de guerra," *Revista de Derecho Internacional* 52 (September 1947):23–46.

515   Sontag, E. "Das Verbrechen gegen die Menschlichkeit," *Schweizerische Zeitschrift für Strafrecht* 64 (1949):201–09.

516   Sottile, Antoine. "Les criminels de guerre, et le nouveau droit pénal international, le seul moyen pour assurer la paix du monde," *Revue de Droit International, de Sciences Diplomatiques et Politiques* 23 (October-December 1945):228–50.

517   _____. "La prescription des crimes des guerre contre l'humanité et le droit pénal international," *Revue de Droit International, de Sciences Diplomatiques et Politiques* 43 (January-March 1965):5–18.

518   Speyer, P. "Les crimes de guerre par omission," *Revue de Droit Pénal et de Criminologie* 30 (1949–1950):903–43.

519   "Symposium: War Crimes Trials; The Nuremberg Trials; Eichmann—International Law?; The War Crimes Trial—A Second Look," *University of Pittsburgh Law Review* 24 (October 1962):73ff.

520   Szilard, L. "My Trial as a War Criminal," *University of Chicago Law Review* 17 (Autumn 1949):79–86.

521   Taft, Donald R. "Punishment of War Criminals," *American Sociological Review* 11 (August 1946):439–44.

522   Tesar, Ottokar. "Die naturrechtlichen Grundlagen der 'Crimes against Humanity,'" in *Gegenwartsprobleme des internationalen Rechts und der Rechtsphilosophie: Festschrift für Rudolf Lann,* edited by D. S. Constantopoulos and Hans Wehberg. Hamburg: Girardet, 1953, pp. 423–46.

523   Truyol y Serra, Antonio. "Crímenes de guerra y derecho natural," *Revista Española de Derecho Internacional* 1 (1948):45–73.

524   Vasalli, G. "Altri grandi processi contro i criminali di guerra," *La Giustizia Penale* 53, pt. 1 (1948):313.

525   _____. "Intorno al fondamento giurdico della punizione dei crimini di guerra," *La Giustizia Penale* 52, pt. 2 (1947):618–26.

526   Veale, Frederick J. P. *Advance to Barbarism: The Development of Total Warfare from Sarajevo to Hiroshima.* London: Mitre Press, 1968.

527   _____. *War Crimes Discreetly Veiled.* New York: Devin-Adair, 1959.

528   Vedovato, Giuseppe. *Diritto internazionale bellico.* Firenze: E. C. Sansoni, 1946.

529   Weber, Wilhelm von. "Internationale Strafgerichtsbarkeit," *Völkerrechtsfragen* 40 (1934):120–36.

530   Wright, Lord. "War Crimes under International Law," *Law Quarterly Review* 62 (January 1946):40–52.

531   Zander, Jens-Peter. *Das Verbrechen im Kriege, ein Völkerrechtlicher Begriff: Ein Beitrag zur Problematik des Kriegsverbrechens.* Würzburg, 1969.

III. Historical Works

Pre-1914

ANCIENT

532 Adcock, Sir F. E. *The Greek and Macedonian Art of War.* Berkeley: University of California Press, 1957.

533 Anderson, J. K. *Military Theory and Practice in the Age of Xenophan.* Berkeley: University of California Press, 1970.

534 Armout, W. S. "Customs of Warfare in Ancient India," *Transactions of the Grotius Society* 8 (1922):71–88.

535 Kautilya. *Kautilya's Arthaśāstra.* Translated by R. Shamasastry. 3d ed. Mysore: Wesleyan Mission Press, 1929.

536 Martin, W. A. P. "Traces of International Law in Ancient China," *International Review* 14 (January 1883):74ff.

537 Pritchett, W. Kendrick. *Ancient Greek Military Practices.* Berkeley: University of California Press, 1971, pt. 1.

538 Reut-Nicolussi, Eduard. "Kriegsverbrechen im Peloponnesischen Krieg," *Österreichische Zeitschrift für Öffentliches Recht* 6 (March 1955): 490–500.

539 Thucydides. *History of the Peloponnesian War.* Translated with an introduction by Rex Warner. Baltimore: Penguin, 1954.

EARLY MODERN EUROPE

General

540 Beeler, John. *Warfare in Feudal Europe, 730–1200.* Ithaca: Cornell University Press, 1971.

541 Oman, Charles. *A History of the Art of War in the Middle Ages.* 2 vols. 2d ed. London: Methuen, 1924.

Trial of Peter von Hagenbach, Breisach, 1474

542 Brauer-Gramm, Hildburg. *Der Landvogt Peter von Hagenbach: Die burgundische Herrschaft am Oberrhein, 1469–74.* Göttingen: Musterschmidt-Verlag, 1957.

543   Heimpel, Hermann. "Peter von Hagenbach und die Herrschaft Burgunds am Oberrheim, 1469–74," *Jahrbuch der Stadt Freiburg im Breisgau* 5 (1942):139–54.

544   _____. "Das Verfahren gegen Peter von Hagenbach zu Breisach, 1474," *Zeitschrift für die Geschichte des Oberrheims* 55 (1942):321–57.

545   Nerlinger, Charles. *Pierre de Hagenbach et la domination bourguignonneen Alsace, 1469–74.* Nancy: Imprimeri de Berger-Leverault, 1890.

546   Schwarzenberger, Georg. "The Breisach War Crime Trial of 1474," *Manchester Guardian,* September 28, 1946.

547   Vaughn, Richard. *Charles the Bold: The Last of the Valois.* New York: Barnes and Noble, 1973.

NAPOLEONIC WARS

548   Bellot, H. Hale. "The Detention of Napoleon Bonaparte," *Law Quarterly Review* 39 (1923):170

549   Nicholson, Harold B. *The Congress of Vienna: A Study in Allied Unity (1812–1822).* New York: Harcourt, Brace, 1946.

550   Stewart, John Hall. "The Imprisonment of Napoleon: A Legal Opinion by Lord Elton," *American Journal of International Law* 45 (July 1951):571–77.

UNITED STATES CIVIL WAR, 1861–1865.

General

551   Arens, Richard. "Vicarious Punishment and War Crimes Prosecution: The Civil War of Alice through the Looking Glass," *Washington University Law Quarterly* 1951 (February 1951):66–70.

552   Halleck, Henry Wager. "Military Tribunals and Their Jurisdiction: Historical Development of the Military Court—Conditions that Confronted the North during Our Civil War," *American Journal of International Law* 5 (October 1911):958–67.

553   Hessetine, William Best. *Civil War Prisons: A Study in War Psychology.* New York: Frederick Unger, 1964.

554   Russ, William A., Jr. "Administrative Activities of the Union Army during the Civil War and after the Civil War," *Mississippi Law Journal* 17 (May 1945):71–89.

555   Strode, Hudson. *Jefferson Davis: Tragic Hero, the Last Twenty-Five Years, 1864–1889.* New York: Harcourt, Brace and World, 1964.

Role of Francis Lieber

556 Baxter, R. R. "Le premier effort moderne de codification du droit de la guerre: François Lieber et l'ordonnance générale No. 100," *Revue Internationale de la Croix-Rouge* 45 (1963):155–76, 217–36.

557 Childress, James F. "Francis Lieber's Interpretation of the Laws of War: General Orders No. 100 in the Context of His Life and Thought," *American Journal of Jurisprudence* 21 (1976):34–70.

558 Coursier, Henri. "Francis Lieber and the Laws of War," *Revue Internationale de la Croix-Rouge* [English supplement, Geneva] 6 (September 1953):156–169.

559 Davis, George B. "Dr. Francis Lieber's Instructions for the Government of Armies in the Field," *American Journal of International Law* 1 (January 1907):13–25.

560 Dyer, Brainard. "Francis Lieber and the American Civil War," *Huntington Library Quarterly* 2 (1939):449–65.

560a Friedel, Frank B. *Francis Lieber: Nineteenth-Century Liberal.* Baton Rouge: Louisiana State University Press, 1948.

561 Gilman, Daniel, ed. *The Miscellaneous Writings of Francis Lieber.* 2 vols. Philadelphia: Lippincott, 1881.

562 Harley, Lewis R. *Francis Lieber: His Life and Political Philosophy.* New York: Columbia University Press, 1899.

563 Holls, Frederick William. *Franz Lieber: Sein Leben und seine Werke.* New York: E. Steiger, 1884.

564 Lieber, Francis. *His Miscellaneous Writings.* 2 vols. Philadelphia: Lippincott, 1880.

565 Nys, Ernest. "Francis Lieber: His Life and Work," *American Journal of International Law* 5 (1911):84–117.

566 Perry, Thomas S. *Life and Letters of Francis Lieber.* Boston: James R. Osgood, 1882.

567 Root, Elihu. "Francis Lieber," *American Journal of International Law* 7 (July 1913):453–69.

568 Shepard, William S. "One Hundredth Anniversary of the Lieber Code," *Military Law Review* 27 (July 1963):157–62.

Andersonville Trial, 1865

569 Chipman, Norton Parker. *The Tragedy of Andersonville: Trial of Captain Henry Wirtz, the Prison Keeper.* San Francisco: Bancroft, 1911.

570   Futch, Ovid L. *History of Andersonville Prison*. Gainsville: University of Florida Press, 1968.

571   Laska, Lewis L., and James M. Smith. "'Hell and the Devil': Andersonville and the Trial of Henry Wirtz, C.S.A., 1865," *Military Law Review* 68 (Spring 1975):77–132.

572   Morsberger, Robert E., and Katherine M. Morsberger. "After Andersonville: The First War Crimes Trial," *Civil War Times Illustrated* 13, no. 4 (1974):30–41.

573   United States, Congress, House of Representatives. *Trial of Henry Wirtz*. 40th Cong., 2d sess. House Executive Doc. 23. Washington, D.C.: GPO, 1868.

PHILIPPINE INSURRECTION, 1899–1901

Documents

574   United States, Congress, Senate. *Affairs in the Philippine Islands*. 57th Cong., 1st sess. Senate Doc. 331. Washington, D.C.: GPO, 1903.

575   _____. *Charges of Cruelty, etc., to the Natives of the Philippines*. 57th Cong., 1st sess. Senate Doc. 205, pt. 1. Washington, D.C.: GPO, 1902.

576   _____. *Trials of Court-Martial in the Philippine Islands in Consequence of Certain Instructions*. 57th Cong., 2d sess. Senate Doc. 213. Washington, D.C.: GPO, 1903.

General

577   Miller, Stuart C. "Our Mylai of 1900: Americans in the Philippine Insurrection," *Trans-Action* 7 (September 1970):19–28.

578   Pomeroy, William J. "'Pacification' in the Philippines, 1898–1913," *France-Asie* 21 (1967):427–46.

579   Schirmer, D. B. "Mylai Was Not the First Time," *New Republic* 164 (April 24, 1971):18–21.

580   Welch, Richard E., Jr. "American Atrocities in the Philippines: The Indictment and the Response," *Pacific Historical Review* 43 (May 1974): 233–53.

World War I, 1914–1918

DOCUMENTS

581   Belgium, Commission d'enquête sur la violation des régles du droit des gens, des lois et des coutumes de la guerre. *Les Atrocités allemandes en Belgique*. Paris, 1914.

582 Bulgaria. *Atrocités grecques en Macedoine pendant de guerre grecobulgare.* Sofia: Imprimerie d'état, 1913.

583 Carnegie Endowment for International Peace, Division of International Law. *Violation of the Laws and Customs of War: Reports of the Majority and Dissenting Reports of American and Japanese Members of the Commission of Responsibilities, Conference of Paris, 1919.* Pamphlet 32. Oxford: Clarendon Press, 1919.

584 France, Foreign Office. *Rapports et procès-verbaux d'enquête de la commission instituée en vue de constater les actes commis par l'ennemi en violation du droit des gens (décret du 23 septembre 1914).* 9 vols. Paris, 1915.

585 Germany, Auswärtiges Amt. *Deutschland Schuldig?* Berlin: Carl Heymanns Verlag, 1919.

586 _____. *German White Book Concerning the Responsibility of the Authors of the War.* Translated by the Carnegie Endowment for International Peace. New York: Oxford University Press, 1924.

587 _____. *Official German Documents Relating to the World War.* Translated by the Carnegie Endowment for International Peace. 2 vols. New York: Carnegie Endowment for International Peace, 1923.

588 Great Britain, Foreign Office. *Evidence and Documents Laid before the Committee on Alleged German Atrocities, Presided over by the Right Honourable Viscount Bryce.* London: HMSO, 1915.

589 *Responsibility for the World War.* Miscellaneous Reading List, no. 25. Washington, D.C.: Carnegie Endowment for International Peace, 1925.

GENERAL

590 Bellot, H. H. L. "War Crimes, Their Prevention and Punishment," *Transactions of the Grotius Society* 2 (1916–1919):31–35.

591 _____. "War Crimes and War Criminals," *Canadian Law Times* 36 (1916):754.

592 _____. "War Crimes and War Criminals," *Canadian Law Times* 37 (1917):9.

593 Colby, Elbridge. "War Crimes," *Michigan Law Review* 23 (1925): 482ff.

594 _____. "War Crimes and Their Punishment," *Minnesota Law Review* 8 (1924):40–58.

595   Exner, F. *Krieg und Kriminalität in Österreich.* Vienna: Holder-Pichler, Tempsky, 1927.

596   Finch, George A. "Jurisdiction of Local Courts to Try Enemy Persons for War Crimes," *American Journal of International Law* 14 (1920):218–23.

597   Garner, James W. *International Law and the World War.* 2 vols. London: Longmans, Green, 1920.

598   Gibbs, P. "War Crimes: The Average Point of View," *Living Age* 304 (March 20, 1920):710–11.

599   Harrison, A. "Punishment of War Guilt," *English Review* 30 (1920): 163–69.

600   Mackay, D. "British War Tribunals," *Central Law Journal* 83 (1916): 422.

601   Merignhac, Alexandre G. J. A. "La responsabilité pénale des actes criminels commis au cours de la guerre 1914–1918," *Revue de Droit International et de Législation Comparée* 1 (1920):34–70.

602   _____. "De la sanction des infractions au droit de gens," *Revue Générale de Droit International Public* 24 (1917):1–5, 55–62.

603   Meurer, Christian. *Völkerrecht im Weltkrieg.* 3 vols. Berlin, 1927.

604   Phillipson, Coleman. *International Law and the Great War.* London: T. Fisher Unwin, 1915.

605   Puttkamer, Ellinor von. "Die Haftung der politischen und militärischen Führung des ersten Weltkriegs für Kriegsurheberschaft und Kriegsverbrechen," *Archiv des Völkerrechts* 1 (May 1949):424–49.

606   Renault, Louis. "De l'application du droit penal aux faits de guerre," *Revue Générale de Droit International Public* 25 (1918):5–29.

607   Roxburgh, Ronald F. "The Sanction of International Law," *American Journal of International Law* 14 (1920):26–37.

608   Schulz, Erich. *Die Kriegsverbrechen: Eine International-strafrechtliche Studie über die Strafauspruchs- und Rechtswidrigkeitslehre, unter Berücksichtigung der Schuld- und Irrtumslehre.* Berlin-Hohenschönhausen: Druck Lokalbiattverlag, 1928.

609   Strisower, Leo. *Der Krieg und die Völkesrechtsordnung.* Vienna: Manz, 1919.

610   Verdross, Alfred. "Kriegsverbrechen und Kriegsverbrecher," *Worterbuch* 1 (1924):775–89.

611 _____ *Die völkerrechtswidrige Kriegshandlung und der Strafanspruch der Staaten.* Berlin: Engelmann, 1920.

GERMAN WAR CRIMES AND WAR CRIMES TRIALS

612 "Aiding War-Criminals to Escape," *Literary Digest* 64 (March 27, 1920):30–31.

613 "Basis of the Extradition Demand," *Current History Magazine of the New York Times* 11, pt. 2 (March 1920):380–84.

614 Bevan, E. R. "Demand for the German War Criminals," *Contemporary Review* 117 (March 1920):305–16.

615 Bissing, Friedrich Wilhelm Freiherr von. *La Terreur en Belgique et dans la Prusse orientale.* Monaco: Imprimeries artistiques réunies, 1915.

616 Carsten, Francis L. "The British Summary Court at Wiesbaden, 1926–1929," *Modern Law Review* 7 (November 1944):215–20.

617 Dumas, Jacques. *Les Sanctions pénales des crimes allemands.* Paris: Rousseau, 1916.

618 Fenwick, Charles G. "Germany and the Crimes of World War," *American Journal of International Law* 23 (October 1929):812–15.

619 Gallinger, August. *The Counterbalance: The Matter of War Criminals from the German Side.* Munich: Süddeutsche Monatshefte, 1922.

620 Garner, James W. "Punishment of Offenders against the Laws and Customs of War," *American Journal of International Law* 14 (1920): 70–94.

621 "German Criminals," *Independent and Weekly Review* 101 (February 21, 1920):286–88.

622 "Germany's Elusive War-Criminals," *Literary Digest* 64 (February 21, 1920):16–17.

623 Harrison, A., and L. Dumont-Wilden. "Punishing the War Criminals," *Living Age* 304 (March 27, 1920):751–62.

624 Hillis, Newell D. *German Atrocities, Their Nature and Philosophy: Studies in Belgium and France during August and July of 1917.* New York: Fleming H. Revell, 1918.

625 Lavisse, Ernest, and Charles Andler. *German Theory and Practice of War.* Translated by L. S. Paris: A. Colin, 1917.

626 Lersner, Kurt Freiherr von. "Die Auslieferung der Deutschen 'Kriegsverbrecher,'" in *Zehn Jahre Versailles,* edited by Heinrich Schnee and Hans Draeger. 3 vols. Berlin: Brückenverlag, 1929–1930, I:545–619.

627   Michelon, Claude. *"Made in Germany": A Compilation of German Atrocities Taken from Official Documents.* Translated by Dora Bosart. Indianapolis: Bobbs-Merrill, 1918.

628   Picton, Harold. *The Better Germany in Wartime.* Manchester, Eng.: National Labour Press, 1918.

629   "Prosecution of German War Criminals," *Contemporary Review* 117 (March 1920):429.

630   "Punishing War Criminals," *Current History Magazine of the New York Times* 11, pt. 2 (March 1920):373-80.

631   Schöller, Peter. *Der Fall Löwen und das Weissbuch: Eine kritische Untersuchung der deutschen Dokumentation über die Vorgänge in Löwen vom 25. bis 28. August 1914.* Cologne: Böhlau, 1958.

632   Scott, James Brown. "The Execution of Captain Fryatt," *American Journal of International Law* 10 (October 1916):865-77.

633   Starr, Merritt. "German Submarine Warfare Violates the Principles of International Law and Treaties Existing between Germany and the United States," *Chicago Legal News* 51 (1918):138.

634   Stülpnagel, Otto von. *Die Wahrheit über die deutschen Kriegsverbrechen.* Berlin: Staatspolitischer Verlag, 1922.

635   Toynbee, Arnold J. *The German Terror in Belgium: An Historical Record.* New York: Doran, 1917.

636   Wolff, T. "War Criminals," *Nation* 26 (1920):799-800.

Leipzig Trials

/ Documents /

637   Great Britain, Foreign Office. *Report of the Proceedings before the Supreme Court in Leipzig.* Cmd. 1450. London: HMSO, 1921.

/ General /

638   "Acquittals That Convict Germany," *Literary Digest* 70 (July 23, 1921):11.

639   Bailey, Gordon Wallace. "Dry Run for the Hangman: The Versailles-Leipzig Fiasco, 1919-1921, Feeble Foreshadow of Nuremberg." Ph.D. dissertation, University of Maryland, 1971.

640   Battle, George Gordon. "Trials before the Leipsic [sic] Supreme Court of Germans Accused of War Crimes," *Virginia Law Review* 8 (1921): 1-26.

641   Breitscheid, R. "Punishment of the War Criminals," *Nation* 113 (October 12, 1921):397.

642 Cluent, Eduard. "Les criminels de guerre devant le Reichsgericht à Leipzig," *Journal de Droit International, de Sciences Diplomatiques et Politiques* 48 (1921):435–41.

643 "German Justice," *Literary Digest* 69 (June 25, 1921):10.

644 "Germany to Try Her Own War-Criminals," *Literary Digest* 64 (February 28, 1920):19.

645 "How Two U-Boat Criminals Were Convicted," *Current History Magazine of the New York Times* 14 (September 1921):948–51.

646 "Leipzig Trials," *Living Age* 310 (July 23, 1921): 241–43.

647 Michelson, Andreas, ed. *Das Urteil im Leipziger U–Boots-Prozess: Ein Fehlspruch? Juristische und militärische Gutachten.* Berlin: Staatspolitischer Verlag, 1922.

648 Mullins, Claude. *The Leipzig Trials: An Account of the War Criminals' Trials and A Study of German Mentality.* London: H. F. and G. Witherby, 1921.

649 ———. "War Criminals' Trials," *Fortnightly Review* 116 (September 1921):417–30.

650 "The Treatment of War Crimes and Crimes Incidental to the War: The Experience of 1918–1922," *Bulletin of International News* 22 (1945): 95–108.

651 "Trial of German Officers," *Independent and Weekly Review* 101 (February 14, 1920):252–53.

652 Wendel, H. "National Martyrs and Matters of Opinion," *Living Age* 311 (October 1, 1921):35–37.

653 Willis, James F. "Prologue to Nuremberg: The Punishment of War Criminals of the First World War." Ph.D. dissertation, Duke University, 1976.

Role of Wilhelm II

654 Balfour, Michael L. G. *The Kaiser and His Times.* Boston: Houghton Mifflin, 1964.

655 Bidou, Henri. "Les mémoires de Guillaume II," *Revue de Paris* 29 (1922):880–85.

656 Eyck, Erich. *Das persönliche Regiment Wilhelms II.* Zurich: Eugen Reutsch Verlag, 1948.

657 France, Ministere de la Guerre. *Examen de la responsabilité pénale de l'Empereur Guillaume II.* Paris, 1918.

658   Frank, R., and F. Fachfahl. *Kann Kaiser Wilhelm II ausgeliefert werden? Zwei Gutachten.* Berlin, 1919.

659   "Germany Debates Trying the Kaiser," *Living Age* 304 (March 13, 1920):626-35.

660   Hanotoux, Gabriel. "Les responsabilités de Guillaume II," *Revue de Paris* 29 (1922):485-90.

661   Larnande, Fernand, and A. De Lapradelle. "Examen de la responsabilité pénale de l'empereur Guillaume II d'Allemagne," *Journal de Droit International, de Sciences Diplomatiques et Politiques* 46 (1919):131-61.

662   Ludwig, Emil. *Wilhelm Hohenzollern: The Last of the Kaisers.* Translated by Ethel Colburn Mayne. New York: Blue Ribbon Books, 1932.

663   Muret, M. "Guillaume II dans le rôle d'Hamlet," *Revue de Paris* 28 (1921):742-55.

664   Piggott, F. T. "Ex-Kaiser and His Officers," *Nineteenth Century* 87 (March 1920):537-54.

665   Viereck, George S. *The Kaiser on Trial.* New York: Greystone Press, 1937.

666   Wilhelm II. *The Kaiser's Memoirs.* Translated and edited by Thomas R. Ybarra. New York: Harper and Bros., 1922.

667   Wright, Quincy. "The Legal Liability of the Kaiser," *American Political Science Review* 13 (1919):120-28.

ROLE OF PROPAGANDA

668   Bruntz, G. B. *Allied Propaganda and the Collapse of the German Empire, 1918.* Stanford: Stanford University Press, 1938.

669   Lasswell, Harold. *Propaganda Technique in the World War.* New York: Peter Smith, 1938.

670   Ponsonby, Arthur (Lord Ponsonby of Schulbrede). *Falsehood in War-Time.* London: George Allen and Unwin, 1942.

671   Read, James Morgan. *Atrocity Propoganda, 1914-1919.* New Haven: Yale University Press, 1941.

672   Squires, James D. *British Propoganda at Home and in the United States from 1914-1917.* Cambridge: Harvard University Press, 1935.

673   Thimme, Hans. *Weltkrieg ohne Waffen: Die Propaganda der Westmächte gegen Deutschland.* Stuttgart: J. B. Gotta'sche, 1932.

673a Viereck, George S. *Spreading Germs of Hate.* New York: Liveright, 1930.

World War II

WARTIME DIALOGUE REGARDING WAR CRIMES TRIALS: OFFICIAL AND UNOFFICIAL

General

674 American Historical Association. *What Shall Be Done with War Criminals.* GI Roundtable, EM11. Washington, D.C.: War Department, 1944.

675 Anderson, A. Arnold. "The Utility of the Proposed Trial and Punishment of Enemy Leaders," *American Political Science Review* 3 (December 1943):1081–1100.

676 Baer, Marcel de. "No Peace for War Criminals," *News from Belgium and the Belgian Congo* 4 (1944):53–56.

677 ———. "The Punishment of War Criminals," *Belgium* 3 (1942): 332–37.

678 ———. "The Treatment of War Criminals: A Lesson from the Past," *Message, Belgian Review* 13 (1942):18–22.

679 ———. "The Treatment of War Criminals: Suggestions for the Future," *Message, Belgian Review* 14 (1942):10–13.

680 Barry, John V. "The Trial and Punishment of Axis War Criminals," *Australian Law Journal* 17 (June 1943):43–49.

681 Bauer, F. *Krigsförbrytarna inför domstol.* Stockholm: Natur och Kultur, 1944.

682 Bial, Louis C. *Vergeltung und Wiedergutmachung in Deutschland: Ein Beitrag zu den Fragen der Bestrafung der Naziverbrecher und der Wiedereinsetzung der Naziopfer in ihre Rechte.* Havana: Editorial Lex, 1945.

683 Bisschop. W. R. *Criminality of War and Its Prevention.* London: Stevens, 1943.

684 Cohn, Sir Ernst J. "The Problem of War Crimes To-day," *Transactions of the Grotius Society* 26 (1940):125–51.

685 Cowles, Willard B. "Trial of War Criminals by Military Tribunals," *American Bar Association Journal* 30 (June 1944):330–33, 362.

686 _____. "Universality of Jurisdiction over War Crimes," *California Law Review* 33 (June 1945):177–218.

687 Creel, George. *War Criminals and Punishment*. New York: Robert M. McBride, 1944.

688 Desmond, Charles S. "Prosecution of Axis Crimes," *New York State Bar Association Bulletin* 67 (1944):362–67.

689 Ewing, Alfred C. "The Ethics of Punishing Germany," *Hibbert Journal* 43 (1945):99–106.

690 Finch, George A. "Retribution for War Crimes," *American Journal of International Law* 37 (January 1943):81–88.

691 Fox, John P. "The Jewish Factor in British Crimes Policy in 1942," *English Historical Review* 92 (January 1977):82–106.

692 Friedmann, W. "International Law and the Present War," *Transactions of the Grotius Society* 26 (1940):221–33.

693 Gault, P. F. "Prosecution of War Criminals," *Journal of Criminal Law and Criminology* 36 (September-October 1945):180–83.

694 Glueck, Sheldon. "Bringing the Nazis to Book," *Saturday Review of Literature* 27 (1944):9–10.

695 _____. "By What Tribunal Shall War Offenders Be Tried?" *Harvard Law Review* 56 (1943):1059–89.

696 _____. "By What Tribunal Shall War Criminals Be Tried?" *Nebraska Law Review* 24 (June 1945):143–81.

697 _____. "Justice for War Criminals," *American Mercury* 60 (March 1945):274–80.

698 _____. "Punishing War Criminals," *New Republic* 109 (1944):706–09; 110 (1944):243–44.

699 _____. "Trial and Punishment of the Axis War Criminals," *Free World* 4 (November 1942):138–46.

700 _____. *War Criminals: Their Prosecution and Punishment*. New York: Knopf, 1944.

701 _____. "War Criminals—Their Prosecution and Punishment: The Record of History," *Lawyers Guild Review* 5 (January-February 1945):1–10.

702 _____. *What Shall Be Done with War Criminals?* Washington, D.C.: GPO, 1944.

703 Goodhart, Arthur L. *What Acts of War Are Justifiable?* Oxford: Clarendon Press, 1940.

704 Gros, André. "Le Châtiment des crimes de guerre," *Cahiers Politiques* 9 (April 1945):49–58.

705 High, Stanley, et al. "Should the German People Be Held Responsible for the Crimes of Their Nazi Leaders?" *Town Meeting* 11, no. 7 (June 14, 1945):3–21.

706 Hoover, Glenn E. "The Outlook for 'War Guilt' Trials," *Political Science Quarterly* 59 (March 1944):40–48.

707 Howard, J. Woodford. *Mr. Justice Murphy: A Political Biography.* Princeton: Princeton University Press, 1968.

708 Hull, Cordell. *The Memoirs of Cordell Hull.* 2 vols. New York: Macmillan, 1948.

709 Inter-American Juridical Committee. *International Juridical Status of Individuals as "War Criminals."* Rio de Janeiro: Inter-American Juridical Committee, 1945.

710 International Committee for Penal Reconstruction and Development. *Report on Rules and Procedure Relating to Punishment of War Crimes Committed in the Course of and Incidental to the Present War.* London: Cambridge University Press, 1943.

711 Jackson, Robert H. "Atrocities and War Crimes: Report to the President," *Department of State Bulletin* 12 (1945):1071–78.

712 _____. "The Challenge of International Lawlessness," *International Conciliation* 374 (November 1941):683–91.

713 _____. "The Rule of Law among Nations," *American Bar Association Journal* 31 (June 1945):290.

714 _____. "War Criminals and International Law: Judicial Proceedings Must Not Be Tied to Predetermined Policy," *Saturday Review of Literature* 28 (June 2, 1945):7–8.

715 Jerome, V. J. "What of the War Criminals?" *Political Affairs* 24 (February 1945):103–44.

716 Lachs, Manfred. *War Crimes: An Attempt to Define the Issues.* London: Stevens, 1945.

717 _____. *"War Crimes-Political Offenses,"* *Juridical Review* 56 (April 1944):27–41.

718   Lauterpacht, Sir Hersh. "The Law of Nations and the Punishment of War Crimes," *British Yearbook of International Law* 21 (1944):58–95.

719   Leahy, William D. *I Was There: The Personal Story of the Chief of Staff to Presidents Roosevelt and Truman Based on His Notes and Diaries.* New York: McGraw-Hill, 1950.

720   Lessner, Ervin, et al. "Should All Germans Be Punished for Nazi Crimes and Atrocities?" *Town Meeting* 10, no. 35 (December 28, 1944): 3–22.

721   Mangoldt, Hermann von. "Das Kriegsverbrechen und seine Verfolgung in Vergangenheit und Gegenwart: Eine völkerrechtliche Studie," *Jahrbuch für Internationales und Ausländisches Öffentliches Recht* 1 (1948):283–334.

722   Manner, George. "The Legal Nature and Punishment of Criminal Acts of Violence Contrary to the Laws of War," *American Journal of International Law* 37 (July 1943):407–35.

723   Moltmann, Günther. *Amerikas Deutschlandpolitik im zweiten Weltkrieg.* Heidelberg: Winter, 1958.

724   _____. "Der Morgenthau Plan als historisches Problem," *Wehrwissenschaftliche Rundschau* 5 (January 1955):15–32.

725   Morgenthau, Henry, Jr. *Germany Is Our Problem.* New York: Harper and Bros., 1945.

726   Morse, Arthur D. *While Six Million Died: A Chronicle of American Apathy.* New York: Random House, 1967.

727   Munro, Hector A. "Plans for the Trial of War Criminals," *Law Journal* 95 (January 6, 1945):5–7.

728   _____. "Trial of Axis War Criminals: The Question of Procedure," *Fortnightly Law Journal* 13 (November 15, 1943):119–22.

729   _____. "The United States and War Criminals," *Law Journal* 95 (1945):231–33.

730   _____. "War Criminals and International Justice," *Law Journal* 95 (June 2, 1945):173–74.

731   National Lawyers Guild (Executive Board). "The Punishment of War Criminals," *Lawyers Guild Review* 4 (November-December 1944): 18–23.

732   "Navy Department Participation in the Prosecution of War Criminals," *Journal of Criminal Law and Criminology* 36 (May-June 1945):39–40.

733 Pella, Vesparian V. "La Justice pénale internationale: Le qu'elle devrait etre (La question des criminels de guerre)," *Revue de Droit International (Sottile-Geneva)* 23 (July-September 1945):85–139.

734 Poljanskij, N. N. (Polyansky). *Mezdunarodnoe pravosudie i prestupniki vojny.* Moscow: Izd-vo Akademii nauk SSSR, 1945.

735 Pritt, D. N. "Trial of War Criminals," *Political Quarterly* 16 (1945): 195–204.

736 _____. "War Criminals," *Labour Monthly* 26 (1944):332–38.

737 "The Punishment of War Criminals" [by National Lawyers Guild], *Lawyers Guild Review* 4 (November-December 1944):18–23. [See entry no. 731.]

738 Radin, Max. "War Crimes and Crimes of War," *Virginia Quarterly Review* 21 (Summer 1945):497–516.

739 Rosenman, Samuel, ed. *The Public Papers and Addresses of Franklin Delano Roosevelt, 1941–1945.* 4 vols. New York: Harper and Bros., 1950.

740 _____. *Working With Roosevelt.* New York: Harper and Bros., 1952.

741 Rowson, S. W. D. "Punishment of War Criminals," *Law Quarterly Review* 60 (July 1944):225–26.

742 Sankey, John S. "War Criminals: Should They Be Tried?" *Fortnightly Law Review* 159 (January 1943):1–8.

743 Schwarzenberger, Georg. *International Law and Totalitarian Lawlessness.* London: Jonathan Cape, 1943.

744 Selling, L. S. "Specific War Crimes," *Journal of Criminal Law and Criminology* 34 (1944):303–10.

745 Sinclair, Upton. "What Shall Be Done with Hitler?" *Free World* 7 (February 1944): 121–24.

746 Stimson, Henry L, and McGeorge Bundy. *On Active Service in Peace and War.* New York: Harper and Bros., 1948.

747 "The Treatment of War Crimes and Crimes Incidental to the War: The Experience of 1918–1922," *Bulletin of International News* 22 (February-March 1945):95–102, 199–208, 251–55, 299–305.

748 "Trial by Executive," *Newsweek* 25 (May 28, 1945).

749 "Trial of the Nazis," *Law Journal* 95 (1945):191.

750   United States, Congress, House of Representatives. *Apprehension and Punishment of War Criminals,* submitted by Luther H. Johnson. 79th Cong., 1st sess. Washington, D.C.: GPO, 1945.

751   ———. *Punishment of War Criminals: Hearings before the Committee on Foreign Affairs on H.J. Res. 93 . . . March 22 and 26, 1945.* 79th Cong., 1st sess. Washington, D.C.: GPO, 1945.

752   United States, Department of State. *Foreign Relations of the United States, 1942: Diplomatic Papers.* 7 vols. Washington, D.C.: GPO, 1960–1963. Vol. I: General.

753   ———. *Foreign Relations of the United States, 1943: Diplomatic Papers.* 6 vols. Washington, D.C.: GPO, 1963–1965. Vol. I: General.

754   ———. *Foreign Relations of the United States, 1944: Diplomatic Papers.* 8 vols. Washington, D.C.: GPO, 1966–1967. Vol. I: General.

755   ———. *Foreign Relations of the United States, 1945: Diplomatic Papers.* 9 vols. Washington, D.C.: GPO, 1967–1969. Vol. II: European Advisory Council; Austria; Germany.

756   United States, Forces, European Theater, General Board. *War Crimes and Punishment of War Criminals.* Study no. 68. N.p., 1945.

757   Vambery, Rustem. "Criminals and War Crimes," *Nation* 160 (May 19, 1945): 567–68.

758   Vedovato, Guiseppe. "La punizione dei Crimini di Guerra," *Rivista di Studi Politici Internazionali* 12 (1945):141–78.

759   "War Crimes," *Solicitor* 9 (February 1942):19–20.

760   Weis, George. "International Criminal Justice in Time of Peace," *Transactions of the Grotius Society* 28 (1942):27–63.

761   Wharton, J. F. "Germany: A Problem in Global Penology," *Saturday Review of Literature* 28 (July 28, 1945):7–10.

762   "What Treatment for War Criminals?" *Information Service* [Federal Council of the Churches of Christ in America] 24 (1945):1–4.

763   Wheeler-Bennett, Sir John, and Anthony Nicholls. *The Semblance of Peace: The Political Settlement after the Second World War.* New York: Norton, 1972.

764   Wilding-White, A. M. "Punishing War Criminals: What Is the Applicable Law?" *Law Journal* 95 (October 13, 1945):331–32.

765   Winner, Percy. "German Road Back: Inquiry into Guilt, Punishment and Expiation," *New Republic* 112 (June 4, 1945):778–81.

766 Wright, Quincy. "War Criminals," *American Journal of International Law* 39 (April 1945):257

Allied Conferences and Declarations

767 "Executions of Hostages by the Nazis: Statement by the President," *Department of State Bulletin* 5 (October 25, 1941):317.

/St. James Conference, London, 1942/

768 Great Britain, Foreign Office. *Punishment for War Crimes.* 2 vols. London: HMSO, 1942.

769 Inter-Allied Information Committee. *Punishment for War Crimes: The Inter-Allied Declaration Signed at St. James' Palace London on 13th January, 1942, and Relative Documents.* London: HMSO, 1942.

770 ———. *Punishment for War Crimes (2): Collective Notes Presented to the Governments of Great Britain, the U.S.S.R., and the U.S.A. and Relative Correspondence.* London: HMSO, 1942.

771 Stransky, Jaroslav. "The Inter-Allied Conference on War Crimes and the Problem of Retribution," *New Commonwealth Quarterly* 7 (1942): 250–57.

772 World Jewish Congress, British Section. *St. James' Conference of the Allied Governments in London and Nazi Anti-Jewish Crimes: Documents Exchanged with the World Jewish Congress.* London: British Section of the World Jewish Congress, 1942.

/Inter-Allied Declaration against Acts of Dispossession, January 5, 1943/

773 Great Britain, Foreign Office. *Inter-Allied Declaration against Acts of Dispossession Committed in Territories under Enemy Occupation or Control.* London: HMSO, 1943.

774 United States, Department of State. *Foreign Relations of the United States, 1943: Diplomatic Papers.* 6 vols. Washington, D.C.: GPO, 1963–1965, I:439–59.

/Cairo and Tehran Conferences, 1943/

775 Fischer, Alexander, ed. *Teheran, Jalta, Potsdam: Die sowjetischen Protokolle von den Kriegskonferenzen der "Grossen Drei."* 2d ed. Cologne: Wissenschaft und Politik, 1973.

776 *Tehran, Jalta, Potsdam: Sbornik dokumentov.* 3d ed. Moscow: Mezdunarodnye otnosenija, 1971.

777 United States, Department of State. *Foreign Relations of the United States: Diplomatic Papers: The Conferences at Cairo and Tehran, 1943.* Washington, D.C.: GPO, 1961.

778   Zieger, Gottfried. *Die Teheran-Konferenz 1943*. Hannover: Niedersächs, Landeszentrale für politische Bildung, 1967.

/Moscow Declaration on Atrocities, November 1, 1943/

779   Barry, John V. "Moscow Declaration on War Crimes," *Australian Law Journal* 17 (December 1943):248–50.

780   "Declaration on German Atrocities," *Department of State Bulletin* 9 (November 6, 1943):311.

781   United Nations Information Organization. *Information Paper No. 1*. London: United Nations Information Organization, Reference Division, 1945.

782   United States, Department of State. *Foreign Relations of the United States, 1943: Diplomatic Papers*. 6 vols. Washington, D.C.: GPO, 1963–1965, I:513–749.

/Washington and Quebec Conferences, 1943/

783   United States, Department of State. *Foreign Relations of the United States: The Conferences at Washington and Quebec, 1943*. Washington, D.C.: GPO, 1970.

/Quebec Conference, 1944/

784   United States, Department of State. *Foreign Relations of the United States: The Conference at Quebec, 1944*. Washington, D.C.: GPO, 1972.

/Yalta Conference, 1945/

785   Clemens, Diane Shaver. *Yalta*. New York: Oxford University Press, 1970.

786   Great Britain, Foreign Office. *Protocol of the Yalta Proceedings*. Cmd. 7088. London: HMSO, 1947.

787   _____. *Report of the Crimea Conference, February 11, 1945*. Cmd. 6598. London: HMSO, 1946.

788   Stettinius, Edward R., Jr. and Walter Johnson, eds. *Roosevelt and the Russians: The Yalta Conference*. Garden City, N.Y.: Doubleday, 1949.

789   United States, Department of State. *Foreign Relations of the United States: Diplomatic Papers: The Conferences at Malta and Yalta, 1945*. Washington, D.C.: GPO, 1955.

/International Conference on Military Trials, London, June 26–August 8, 1945/

Documents

790   Great Britain, Ministry of Information. *A Catalogue of Crime: An Outline Indictment of German War Guilt, Criminal War Aims and War-Time Excesses*. London: Ministry of Information, 1945.

791 Great Britain, Parliament. *Agreement by the Government of the United Kingdom of Great Britain and Northern Ireland, the Government of the United States of America, the Provisional Government of the French Republic and the Government of the Union of Soviet Socialist Republics for the Prosecution and Punishment of the Major War Criminals of the European Axis: London, 8th August 1945.* Cmd. 6668. London: HMSO, 1945.

792 United States, Department of State. *Report of Robert H. Jackson, United States Representative to the International Conference on Military Trials, London, 1945.* State Department Pub. no. 3080. Washington, D.C.: GPO, 1949.

General

793 Alderman, S. S. "Negotiating the Nuremberg Trial Agreements, 1945," in *Negotiating with the Russians,* edited by Raymond Dennett and Joseph E. Johnson. Boston: World Peace Foundation, 1951.

794 Ivrakis, S. C. *Soviet Concepts of International Law, Criminal Law and Criminal Procedure at the International Conference on Military Trials.* London, 1945.

795 Kilmuir, Earl of (Sir David Maxwell Fyfe). *Political Adventure: The Memoirs of the Earl of Kilmuir.* London: Weidenfeld and Nicolson, 1964.

796 Ratz, Paul. "Über die völkerrechtlichen Grundlagen des Londoner Status vom 8. August 1945 und Kontrollratsgesetzes Nr. 10," *Archiv des Völkerrechts* 3 (May 1952):275–99.

/Potsdam Conference, 1945/

797 Deuerlein, Ernst. *Potsdam 1945: Ende und Anfang.* Cologne: Wissenschaft und Politik, 1970.

798 ———, ed. *Potsdam 1945: Quellen zur Konferenz der "Grossen Drei."* Munich: Deutsche Taschenbuch Verlag, 1963.

799 Faust, F. *Die Potsdamer Abkommen und seine völkerrechtliche Bedeutung.* 2d ed. Frankfurt am Main: Metzner, 1960.

800 Feis, Herbert. *Churchill-Roosevelt-Stalin: The War They Waged and the Peace They Sought.* 2d ed. Princeton: Princeton University Press, 1967.

801 ———. *Zwischen Krieg und Frieden: Das Potsdammer Abkommen.* Frankfurt am Main: Athenäum, 1962.

802 France, Ministry of Information. *Accord du 8 août 1945 Statut de Tribunal Militaire International, articles et documents.* Nouvelle Serie no. 348. Paris: Ministry of Information, 1945.

803 Poljanskij, N. N. (Polyansky). "The Berlin Conference and the War Criminals," *USSR Embassy Information Bulletin* 5 (September 1, 1945): 1–2.

804 "Tripartite Conference at Berlin [Potsdam Conference]," *Department of State Bulletin* 13 (August 5, 1945):153–61.

805 United States, Department of State. *Foreign Relations of the United States: Diplomatic Papers: The Conference of Berlin (The Potsdam Conference), 1945.* 2 vols. Washington, D.C.: GPO, 1960.

/United Nations War Crimes Commission, 1942–1947 (See under IV. Subsidiary Issues/The United Nations and War Crimes)/

/"Saboteur's Case" (*Ex Parte Quirin,* 319 US 1 [1942])/

806 Battle, George Gordon. "Military Tribunals," *Virginia Law Review* 29 (December 1942):255–71.

807 Cramer, Myron C. "Military Commissions: Trial of the Eight Saboteurs," *Washington Law Review* 17 (November 1942):247–55.

808 Cushman, Robert E. "The Case of the Nazi Saboteurs," *American Political Science Review* 36 (December 1942):1082–91.

809 Hyde, Charles Cheney. "Aspects of the Saboteur Case," *American Journal of International Law* 37 (1943):88–91.

810 Kraus, Rose. "Saboteurs and Military Justice," *St. John's Law Review* 17 (November 1942):29–34.

811 M. L. C., Jr. "The Military Commission in 1942," *Virginia Law Review* 29 (December 1942):317–38.

812 "Military Trial of Saboteurs," *Indiana Law Journal* 18 (April 1943): 246–47.

813 Schilling, G. T. "Constitutional Law—Saboteurs and the Jurisdiction of Military Commissions," *Michigan Law Review* 41 (December 1942):481–95.

International Military Tribunal: Nuremberg, November 14, 1945–October 1, 1946

PRIMARY EVIDENTIARY DOCUMENTS

American Editions

814 IMT. *Trial of the Major War Criminals before the International Military Tribunal, Nuremberg, 14 November 1945–1 October 1946.* 42 vols. Nuremberg: IMT, 1947

815 United States Office of Chief Counsel for Prosecution of Axis Criminality. *Nazi Conspiracy and Aggression.* 8 vols. 2 supplements. Washington, D.C.: GPO, 1946–1948.

British Edition

816 IMT. *The Trial of German Major War Criminals: Proceedings of the International Military Tribunal Sitting at Nuremberg, Germany, 20th November, 1945 to 1st December, 1945—Taken from the Official Transcript.* 21 vols. London: HMSO, 1946.

French Edition

817 Le Procès des Grands Criminels de Guerre devant le Tribunal Militaire International de Nuremberg. 41 vols. Paris: Imprimerie Nationale, 1947–1949.

German Edition

818 *Der Prozess gegen die Hauptkriegsverbrecher vor dem Internationalen Militärgerichtshof, 14. November 1945 bis 1. Oktober 1946.* 42 vols. Nuremberg: IMT, 1947–1949.

OFFICIAL DOCUMENTS: GENERAL

819 Biddle, Francis. "Report from Francis Biddle to President Truman, *Department of State Bulletin* 15 (November 24, 1946):954–57.

820 Czechoslovakia, Ministry of Information. *Ceskoslovensko a Norimberský process: Hlvanî Dokumenty Norimberského Procesu o Zlocinech Nacistù proti Ceskoslovensku.* Prague: Ministry of Information, 1946.

821 *Exposés introductifs de M. le Juge Jackson, Sir Hartley Shawcross et le Général R. Rudenko: Introduction de M. Champetier de Ribes.* Paris: Office français d'Édition, 1946.

822 Fite, Katherine B. *The Nürnberg Judgment: A Summary.* Department of State Pub. no. 2727. Washington, D.C.: GPO, 1947.

823 France, Ministère de l'Information. *Service de recherche des crimes de guerre ennemis: Le procès de Nuremberg: L'accusation alliée.* Paris: Office français d'Édition, 1946.

824 ———. *Service de recherche des crimes de guerre ennemis: Le procès de Nuremberg: L'accusation française.* 2 vols. Paris: Office français d'Édition, 1946.

826 Great Britain, Foreign Office. *Judgment of the International Military Tribunal for the Trial of German Major War Criminals.* Misc. no. 12. Cmd. 6964. London: HMSO, 1946.

827 _____. *The Trial of the German Major War Criminals: Opening Speeches of the Chief Prosecutors.* London: HMSO, 1946.

828 Great Britain, War Office. *Regulations for the Trial of War Criminals: Royal Warrant, June 14, 1945.* London: War Office, 1945.

829 IMT. *The Trial of German Major War Criminals by the International Military Tribunal Sitting at Nuremberg, Germany (Commencing 20th November, 1945): Opening Speeches of the Chief Prosecutors for the United States of America, the French Republic, the United Kingdom of Great Britain and Northern Ireland and the Union of Soviet Socialist Republics.* London: HMSO, 1946.

830 _____. *The Trial of German Major War Criminals by the International Military Tribunal Sitting at Nuremberg, Germany (Commencing 20th November, 1945): Speeches of the Chief Prosecutors for the United States of America, the French Republic, the United Kingdom of Great Britain and Northern Ireland and the Union of Soviet Socialist Republics, at the Close of the Case against the Individual Defendants.* London: HMSO, 1946.

831 _____. *The Trial of German Major War Criminals by the International Military Tribunal Sitting at Nuremberg, Germany (Commencing 20th November, 1945): Speeches of the Prosecutors for the United States of America, the French Republic, the United Kingdom of Great Britain and Northern Ireland and the Union of Soviet Socialist Republics at the Close of the Case against the Indicted Organisations.* London: HMSO, 1946.

832 IMT, Secretariat. *Documents Constituting Basic Authority War Crimes Trials.* Nuremberg: IMT, Secretariat, 1947.

833 _____. *Le Procès des Grands Criminels de Guerre devant le Tribunal Militaire International, Nuremberg, 14 nov. 1945–1er oct. 1946: Textes officiel en langue française.* 3 vols. Nuremberg: IMT, Secretariat, 1947.

834 Jackson, Robert H. "Final Report to the President from Supreme Court Justice Jackson," *Department of State Bulletin* 13 (October 27, 1946):771–76.

835 _____. *Trial of German War Criminals: Opening Address by R. H. Jackson.* Washington, D.C.: GPO, 1946.

836 *Jugement rendu par le Tribunal Militaire International au cours de ses audiences tenues les 30 septembre et 1er october 1946 dans le procès des Grands Criminels de Guerre.* Paris: Imprimerie des Journaux officiels, 1946.

837 Truman, Harry S. *Public Papers of the President of the United States, Harry S. Truman: Containing the Public Messages, Speeches, and Statements by the President, January 1 to December 31, 1946.* Washington, D.C.: GPO, 1962.

838 United Nations, Secretary General. *The Charter and Judgement of the Nürnberg Tribunal, History and Analysis: Memorandum by the Secretary-General of the United Nations.* A/CN.4/5. Lake Success, N.Y.: United Nations General Assembly, International Law Commission, 1949.

839 United Nations, War Crimes Commission. *Charges by the European and the United States Governments against German, Italian and Japanese War Criminals.* 41 vols. London: HMSO, 1944–1947.

840 United States, Army, Judge Advocate General. *Report of the Deputy Judge Advocate for War Crimes, European Command, June 1944 to July 1948.* N.p., 1948.

841 United States, Department of State. *Germany, 1947–1949: The Story in Documents.* State Department Pub. no. 3556. Washington, D.C.: GPO, 1950.

842 _____. *Trail of War Criminals: 1. Report of Robert H. Jackson to the President; 2. Agreement Establishing an International Military Tribunal; 3. Indictment.* State Department Pub. no. 2420. Washington, D.C.: GPO, 1945.

843 United States, Naval War College. *International Law Documents, 1946–1947.* Washington, D.C.: GPO, 1948.

DOCUMENTS COLLECTIONS: UNOFFICIAL

844 Martínez, José Agustín. *Los procesos penales de la postguerra: Documentos para la historia contemporánea.* Madrid: Ediciones y Publicaciones Españolas, 1955.

845 Osmańcsyk, Edmund Jan. *Dokumenty Pruskie.* Warsaw: Czytelnik, 1947.

846 Piotrowski, Stanislaw, ed. *Sprawy polskie przed Miedzynarudowym Trybunaem Wojennym w Norymberdze.* 2d ed. Warsaw: Wydawn. Prawnicze, 1957.

847 Vicar, G. *Le livre noir: 100 documents prodigieux sur le plus grand procès de l'histoire.* Paris: Editions du Bateau Irre, 1946.

OFFICIAL MICROFILM PUBLICATIONS

United States National Archives: World War II War Crimes Records, Record Group 238

/Document Series and Interrogation Records Assembled by the Office of Chief Counsel for War Crimes, 1945–1949/

848 *Records of the U.S. Nuernberg War Crimes Trials: NG Series, 1933–1948.* T1139. 70 rolls.

849 *Records of the U.S. Nuernberg War Crimes Trials: NI Series, 1933–1948.* T301. 164 rolls.

850   *Records of the U.S. Nuernberg War Crimes Trials: NM Series, 1874–1946.* M936. 1 roll.

851   *Records of the U.S. Nuernberg War Crimes Trials: NOKW Series, 1933–1947.* T1119. 47 rolls.

852   *Records of the U.S. Nuernberg War Crimes Trials: NP Series, 1943–1946.* M942. 1 roll.

/ Records of the International Military Tribunal Described in National Archives Preliminary Inventory No. 21/

853   *Diary of Hans Frank.* T992. 12 rolls.

854   *Mauthausen Death Books.* T990. 2 rolls.

855   *Prosecution Exhibits Submitted to the International Military Tribunal.* T988. 54 rolls.

856   *United States Trial Briefs and Document Books.* T991. 1 roll.

857   *War Diaries and Correspondence of General Alfred Jodl.* T989. 2 rolls.

United States National Archives: General Records of the Department of State, Record Group 59

858   *Records of the Department of State Special Interrogation Mission to Germany, 1945–1946.* M679. 3 rolls.

United States National Archives: Records of the U.S. Army Commands, 1942–, Record Group 338

859   *German Documents among the War Crimes Records of the Judge Advocate Division, Headquarters, United States Army, Europe.* T1021. 20 rolls.

GUIDES AND BIBLIOGRAPHIES

860   Conover, Helen F., comp. *The Nazi State, War Crimes, and War Criminals.* Washington, D.C.: Library of Congress, 1945.

861   Franklin, Mitchell. "Sources of International Law Relating to Sanctions against War Criminals," *Journal of Criminal Law and Criminology* 36 (September-October 1945):153–79.

862   German Association of Comparative Law. *Bibliography of German Law in English and German: A Selection* [through December 31, 1963]. Karlsruhe: Verlag C. F. Müller, 1964.

863   _____. *Bibliography of German Law in English and German: A Selection.* Supplement, 1964–1968. Karlsruhe: Verlag C. F. Müller, 1969.

864 Halley, Fred G., comp. *Preliminary Inventory of the Records of the United States Counsel for the Prosecution of Axis Criminality.* Preliminary Inventory no. 21. Washington, D.C.: National Archives, 1949.

865 Hersch, Gisels, comp. *A Bibliography of Geneva Studies, 1945–1971.* Bloomington: Indiana University Press, 1972.

866 IMT. *Inventory of International Military Tribunal Archives, Nuremberg, as Transferred to International Court of Justice, The Hague.* Nuremberg: IMT, n.d.

867 Kempner, Robert M. W. "Nuremberg Trials as Sources of Recent German Political and Historical Materials," *American Political Science Review* 44 (June 1950):447–59.

868 Kosicki, Jerzy. *Bibliografiá piśmiennictwa polskiego za lata 1944–1953 o hitlerowskich zbrodniach wojennych.* Warsaw: Wydawn. Prawnicze, 1955.

869 Michel, H. "Les principales sources françaises de l'histoire de la deuxième guerre mondiale," *Revue Historique* 200 (October-December 1948):206–19.

870 Neumann, Inge S., with additional material furnished by the Wiener Library, Robert A. Rosenbaum, ed. *European War Crimes Trials: A Bibliography.* New York: Carnegie Endowment for International Peace, 1951.

871 Niebergall, Fred. "Brief Survey Concerning the Records of the War Crimes Trials Held in Nürnberg, Germany," *Law Library Journal* 42 (1949):87–90.

872 ———. "The Documents of Nuremberg," *Wiener Library Bulletin* 42 (March 1949):9.

873 Scanlon, Helen Lawrence, comp. *A Select List of Books and Articles Defining War Crimes under International Law and Discussing Their Trial and Punishment.* Washington, D.C.: Carnegie Endowment for International Peace, 1945.

874 Taylor, Telford. "Outline of the Research and Publication Possibilities of the War Crimes Trials," *Louisiana Law Review* 9 (May 1949): 496–508.

875 United Nations. *Guide to Records of the War Crimes Trials Held in Nürnberg, Germany, 1945–1949, Prepared in Archives Section, Communications and Records Division.* United Nations Archives Reference Guide no. 7/rev. 1. Lake Success, N.Y.: United Nations, Archives Section, 1949.

876   United States National Archives. *Records of the United States Nuernberg War Crimes Trials Interrogations, 1946–1949.* Washington, D.C.: National Archives, 1977.

877   Wiener Library. *Catalogue of Nuremberg Documents.* London: Wiener Library, 1961.

878   Wolfe, Robert, ed. *Captured German and Related Records: A National Archives Conference.* Athens: Ohio University Press, 1974.

GUIDES TO GERMAN SOURCE MATERIAL

879   Brennecke, Gerhard, comp. *Die Nürnberger Geschichtsentstellung: Quellen zur Vorgeschichte und Geschichte des 2. Weltkrieges aus den Akten der deutschen Verteidigung.* 2d ed. Tübingen: Verlag der Deutschen Hochschullehrer Zeitung, 1970.

880   Mommsen, Wolfgang. "Die Akten der Nürnberger Kriegsverbrechenprozesse und die Möglichkeiten ihrer historischen Auswertung," *Der Archivar* 3 (1950):14–25.

881   Puchner, Otto. "Der Bestand 'Nürnberger Prozesse' im Staatsarchiv Nürnberg," *Wehrwissenschaftliche Rundschau* 6 (February 1956):93–97.

882   Seraphim, Hans-Günther. "Die Dokumentenedition der amtlichen deutschen Ausgabe der Verfahrens gegen die Hauptkriegsverbrecher," *Europa-Archiv* 5 (September 5, 1950):3307–10.

883   _____. "Der Index der amtlichen deutschen Ausgabe des Prozesses die Haptkriegsverbrecher," *Europa-Archiv* 5 (May 20, 1950):3028–31.

884   Vogel, Rolf, ed. *Ein Weg aus der Vergangenheit: Eine Dokumentation zur Verjahrungsfrage zu den NS-Prozessen.* Frankfurt am Main: Ullstein, 1969.

GERMAN LAW AND GOVERNMENT

885   Control Commission for Germany, British Element, Office of Legal Advisor. *The German Penal Code of 1871 (with Introductory Act of 1870), Amended to May, 1950, as Effective in the British Occupation Zone of W. Germany and the British Sector of Berlin.* N.p., 1950.

886   Emerson, Rupert. *State and Sovereignty in Modern Germany.* New Haven: Yale University Press, 1928.

887   Fischer, Diana Davis. "National Socialist Germany and International Law." Ph.D. dissertation. University of Washington, 1973.

888   Harvey, C. P. "Sources of Law in Germany," *Modern Law Review* 11 (1948):196–213.

889 Hoche, Werner, comp. *Die Gesetzgebung des Kabinetts Hitler.* 30 vols. Berlin: F. Vahlen, 1933-1937.

890 ———. *Verordnung zum Schutze des deutschen Volks vom 4. Februar 1933.* Berlin: F. Vahlen, 1933.

891 Hoefer, Frederick. "The Nazi Penal System," *Journal of Criminal Law and Criminology* 35 (March-April 1945):385-93.

892 Huber, Ernst Rudolf. *Verfassungsrecht des Grossdeutschen Reiches.* 2d ed. Hamburg: Hanseatische Verlag Anstalt, 1939.

893 Morstein Marx, Fritz. *Government in the Third Reich.* 2d rev. ed. New York: McGraw-Hill, 1937.

894 United States, Department of War. *The Statutory Criminal Law of Germany.* Pamphlet no. 31-122. Washington, D.C.: Department of War, 1946.

895 Waltzog, Alfons. *Recht der Landkriegsführung: Die wichtigsten Abkommen des Landkriegsrechts.* Berlin: F. Vahlen, 1942.

THE TRIAL: GENERAL

896 Albrecht, R. G. *Defense Record.* Nuremberg, 1946.

897 Alexander, Charles W., and Anne Keeshan. *Justice at Nuremberg: A Pictoral Record of the Trial of Nazi War Criminals by the International Tribunal at Nuremberg, Germany, 1945-1946.* New York: Marvel Press, 1946.

898 Alexandov, G. N. "Looking Back to Nuremberg," *New Times* 43 (1965):16; 44 (1965):20; 47 (1965):16.

899 ———. *Sud istorii.* Moscow: Izd. Politischeskoi Lit., 1966.

900 Amaudruz, G. A. *UBU-Justicier au premier procès de Nuremberg.* Paris: Les Actes des Apotres, 1949.

901 Anders, Karl. *Im Nürnberger Irrgarten.* Nuremberg: Nest-Verlag, 1948.

902 Andrus, Burton C. *I Was the Nuremberg Jailer.* New York: Coward-McCann, 1969.

903 Appleman, John Alan. *Military Tribunals and International Crimes.* Indianapolis: Bobbs-Merrill, 1954.

904 April, Nathan. "An Inquiry into the Judicial Basis for the Nuremberg War Crime Trial," *Minnesota Law Review* 30 (April 1946):313-31.

905 Audric, John. "The Germans Do Not Know of the Nuremberg Trials," *Justice of the Peace* 110 (February 16, 1946):110.

906 Bader, Karl S. "Nürnberger Prozess," *Deutsche Rechtszeitschrift* 1 (November 1946):140–42.

907 _____. "Umschau-Zum Nürnberger Ärzteprozess," *Deutsche Rechtszeitschrift* 2 (1947):401–02.

908 _____. "Zum Nürnberger Urteil," *Deutsche Rechtszeitschrift* 1 (1946):183–95.

909 Balmer-Basilius, H. R. "Nürnberg und das Weltgewissen," *Friedens-Warte* 46 (1946):289–93.

910 Balzas, A. "Nurnbergerdommens retlige bergrundelse," *Nordisk Tiddskrift for International Ret* 18 (1947–1948):24–31.

911 _____. "Die rechtliche Begründung des Nürnberger Urteils," *Friedens-Warte* 46 (1946):369–75.

912 Bardèche, Maurice. *Neuremberg, het beloofde land.* Atwerp: Dauperta, 1951.

913 _____. *Nuremberg: Ill ou les faux monnayeurs.* Paris: Les sept couleurs, 1950.

914 _____. *Nuremberg: Ou, la terre promise.* Paris: Les sept couleurs, 1948.

915 _____. *Die Politik der Zerstörung—Nürnberg oder Europa.* Göttingen: Plesse Verlag, 1950.

916 Bauer, Fritz. *Die Kriegsverbrecher vor Gericht.* Neue internationale Bibliothek 3. Zurich: Europa Verlag, 1945.

917 _____. *Rättegången i Nürnberg.* Stockholm: Kooperativa för-bundets bokförlag, 1946.

918 Bednarek, Irena. *Fanfary i werble Posłowie: Włodzimierz Janiurek.* Katowice: Ślask, 1964.

919 _____. *Kulisy Wielkiej Zbrodni.* 2d ed. Katowice: Ślask, 1961.

920 Berg, Frederick. *Nürnberg-prosessen fra uke til uke.* Translated by Torleiv Opstad. Oslo: E. G. Mortensen, 1946.

921 _____. *Os julgamentos de Nuremberg.* 2 vols. Pôrto: Edicôes AOV, 1947.

922 Bernays, Murray C. "Legal Basis of the Nürnberg Trials," *Survey Graphic* 35 (January 1946):4–9; 35 (November 1946):390–91.

923 ———. "Letters to Fortune: The Nürnberg Novelty," *Fortune* 33 (February 1946):10-11.

924 ———. "Nuremberg: Its Justification and Lessons," *West Virginia Bar Association Report* 62 (1946):68-83.

925 ———. "Nuremberg: Its Vindication of Western Justice, Its Profound Lessons in Moral Leadership, and Its Deterrence to Future Aggression," *Survey Graphic* 35 (1946):390-91.

926 Bernstein, Victor H. *Final Judgment: The Story of Nuremberg.* New York: Boni and Gaer, 1947.

927 Bertrand, C.-A. "Les procès de Nuremberg," *Revue du Barreau de la Province Québec* 8 (November 1948):477-88.

928 Bial, Louis C. "The Nürnberg Judgment and International Law," *Brooklyn Law Review* 13 (February 1947):34-49.

929 Bogatsvo, Julius. *I Nazisti dopo il nazismo: Dove sono, cosa fanno oggi gli ex-gerarchi nazisti.* Milan: G. De Vecchi, 1972.

930 Bogoslovsky, B. "The Nuremberg Trials," *New Jersey State Bar Association Year Book* (1946):72-85.

931 Boissier, Pierre. *L'épée dans la balance.* Geneva: Éditions labor et Fides, 1953.

932 Bosch, William J. *Judgment on Nuremberg: American Attitudes toward the German War-Crime Trials.* Chapel Hill: University of North Carolina Press, 1970.

933 Brand, James T. "Crimes against Humanity and the Nürnberg Trials," *Oregon Law Review* 28 (February 1949):93-119.

934 Brandt, Willy [of Karl Frahm]. *Nürnberg-Norge-dommen.* Oslo: Aschehoug, 1946.

935 Brottet mot Freden. *Domen i Nürnberg.* Stockholm: Natur och Kultur, 1946.

936 Brown, John Mason. "Nuremberg—Century of Progress," *Saturday Review of Literature* 29 (August 24, 1946):20-24.

937 Calvocoressi, Peter. *Nuremberg: The Facts, the Law and the Consequences.* New York: Macmillan, 1948.

938 Carjeu, P. *Le jugement du Tribunal Militaire de Nuremberg.* Paris: Institut de Criminologie, 1951.

939   Carter, Edward F. "The Nuremberg Trial: A Turning Point in the Enforcement of International Law," *Nebraska Law Review* 28 (March 1949):370-86.

940   Cartier, Raymond. *Les secrets de la guerre dévoilés a Nuremberg.* Paris: Arthémé Fayard, 1947.

941   Carton de Wiart, H. "Grands criminels de guerre," *Revue de Droit International (Sottile-Geneva)* 24 (April-September 1946):41-43.

942   "The Chalice of Nuremberg," *Time* 46 (December 10, 1945):25-28.

943   Chalufour, A. "Le procès de Nuremberg et le droit international," *Annuaire de l'Association des Auditeurs et Anciens Auditeurs de l'Académie de Droit International de La Haye* 28 (1958):26-38.

944   Chamberlin, William Henry. "Don't Call It Justice," *Forum* 104 (December 1945):329-31.

945   Crouchuet, R. *Le procès de Nuremberg: Les criminels nazis devant leurs juges.* Paris: Hachette, 1947.

946   Cyprian, Tadeusz. *Nieznana Norymberga: Dwanaście Procesów Norymberskich.* Warsaw: Książka i Wiedza, 1965.

947   _____. *Sprawy polskie w procesie norymberskim.* Poznan: Instytut zachodni, 1956.

948   Davidson, Eugene. "The Nuremberg Trials and One World," in *Issues and Conflicts, Studies in Twentieth Century American Diplomacy,* edited by George L. Anderson. Lawrence: University of Kansas Press, 1959.

949   _____. *The Trial of the Germans.* New York: Macmillan, 1966.

950   Dawson, John. Review of *Nuremberg Trial and Aggressive War,* by Sheldon Glueck. *American Sociological Review* 12 (February 1947): 124-25.

951   Dean, G. "Trial of the Major European War Criminals," *New Jersey Realty Title News* 1 (1945):4-6.

952   Descheemaeker, Jacques. *Le tribunal militaire international des grands criminels de guerre.* Paris: Éditions A. Pedone, 1947.

953   _____. "Le Tribunal militaire international des grands criminels de guerre," *Revue Générale de Droit International Public* 50 (1946): 210-311.

954   Dickler, Gerald. *Dreizehn Prozesse, die Geschichte machten.* Munich: Rütten and Loening, 1964.

955 Dimock, Edward J. "Factual Outline of the Indictment of War Criminals," *American Bar Association Journal* 31 (December 1945):638–41, 646–47.

956 Doman, Nicholas R. "Political Consequences of the Nuremberg Trial," *Annals of the American Academy of Political and Social Science* 246 (July 1946):81–90.

957 Donati, A. "Il processo di Norimberga e il diritto penale internazionale," *Stato Moderno* 2 (1945):350–51.

958 Dupays, Paul. *Au Palais de Nuremberg, Chronique Historique: Au Tribunal International Militaire, mi-avril-mai 1946.* Paris: Éditions de la Critique, 1952.

959 _____. *Au Temple de Thémis, Chronique Historique: Justice à Laneberg à Nuremberg, mi-mars à mi-avril 1946.* Paris: Éditions de la Critique, 1946.

960 _____. *Grands Chefs du Nazisme, Chronique Historique: Tribunal International de Nuremberg, mi-mars à mi-avril 1946.* Paris: Éditions de la Critique, 1946.

961 _____. *Justice Chronique Historique: Tribunal International de Nuremberg, mi-juin à mi-octobre, 1946.* Paris: Éditions de la Critique, 1952.

962 _____. *Ne Fais pas à Autrui . . . Chronique Historique: Tribunal International de Nuremberg, janvier-mars, 1946.* Paris: Éditions de la Critique, 1952.

963 Eccard, F. "La signification suprême du procès de Nuremberg," *Revue de Droit International (Sottile-Geneva)* 24 (April-September 1946): 82–84.

964 Ecer, Bohuslav, ed. *Norimberský Sond.* Prague: Orbis, 1946.

965 Eckert, J. *Schuldig oder entlastet?* Munich: Rechts- und Wirtschaftsverlag, Dr. Gruber, 1947.

966 Egbert, L. D. "L'accusation américaine au tribunal militaire international," *Nouvelle Revue de Droit International Privé* 13 (1946):419–29.

967 Ehard, Hans. "The Nuremberg Trials against the Major War Criminals and International Law," *American Journal of International Law* 43 (April 1949):223–45.

968 Ehrenberg, Ilja (Erenburg). "History's Morality: The Nuremberg Trial," *USSR Embassy Information Bulletin* 5 (December 8, 1945):1–3, 7.

969 _____. *Menschen, Jahre, Leben.* Translated from Russian by Alexander Kaempfe. 2 vols. Munich: Kindler, 1965.

970 _____. "The Nuremberg Trial," *Answer* 4 (1946):11–12, 16.

971 Emmet, Christopher. "Verdict on Nuremberg," *Commonweal* 45 (November 22, 1946):138–41.

972 Erades, L. "Volkenrechtelijke aspecten van het Nurenbergse vonnis," *Rechtsgeleerd Magazijn Themis* 67 (1949):249–98.

973 Eulan, Heinz. "The Nuremberg War-Crime Trials: Revolution in International Law," *New Republic* 113 (November 12, 1945):625–28.

974 Fernández de la Mora, G. "Las aporias de Nuremberg," *Arbor* 18 (April 1951):537–62.

975 Finch, George A. "The Nuremberg Trial and International Law," *American Journal of International Law* 41 (January 1947):20–37.

976 Forbes, Gordon W. "Some Legal Aspects of the Nuremberg Trial," *Canadian Bar Review* 24 (August-September 1946):584–99.

977 Franco Sodi, C. *Racismo, antiracismo y justicia penal: El Tribunal de Nuremberg.* Mexico City: Botas, 1946.

978 Gallagher, Richard. *Nuremberg: The Third Reich on Trial.* New York: Avon, 1961.

979 Gallus, Galieni. *Nuremberg and After.* Newton, Wales: Montgomeryshire Printing, 1946.

980 Genêt [Janet Flanner]. "Letter from Nuremberg," *New Yorker* 21 (January 5, 1946):46–50.

981 _____. "Letter from Nuremberg," *New Yorker* 22 (March 30, 1946):68–74.

982 Genton, J. "Le Tribunal Militaire International: Compétence réelle: Les solutions données par le Statut du 8 août 1945," *Revue de Droit Pénal et de Criminologie* 28 (1947–1948):477–561.

983 Gibb, Andrew Dewar. *Perjury Unlimited: A Monograph on Nuremberg.* Edinburgh: W. Green, 1954.

984 Glueck, Sheldon. "The Nuremberg Trial and Aggressive War," *Harvard Law Review* 59 (February 1946):396–546.

985 _____. *The Nuremberg Trial and Aggressive War.* New York: Knopf, 1946.

986 Gollancz, Victor. *Unser bedrohtes Erbe.* Zurich: Atlantis–Verlag, 1947.

987 Goodhart, Arthur L. "The Legality of the Nuremberg Trials," *Juridical Review* 58 (April 1946):1–19.

988 ———. "Questions and Answers Concerning the Nuremberg Trials," *International Law Quarterly* 1 (Winter 1947):525–31.

989 Goutel, Eric de; Francis Mercury; Pierre Nouaille; and Lucien Viéville; comps. *Le Procès de Nuremberg.* . . . Paris: F. Beauval, 1969.

990 Greenfell, Russell. *Unconditional Hatred: German War Guilt and the Future of Europe.* New York: Devin-Adair, 1953.

991 Gregory, Tappan. "Murder Is Murder and the Guilty Can Be Punished," *American Bar Association Journal* 32 (September 1946): 544–49.

992 ———. "The Nuremberg Trials," *Connecticut Bar Journal* 21 (January 1947):2–20.

993 ———. "The Nuremberg Trials," *Illinois Bar Journal* 34 (June 1946):469–82.

994 Grew, Joseph C. "Cooperation with the United States Chief Counsel for the Prosecution of Axis Criminality," *Department of State Bulletin* 12 (July 1, 1945):40.

995 Grewe, Wilhelm, and Otto Küstler. *Nürnberg als Rechtfrage: Eine Diskussion.* Stuttgart: E. Klett, 1947.

996 Gross, Leo. "The Punishment of War Criminals: The Nuremberg Trial," *Nederlands Tijdschrift voor International Recht* 2 (October 1955): 356–74; 3 (January 1956):10–24.

997 Grundinsk, Ulrich. "Das Formalrecht des Nürnberger Strafverfahrens." Doctor of Law dissertation, Erlangen University, 1949.

998 Gründler, Gerhard E., and Arnim von Manikowsky. *Das Gericht der Sieger.* Oldenburg: Gerhard Stalling, 1967.

999 Gutzwiller, M. "Um das Urteil von Nürnberg," *Schweizer Rundschau* 46 (1946):687–92.

1000 Haensel, Carl. *Das Gericht vertagt sich: Aus dem Tagebuch eines Nürnberger Verteidigers.* Hamburg: Classen, 1950.

1001 ———. "Nürnberger Probleme," *Deutsche Rechtszeitschrift* 1 (September 1946):67–69.

1002 ———. "Zum Nürnberger Urteil: Schuldprinzip und Gruppenkriminalität," *Süddeutsche Juristenzeitung* 2 (1947):19–25.

1003 ———. "Das Urteil im Nürnberger Juristenprozess," *Deutsche Rechtszeitschrift* 3 (February 1948):40–43.

1004 Harris, Whitney, R. "The Nuremberg Trial," *State Bar Journal of California* 22 (March-April 1947):76–97.

1005 ———. Review of *Nuremberg Trials,* by August von Knieriem. *American Journal of International Law* 54 (April 1960):443–44.

1006 ———. *Tyranny on Trial: The Evidence at Nuremberg.* Dallas: Southern Methodist University Press, 1954.

1007 Härtle, Heinrich. *Freispruch für Deutschland: Unsere Soldaten vor dem Nürnberger Tribunal.* Göttingen: K. W. Schütz, 1965.

1008 Hauser, Ernest O. "The Backstage at Nuremberg," *Saturday Evening Post* (January 19, 1946):18, 19, 137.

1009 Heinze, Kurt, and Karl Schilling, eds. *Die Rechtsprechung der Nürnberger Militärtribunale.* Bonn: Girardet, 1952.

1010 Heydecker, Joe J., and Johannes Leeb. *The Nuremberg Trial: A History of Nazi Germany as Revealed through the Testimony at Nuremberg.* Translated and edited by R. A. Downie. Cleveland: World Publishing, 1962.

1011 Hirsch, Felix. "Lessons of Nuremberg," *Current History* 11 (October 1946):312–18.

1012 Hirsch, Rudolf. *Zeuge in Ost und West.* Rudolstadt: Greifenverlag, 1965.

1013 Hoegner, Wilhelm. *Der schwierige Aussenseiter: Erinnerungen ein Abgeordneten, Emigranten und Ministerpräsidenten.* Munich: Isar-Verlag, 1959.

1014 Hoffmann, J. R. "Nazi War Crimes and Criminals," *Dicta* 23 (1946):30–31.

1015 Hula, Erich. "Punishment for War Crimes," *Social Research* 13 (March 1946):1–23.

1016 "Indictment of War Criminals," *American Bar Association Journal* 31 (December 1945):645–46, 673.

1017 Jaffe, Sidney E. "Natural Law and the Nuremberg Trial," *Nebraska Law Review* 26 (November 1946):90–95.

1018 Janeczek, Edward J. *Nuremberg Judgment in the Light of International Law.* Geneva: Imprimeries Populaires, 1949.

1019 Jescheck, Hans Heinrich. "Nürnberger Prozesse," in *Wörterbuch des Völkerrechts,* edited by Hans-Jürgen Schlochauer. 2 vols. Berlin: Walter de Gruyter Verlag, 1961, II: 638–43.

1020 _____. *Die Verantwortlichkeit der Staatsorgane nach Völkerrecht: Eine Studie zu den Nürnberger Prozessen.* Bonn: L. Röhrscheid, 1952.

1021 Jones, E. F. "Rola delegacji polskiej w procesie norymberkim," *Pantswo i Prawo* 3 (1948):111–12.

1022 Judson, H. "Fascism on Trial at Nürnberg," *Department of State Bulletin* 14 (1946):250–56.

1023 Kahn, Leo. *Nuremberg Trials.* New York: Ballantine Books, 1972.

1024 Kalnoky, Countess Ingeborg, with Ilona Herisko. *Guest House: A Nuremberg Memoir.* Indianapolis: Bobbs-Merrill, 1974.

1025 Karsten, T. L., and J. H. Mathias. "Judgment at Nuremberg," *New Republic* 115 (October 21, 1946):115.

1026 Kelson, Hans. "Will Judgment in the Nuremberg Trial Constitute a Precedent in International Law?" *International Law Quarterly* 1 (Summer 1947):153–71.

1027 Kempner, Robert M. W. *Das Dritte Reich im Kreuzverhör: Aus den unveröffentlichen Vernehmungsprotokollen des Anklägers Robert M. W. Kempner.* Munich: Bechtle, 1969.

1028 Kennedy, John F. *Profiles in Courage.* New York: Harper, 1956.

1029 Kenny, John P. *Moral Aspects of Nuremberg.* Washington, D.C.: Pontifical Faculty of Theology, Dominican House of Studies, 1949.

1030 Kirchner, C. "Das Nürnberger Urteil und der Par. 267 Abs. 1 Strafprozessordnung," *Die Spruchgerichte* 2 (1948):199–200.

1031 Klafowski, Alfons. *The Nuremberg Principles and the Development of International Law.* Warsaw: Zachodnia Agencja Prasowa, 1966.

1032 Klefisch, Theodor. "Gedanken über Inhalt und Wirkung des Nürnberger Urteils," *Juristische Rundschau* 1 (1947):45–49.

1033 Knepflé, G. A. *In naam der menschheid: De wereld spreekt vonnis over Nazi-Duitschland: Nuremberg 1945-1946.* Amsterdam: Uitgererij Buijten Schipperheijn, 1946.

1034 Knieriem, August von. *The Nuremberg Trials.* Translated by Elizabeth D. Schmitt. Chicago: Henry Regnery, 1959.

1035 _____. *Nürnberg: Rechtliche und menschliche Probleme.* Stuttgart: E. Klett, 1953.

1036 Koehler, F. *Geheime Kommandosache: Aus den Dokumenten des Nürnberger Prozess gegen die Hauptkriegsverbrecher.* Berlin: Kongress-Verlag, 1956.

1037 Kommiten for Utrikespolitisk Upplysning, Stockholm. *Nürnbergprocessen.* Stockholm: Kooperativa förbundets bokförlag, 1946.

1038 Konvitz, Milton R. "Will Nuremberg Serve Justice?" *Commentary* 1 (January 9, 1946):9–15.

1039 Kramarz, H. "Täter und Teilnehmer im Urteil des Internationalen Militärgerichtshofs zu Nürnberg." Doctor of Law dissertation, Erlangen University, 1952.

1040 Kranzbühler, Otto. "Nürnberg als Rechtsproblem," in *Um Recht und Gerechtigkeit: Festgabe fur Erich Kaufmann.* Stuttgart: W. Kohlhammer, 1950.

1041 _____. *Rückblick auf Nürnberg.* Hamburg: Zeit Verlag, 1949.

1042 Kraus, Herbert. *Gerichtstag in Nürnberg.* Hamburg: Gesetz und Recht Verlag, 1947.

1043 Lachs, Manfred. "Le jugement de Nuremberg," *Revue Internationale de Droit Pénal* 17 (1946):398–404.

1044 Lande, A. *The Legal Basis of the Nürnberg Trial.* New York: Interim International Service, 1945.

1045 Latersner, Hans. *Plädoyer vor dem internationalen Militärgerichtshof zu Nürnberg.* Nürnberg: Wilhelm Muhler, 1946.

1046 Lauer, Lawrence. "The International War Criminal Trials and the Common Law of War," *St. John's Law Review* 20 (November 1945): 18–24.

1047 Lawrence, Lord Justice G. "The Nuremberg Trial," *International Affairs* 23 (April 1947):151–59.

1048 Lazard D. *Le procès de Nuremberg: Récit d'un témoin.* Paris: Les Éditions de la Nouvelle France, 1947.

1049 "Legality of Nuremberg," *Duquesne University Law Review* 4 (1965):146–62.

1050 Lener, S. "Diritto e politica nel processo di Norimbergen," *Civiltà Cattolica* 97 (1946):92–106.

1051 ———. "Dal mancato giudizio del Kaiser al processo di Norimbergen," *Civiltà Cattolica* 97 (1946):857–907.

1052 Leventhal, Harold; Sam Harris; John M. Woolsey, Jr.; and Warren F. Farr. "The Nuremberg Verdict," *Harvard Law Review* 60 (July 1947): 857–907.

1053 Liebenthal, Gerhard F. *Domen: Ett Dokument i Bild och Skrift om Krigsförbrytarprocessen i Nürnberg.* Stockholm: Åhlen and Åkerlund, 1946.

1054 Lindberg, Hugo. *En dag i Nürnberg.* Stockholm: Wahlström and Widstrand, 1946.

1055 Lippe, Viktor Freiherr von der. *Nürnberger Tagebuchnotizen: November 1945 bis Oktober 1946.* Frankfurt am Main: F. Knapp, 1951.

1056 Lippmann, Walter. "The Meaning of the Nuremberg Trial," *Ladies' Home Journal* 63 (June 1946):32, 188–90.

1057 Lüders, Karl-Heinz. "Zum Nürnberger Urteil: Strafgerichtsbarkeit über Angehörige des Feindstaats," *Süddeutsche Juristenzeitung* 1, no. 8/9 (1946):216–18.

1058 Lunau, Heinz. *The Germans on Trial.* New York: Storm Publishers, 1948.

1059 McConnell, G. R. "The Trial of War Criminals at Nuremberg," *Wyoming Law Journal* 1 (December 1946):3–12.

1060 McIntyre, Dina Ghandy. "The Nuremberg Trials," *University of Pittsburgh Law Review* 24 (October 1962):73–116.

1061 "Majestic Justice," *Christian Century* 63 (October 16, 1946):1238–40.

1062 Małcuzyński, Karol. *Oskarzeni nie przyznają się do winy.* Warsaw: Zachodnia Agencja Prasowa, 1966.

1063 Mann, Eric. *Germany Prepares for War: The Case against Germany.* Des Moines: Advertisers Press, 1944.

1064 Maridikas, George S. "Un précédent du procès de Nuremberg tiré de l'histoire de la Grèce ancienne," *Revue Hellénique de Droit International* 5 (January–June 1952):1–16.

1065 Marshall, James. Review of *Nuremberg Trial and Aggressive War,* by Sheldon Glueck. *Saturday Review of Literature* 28 (September 21, 1946):9–10.

1066 Martin, G. S. "Epilogue at Nuremberg: August 31, the Last Day of the Trial, Its Drama and Essence," *Free World* 12 (1946):23–25.

1067 Martínez, José Agustín. *El juicio de Nuremberg*. Havana: J. Montero, 1949.

1068 Martius, G. "Das Nürnberger Urteil vom 30. September–1. Oktober 1946 in völkerrechtlicher Beziehung," *Neue Justiz* 1 (1947):91–98.

1069 Maunoir, Jean-Pierre. *La répression des crimes de guerre devant les tribunaux français et alliés*. Geneva: Éditions Médecine et Hygiène, 1956.

1070 Mayda, Giuseppe. *Il processo di Norimberga*. Milan: A. Mondadori, 1972.

1071 Mendelssohn, Peter de. "America's Case at Nuremberg," *Nation* 161 (December 15, 1945):652–54.

1072 Merle, Marcel. *Le procès de Nuremberg et le châtiment des criminels de guerre*. Paris: Éditions A. Pedone, 1949.

1073 Moley, Raymond. "Making History at Nuremberg," *Newsweek* 28 (September 30, 1946):96.

1074 Montero, Mario. "El Tribunal de Nuremberg," *Revista Peruana de Derecho Internacional* 8 (May-August 1948):128–45.

1075 Morgan, John H. *The Great Assize: An Examination of the Law of the Nuremberg Trials*. London: J. Murray, 1948.

1076 Morley, Felix. "The Case for Taft," *Life* 24 (February 9, 1948): 51–66.

1077 "Morning after Judgment Day," *Time* 48 (October 14, 1946):32.

1078 Morris, James. "Major War Crimes Trial in Nürnberg," *North Dakota Bar Briefs* 25 (April 1949):97–109.

1079 Musmanno, Michael A. *The Eichmann Kommandos*. Philadelphia: Macrae Smith, 1961.

1080 Nash, Arnold. "The Nuremberg Trials," *Christian Century* 63 (September 25, 1946):1148–50.

1081 Neave, Airey M. S. *They Have Their Exits*. London: Hodder and Stoughton, 1953.

1082 Niebuhr, Reinhold. "A Report on Germany," *Christianity and Crisis* 2 (October 14, 1946):6–13.

1083 _____. "Victor's Justice," *Common Sense* 15 (January 1946):6–9.

1084 "Note on the Nuremberg Trials," *Law Quarterly Review* 62 (1946): 229–33.

1085 "Notes from Nürnberg," *Time* 47 (February 25, 1946):26.

1086 "Nuremberg and History," *Opinion* 16 (September 1946):8.

1087 "Nuremberg Blot," *Newsweek* 28 (October 14, 1946):8.

1088 "The Nuremberg Judgment," *Living Church* 113 (October 13, 1946):18.

1089 "The Nuremberg Trials," *Ave Maria* 67 (March 31, 1948):323.

1090 "The Nuremberg Trials" [by Arnold Nash], *Christian Century* 63 (September 25, 1946):1148–50. [See entry no. 1080.]

1091 "The Nuremberg Trials," *International Review* 19 (July 1946): 99–100.

1092 "The Nuremberg Trials," *Opinion* 16 (December 1945):5–6.

1093 "Nuremberg Tribunal Verdicts Due Next Week," *Army and Navy Bulletin* 2 (September 21, 1946):10.

1094 "The Nuremberg Verdicts," *Churchman* 160 (November 1946):4.

1095 "Nürnberg: Are We Sowing to Reap the Same Whirlwind Again?" *Life* 21 (October 14, 1946):36.

1096 "The Nürnberg Confusion," *Fortune* 34 (December 1946):120–21.

1097 "The Nürnberg Debate," *Time* 48 (October 14, 1946):29.

1098 *Nürnberg 1946: Het proces tegen de duitse oorlogsmisdadigers.* Brussels: Reinaert, 1962.

1099 "The Nürnberg Novelty" [by Rustem Vambery], *Fortune* 32 (December 1945):140–41. [See entry no. 1183.]

1100 O'Brien, Howard V. "Lessons from Nuremberg," *Forum* 106 (November 1946):443.

1101 Occhi, A. D. *Il processo di Norimbergan.* Seconda guerra mondiale collezione de memoire, diari e studi., vols. 17–18. Milan: Rizzoli, 1947.

1102 "One for Fifteen," *Time* 46 (December 10, 1945):28.

1103 Oscar, Friedrich (Olmes). *Über Galgen wächst kein Gras: Die Fragwürdige Kulisse der Kriegsverbrecherprozesse im Spiegel unbekann ter Dokumente.* Brunswick: Erasmus-Verlag, 1950.

1104 Ottolenghi, G. "Le problème des criminels de guerre," *Revue de Droit International (Sottile-Geneva)* 24 (January-March 1946):1–16.

1105 "Our Law Was Broken," *Commonweal* 45 (November 29, 1946): 164–66.

1106 Pannenbecker, O. *Geheim! Dokumentarische Tatsachen aus dem Nürnberger Prozess.* Düsseldorf: Bastion Verlag, 1947.

1107 ———. "The Nuremberg War-Crimes Trial," *De Paul Law Review* 14 (Spring-Summer 1965):348–58.

1108 Peklis, Alexander H. "To the Nuremberg Court," *New Republic* 115 (August 26, 1946):232–33.

1109 Peretti-Griva, D. R. "A proposito del processo di Norimberga," *Il foro padano* 2 (1946):183ff.

1110 Pergler, Charles. "War Crimes and War Criminals," *Journal of the Bar Association of the District of Columbia* 13 (September 1946): 385–92.

1111 Pheleger, Herman. "Nuremberg—A Fair Trial?" *Atlantic Monthly* 177 (April 1946):60–65.

1112 ———. "The Nuremberg Trials," *California State Bar Proceedings* 19 (1946):72–80.

1113 Podkowlnski, Marian. *W cieniu norymberskiel Temidy: Z notatek korespondenta.* Warsaw: Czytelnik, 1954.

1114 Polevoy, Boris N. *V konste kontsov.* Moscow, 1969.

1115 Poliakov, Leon, comp. *Le procès de Nuremberg.* Paris: Julliard, 1971.

1116 Polyansky, N. (Poljanskij). "The Soviet Prosecution's Case at Nuremberg," *New Times* 4 (1946):3–6.

1117 Poroy, Nazim. *Nüremberg Dâvasi.* Ankara: Milli Egitim Basimevi, 1948.

1118 "Le procès de Nuremberg: Les grands criminels de guerre," *Revue de Droit International, de Sciences Diplomatiques et Politiques* 23 (1945): 278–86; 24 (1946):112–37.

1119 Radin, Max. "Justice at Nuremberg," *Foreign Affairs* 24 (April 1946):369–84.

1120 Rappaport, E. S. "Le troisème Nuremberg," *Revue de Droit International (Sottile-Geneva)* 24 (April-September 1946):44–46.

1121 "Recalling Nuernberg Trials," *Ave Maria* 71 (April 26, 1952):514.

1122 Redley, Adolphus G. "International Law at the Crossroads," *South Atlantic Quarterly* 45 (October 1946):165–75.

1123 "The Results of Nuremberg," *New Republic* 115 (October 14, 1946): 467–68.

1124 Reuter, Paul. "Nürnberg 1946—The Trial," *Notre Dame Lawyer* 23 (November 1947):76–97.

1125 Rheinstein, Max. Review of *The Nuremberg Trial and Aggressive War,* by Sheldon Glueck. *University of Chicago Law Review* 14 (February 1947):319–21.

1126 Reithmuller Vaccaro, Julio H. *El proceso de Nuremberg desde el punto de vista jurídico.* Santiago: Editorial Universitaria, 1962.

1127 Ringsted, H. V. "Nazi Terror in Denmark as Exposed at the Nuremberg Trial," *Danish Foreign Office Journal* 2 (1946):11–115.

1128 Rome, M. E. "Trials at Nuremberg," *Maryland State Bar Association Report* 51 (1946):183–95.

1129 Rothe, Wolf Dieter, comp. *Die Endlösung der Judenfrage.* 1 vol. to date. Frankfurt am Main: Bierbaum, 1974.

1130 Rubin, Eli. *Nuremberg Trial: Germany before Her Judges.* London: Transatlantic Authors, 1945.

1131 Rudenko, Roman A. *Die Gerechtigkeit fordert für alle Hauptkriegsverbrecher nur eine Strafe, die Todesstrafe: General Rudenkos Schlussrede in Nürnberg.* Berlin: Verlag Tägliche Rundschau, 1947.

1132 ———. *Die Gerechtigkeit nehme ihren Lauf! Die Reden des sowjetischen Hauptanklägers R. A. Rudenko im Nürnberger Prozess der deutschen Haptkreigsverbrecher.* Berlin: Verlag der Sowjetischen Militärverwaltung in Deutschland, 1946.

1133 ———. *Niurnbergskii process nad glavnymi nemete kimi voennymi prestupnikami: Sbornik materialov v vemi tomakh pod obschchei red. R. A. Rudenko.* 7 vols. Moscow: Gos. izd-vo iurid. lit-ry, 1957–1961.

1134 Russell of Liverpool, Baron. *The Scourge of the Swastika: A Short History of Nazi War Crimes.* London: Cassell, 1954.

1135 Saurel, Louis. *Le procès de Nuremberg.* 2d rev. ed. Paris: Éditions Rouff, 1967.

1136 Schick, Franz B. "New Crimes? Legal Basis of the Nuremberg Trials," *Free World* 11 (1946):39–42.

1137 ———. "The Nuremberg Trial and the Development of an International Criminal Law," *Juridical Review* 59 (December 1947):192–207.

1138 ———. "The Nuremberg Trial and the International Law of the Future," *American Journal of International Law* 41 (October 1947):770–94.

1139 Schmidt, Paul. *Der Statist auf der Galerie 1945 bis 1950: Erlebnisse, Kommentare, Vergleiche.* Bonn: Athenäum, 1951.

1140 Schneider, Peter, and Hermann Josef Meyer, eds. *Rechtliche und politische Aspekte der NS-Verbrecherprozesse Kolloquium: 5 Vorträge von Fritz Bauer.* Mainz: Johannes-Gutenberg-Universität, 1968.

1141 Schneider, Rolf. *Prozess in Nürnberg (Ein Dokumentarstück): Mit einem Anhang: Auszüge aus dem "Nürnberger Tagebuch" vom G. M. Gilbert.* Frankfurt am Main: Fischer-Bücherei, 1968.

1142 Schönborn, Erwin. *Soldaten Verteidigen ihre Ehre.* Frankfurt am Main: Bierbaum, 1974.

1143 Schwarzenberger, Georg. "The Judgment of Nuremberg," *Tulane Law Review* 21 (March 1947):329–61.

1144 ———. "The Judgment of Nuremberg," *Year Book of World Affairs* 2 (1948):94–124.

1145 Sears, Charles B. "The International Military Tribunal," *New York State Bar Association Bulletin* 71 (1948):196–204.

1146 "The Senator Takes a Chance," *Catholic World* 169 (November 1946):97–99.

1147 "Settling the Issue of War Guilt, Conclusive Verdict against Nazis," *U.S. News and World Report* 21 (October 11, 1946):24–25.

1148 Shapiro, William E., project editor. *Trial at Nuremberg, by the Staff of CBS News.* New York: Franklin Watts, 1968.

1149 Sheean, Vincent. "Error in Translation: Nuremberg and Menschlichkeit," *United Nations World* 1 (September 1947):28–29.

1150 Shirer, William L. "Civilization, Plaintiff: Review of Authentic Recorded Highlights of the Nuremberg Trial," *Saturday Review of Literature* 31 (May 29, 1948):41.

1151 Smith, Willis. "The Nuremberg Trial," *American Bar Association Journal* 32 (July 1946):390–96.

1152 Snyder, Louis L. Review of *Nuremberg Diary,* by G. M. Gilbert. *American Historical Review* 53 (October 1947):166–67.

1153 Steinbauer, Gustav. *Ich war Verteidiger in Nürnberg: Ein Dokumentenbeitrag zum Kampf um Österreich.* Klagenfurt: Kaiser, 1950.

1154 Stephens, Robert G., Jr. "Aspects of the Nuremberg Trial," *Georgia Bar Journal* 8 (February 1946):262–67; 8 (May 1946):375–83; 9 (August 1946):57–65.

1155 Stimson, Henry L. "The Nuremberg Trial, Landmark in Law," *Foreign Affairs* 25 (January 1947):179–89.

1156 Stöcker, Jakob. *Vor dem Tribunal des Weltgerichts: Auf dass Gerechtigkeit werde! Streiflicher zum Nürnberger Prozess.* Hanover: Verlag das Andere Deutschland, 1946.

1157 Storey, Robert G. "Legal Aspects of the Trial of Major War Criminals at Nuremberg," *Louisiana State Bar Association Journal* 5 (October 1946):67–81.

1158 ———. "The Nuremberg Trials," *Tennessee Law Review* 19 (December 1946):517–25.

1159 Süskind, W. E. *Die Mächtigen vor Gericht: Nürnberg 1945/46 am Ort und Stelle erlebt.* Munich, 1963.

1160 Swanson, Roy Arthur. "Frontier Decadence," *Minnesota Review* 3, no. 2 (Winter 1963):192–204.

1161 Swearingen, Victor C. "Nuremberg War Crime Trials," *Kentucky State Bar Journal* 12 (December 1947):11–20.

1162 Szabo, Imre. *A Nünbergi per és a namzetközi büntetöjog.* Budapest: Officina, 1946.

1163 Taft, Robert A. "Equal Justice under Law," *Vital Speeches* 13 (November 1, 1946):44–48.

1164 ———. "The Republican Party," *Fortune* 39 (April 1949):108–18.

1165 Tatage, Paul W. "The Nuremberg Trials: 'Victor's Justice'?" *American Bar Association Journal* 36 (March 1950):247–48.

1166 Taylor, Telford. "The Nuremberg Trials," *Columbia Law Review* 55 (April 1955):488–525.

1167 ———. *Nuremberg Trials, War Crimes and International Law.* New York: Carnegie Endowment for International Peace, 1949.

1168 ———. "Nuremberg War Crimes Trials," *International Conciliation* 450 (April 1949):243–371.

1169 ———. "The Nuremberg War Crimes Trials: An Appraisal," *Proceedings of the Academy of Political Science* 23 (1948/1950):239–54.

1170 ———. *Die Nürnberger Prozesse: Kriegsverbrechen und Völkerrecht.* Zurich: Europa Verlag, 1950.

1171 ———. "The Use of Captured German and Related Records in the Nürnberg War Crimes Trials," in *Captured German and Related Records: A National Archives Conference,* edited by Robert Wolfe. Athens: Ohio University Press, 1974, pp. 92–100.

1172 Teitgen, M. "Le jugement de Nuremberg," *Revue de Droit International (Sottile-Geneva)* 24 (October–December 1946):161–73.

1173 Torgesen, Rolf N. "The Nuremberg Trials," *Norseman* 4 (1946): 391–99.

1174 ———. "The Nuremberg Trials," *Tidsskrift for Rettsvitenskap* 59 (1946):344–57.

1175 Trainin, Aaron N. "Le Tribunal militaire international et le procès de Nuremberg," *Revue Internationale de Droit Pénal* 17 (1946):263–76.

1176 ———. "Wspoluczestnictwo w przestepstwach miedzynarodowych a proces norymberski," *Pantswo i Prawo* 3 (1948):77–86.

1177 "Trial by Victory," *Time* 48 (August 5, 1946):3.

1178 Truman, Harry S. "Prosecution of Major Nazi War Criminals," *Department of State Bulletin* 15 (October 27, 1946):954.

1179 ———. "Reply of President Truman to Justice Jackson," *Department of State Bulletin* 15 (October 27, 1946):776.

1180 Tushins, J. W. "The Nuremberg Trial of World War II Criminals," *Law Society Journal* 12 (November 1946):321–26.

1181 Utley, Freda. *The High Cost of Vengeance.* Chicago: Henry Regnery, 1949.

1182 Vambery, Rustem. "The Law of the Tribunal," *Nation* 163 (October 12, 1946):400–01.

1183 ———. "The Nürnberg Novelty," *Fortune* 32 (December 1945): 140–41.

1184 Veale, F. J. P. *El Crimen de Nuremberg.* Translated by Pablo Uriate. Barcelona: Editorial Ahr, 1955.

1185 "Le verdict de Nuremberg," *Revue de Droit International (Sottile-Geneva)* 24 (1946):260–64.

1186 Versfelt, W. J. B. "Het Nuerenberger proces en zijn belang," *Etudes Internationales* 1 (1948):483–99.

1187 Vinde, Victor. *Nürnberg i blixtljus.* Stockholm: Bonnier, 1946.

1188 Voight, F. A. "Nuremberg," *Nineteenth Century and After* 140 (November 1946):252–58.

1189 Wahl, E. *Il processo di Norimberga.* Milan: Lucchi, 1946.

1190 Walden, Jesco von. . . . *und morgen die ganze Welt? Die Verschwörung der Baunen Paladine.* Berlin: Kongress-Verlag, 1960.

1191 Walm, Nora. "Crime and Punishment," *Atlantic Monthly* 177 (January 1946):43–47.

1192 Walsh, Edmund A. "Comments and Corollaries," *America* 76 (November 9, 1946):151–54.

1193 Wechsler, Herbert. "*Fortune* Letters—Nuremberg Defended," *Fortune* 35 (April 1947):29–32.

1194 _____. "The Issues of the Nuremberg Trial," *Political Science Quarterly* 62, no. 1 (March 1947):11–26.

1195 West, Rebecca. *A Train of Powder.* New York: Viking Press, 1955.

1196 White, William Smith. *The Taft Story.* New York: Harper, 1954.

1197 "Will Nuremberg Stop New Aggressors?" *Saturday Evening Post* (November 2, 1946):164.

1198 Witenberg, J. C. "De Grotius à Nuremberg: Quelques réflexions," *Revue Générale de Droit International Public* 51 (1947):89–112.

1199 Wolf, J. *Les Fondements du Tribunal Militaire International: Considération sur le procès de Nuremberg.* Brussels: Larcier, 1946.

1200 Wolf, R. B. "The Trial at Nuremberg," *Case and Comment* 51 (July-August 1946):23–26.

1201 Wright, Quincy. "Legal Positivism and the Nuremberg Judgment," *American Journal of International Law* 42 (April 1948):405–14.

1202 _____. "The Nuremberg Trial," *Journal of Criminal Law and Criminology* 37 (March-April 1947):477–78.

1203 _____. "The Nuremberg Trials," *Chicago Bar Review* 27 (1946): 201–09.

1204 Wyzanski, Charles E., Jr. "Dangerous Precedent," *Atlantic Monthly* 177 (April 1946):66–70.

1205 _____. "Nuremberg in Retrospect," *Atlantic Monthly* 178 (December 1946):56–59.

1206   Zienau, Oswald. "Rechtsprechung in Nürnberg," *La Oltra Alemania* 150 (September 1947):6–7.

THE DEFENDANTS

General

1207   Bayles, William D. *Caesars in Goose Step.* New York: Harper and Bros., 1940.

1208   Courier, Gabriel. "Hanging," *Christian Herald* 69 (October 1946): 10.

1209   Dutch, Oswald. *Hitler's Twelve Apostles.* New York: Robert M. McBride, 1940.

1210   Fishman, Jack. *The Seven Men of Spandau.* New York: Rinehart, 1954.

1211   Gereke, Henry F. "I Walked to the Gallows with the Nazi Chiefs." Edited by M. Sinclair. *Saturday Evening Post* (September 1, 1951):17–19, 57–58.

1212   Gilbert, G. M. *Nuremberg Diary.* New York: Farrar, Strauss and Cudahy, 1947.

1213   Graven, Jean. "Vingt ans après: La libération des prisonniers de Spandau," *Revue de Droit Pénal et de Criminologie* 27 (1946–1947): 436–60.

1214   Howard, T. "Eight Eyes on Seven Faces: Report from Inside Spandau," *Newsweek* 30 (August 18, 1947):32–33.

1215   Kelly, Douglas M. "Preliminary Studies of the Rorschach Records of the Nazi War Criminals," *Rorschach Research Institute* 10 (June 1946): 45–48.

1216   _____. *Twenty-Two Cells in Nuremberg: A Psychiatrist Examines the Nazi Criminals.* New York: Greenberg, 1947.

1217   Kirkpatrick, Ivone. *The Inner Circle: Memoirs.* London: Macmillan, 1959.

1218   "Last Ride: Former Nazi Leaders," *Newsweek* 30 (July 28, 1947):32.

1219   Lerner, Daniel, with Ithiel de Sola Pool and George K. Schueller. *The Nazi Elite.* Hoover Institution, Series B. Stanford: Stanford University Press, 1951.

1220   "Living Symbols: Spandau Prisoners," *Newsweek* 66 (November 8, 1965):53.

1221 "Nazi Leaders Hang for War Crimes," *Lutheran Outlook* 15 (October 1946):294–95.

1222 "No Escape for the Seven Prisoners of Spandau," *Newsweek* 43 (March 1, 1954):36.

1223 Nova, Fritz. "The National Socialist Fuehrerprinzip and Its Background in German Thought." Ph.D. dissertation, University of Pennsylvania, 1943.

1224 "Nuremberg: Last Laugh," *Newsweek* 28 (October 28, 1946):45–47.

1225 "Nuremberg: The Acquitted," *Newsweek* 28 (October 14, 1946):57–58.

1226 "Reich: Until Dead," *Newsweek* 28 (October 21, 1946):54.

1227 "Russia vs. Newsweek: How the Surviving Nuremberg War Criminals Are Living in Spandau Prison," *Newsweek* 30 (November 3, 1947): 36–38.

1228 Schuster, George N. "Hanging at Nuremberg: The Truth Was Not Allowed to Emerge," *Commonweal* 45 (November 15, 1946):110–13.

1229 Vercel, Michel C. *Les rescapés de Nuremberg: Les "seigneurs de la guerre" après le verdict.* Paris: Éditions Albin Michel, 1966.

1230 "We Furnish the Hangman," *Ave Maria* 64 (November 7, 1946): 580–81.

1231 Ziegler, Hans Severus, comp. *Grosse Prüfung: Letzte Briefe und letzte Worte Todgeweihter.* Hanover: National-Verlag, 1972.

Military Defendants

1232 Assmann, Kurt. "Hitler and the German Officer Corps," *United States Naval Institute Proceedings* 82 (May 1956):509–20.

1233 Craig, Gordon A. "The Army and National Socialism, 1933–1945: The Responsibility of the Generals," *World Politics* 3 (November 1949): 426–38.

1234 Härtle, Heinrich. *Freispruch für Deutschland: Unsere Soldaten vor dem Nürnberger Tribunal.* Göttingen: K. W. Schütz, 1965.

1235 Latersner, Hans. *Verteidigung deutscher Soldaten: Plädoyers vor alliierten Gerichten.* Bonn: Girardet, 1950.

1236 Moll, Otto E. *Die deutschen Generalfeldmarschälle, 1939–1945.* 2d ed. Rastatt: Pabel, 1962.

1237   Nelte, Otto. *Die Generale: Das Nürnberger Urteil und die Schuld der Generale.* Hanover: Verlag das Andere Deutschland, 1947.

1238   Ruge, Friedrich. *Der Seekrieg: The German Navy's Story, 1939–1945.* Translated by M. G. Saunders. Annapolis: United States Naval Institute, 1957.

1239   Siewert, Curt. *Schuldig? Die Generale unter Hitler.* Bad Nauheim: Podzun-Verlag, 1968.

/ Karl Dönitz /

1240   Assmann, Kurt. "Der deutsche U-Bootkrieg und die Nürnberger Rechtsprechung," *Marine Rundschau* 50 (1953):2–8.

1241   Dönitz, Karl. *Die Fahrten der "Breslau" im Schwarzen Meer.* Berlin: Ullstein, 1917.

1242   _____. *Mein wechselvolles Leben.* Göttingen: Musterschmidt-Verlag, 1968.

1243   _____. *Memoirs: Ten Years and Twenty Days.* Translated by R. H. Stevens. London: Weidenfeld and Nicolson, 1959.

1244   _____. *Die U-bootswaffe.* 4th ed. Berlin: Mittler, 1943.

1245   Lüdde-Neurath, Walter. *Regierung Dönitz: Die letzten Tage des Dritten Reiches.* Göttingen: Musterschmidt-Verlag, 1953.

1246   Peillard, Leonce. *The Laconia Affair.* New York: Putnam, 1963.

1247   Steinert, Marlis G. *Twenty-three Days: The Final Collapse of Nazi Germany.* New York: Walker, 1969.

1248   Thompson, H. K., Jr., and Henry Strutz. *Doenitz at Nuremberg: A Reappraisal: War Crimes and the Military Professional.* New York: Amber Publishing, 1976.

/ Hermann Göring /

1249   Bewley, Charles. *Hermann Goering and the Third Reich.* New York: Devin-Adair, 1962.

1250   Bross, Werner. *Gespräche mit Hermann Göring während des Nürnberger Prozesses.* Flensburg: Christian Wolff Verlag, 1950.

1251   "Fat, Satisfied, Vulgar," *Newsweek* 25 (May 21, 1945):54–56.

1252   Gilbert, G. M. "Hermann Goering: Amiable Psychopath," *Journal of Abnormal and Social Psychology* 43 (April 1948):211–29.

1253   Göring, Emmy. *My Life with Goering.* London: David Bruce and Watson, 1972.

1254   Göring, Hermann. *Aufbau einer Nation.* Berlin: Mittler, 1934.

1255 Gritzbach, Erich. *Hermann Göring: Werk und Mensch.* Munich: Zentralverlag der NSDAP, 1941.

1256 Lee, Asher. *Goering, Air Leader.* New York: Hippocrene Books, 1972.

1257 Manvell, Roger, and Heinrich Fraenkel. *Goering.* New York: Simon and Schuster, 1962.

1258 Mosley, Leonard. *The Reich Marshall: A Biography of Hermann Goering.* Garden City, N.Y.: Doubleday, 1974.

/ Alfred Jodl/

1259 "Eisenhower Reports on ETO Tour," *Army and Navy Bulletin* 2 (October 26, 1946):2.

1260 Warlimont, Walter. *Inside Hitler's Headquarters, 1939–1945.* Translated by R. H. Barry. New York: Praeger, 1964.

/ Wilhelm Keitel/

1261 Keitel, Wilhelm. Edited by Walter Görlitz and translated by David Irving. *The Memoirs of Field-Marshall Keitel.* New York: Stein and Day, 1966.

1262 Mueller, Gene A. "Wilhelm Keitel: Chief of the Oberkommando der Wehrmacht, 1938–1945." Ph.D. dissertation, University of Idaho, 1973.

1263 Schmeller, Helmut J. *Hitler and Keitel: An Investigation of the Influence of Party Ideology on the Command of the Armed Forces in Germany between 1938–1945.* Ft. Hays: Kansas State College, 1970.

/ Erich Raeder/

1264 Assmann, Kurt. "Grossadmiral Dr. hc. Raeder und der Zweite Weltkrieg," *Marine Rundschau* 58 (February 1961):3–17.

1265 Gemzell, Carl-Axel. *Raeder, Hitler und Skandinavien.* Frankfurt am Main: Bernard und Graefe Verlag, 1965.

1266 Martienssen, Anthony K. *Hitler and His Admirals.* London: Secker and Warburg, 1948.

1267 Raeder, Erich. *My Life.* Translated by Henry W. Drexel. Annapolis: United States Naval Institute, 1960.

Government Defendants

/ Hans Frank/

1268 Du Prel, Max Freiherr. *Das Generalgouvernment.* Würzburg, 1942.

1269 Frank, Hans. *Im Angesicht des Galgens.* Munich: Friedrich Alfred Beck Verlag, 1953.

1270 _____. *Friedrich Nietzsche.* Krakow: Burgverlag, 1944.

1271 _____. *Das Führerprinzip in der Verwaltung.* Krakow: Burgverlag, 1944.

1272 _____. *Neues deutsches Recht.* Munich: Zentralverlag der NSDAP, 1936.

1273 _____. *Die Technik des Staates.* Berlin: Der Rechtsverlag, 1942.

1274 Klessmann, Cristoph. "Der Generalgouveneur Hans Frank," *Vierteljahrshefte für Zeitgeschichte* 19 (1971):245–60.

1275 Präg, Werner, and Wolfgang Jacobmeyer, eds. *Das Diensttagebuch des deutschen Generalgouverneurs in Polen 1939–1945.* Stuttgart: Deutsche Verlags-Anstalt, 1976.

1276 Weh, Albert. *Übersicht über das Recht des Generalgouvernments.* 2d ed. Krakow: Burgverlag, 1944.

/Wilhelm Frick/

1277 Fabricius, Hans. *Reichsinnernminister Dr. Frick: Der revolutionäre Staatsmann.* Berlin: Deutsche Kulturwacht, 1939.

1278 Frick, Wilhelm. *Freiheit und Bindung der Selbstverwaltung.* Munich: Zentralverlag der NSDAP, 1937.

1279 _____. *Die Nationalsozialisten im Reichstag, 1924–1928.* Munich: Zentralverlag der NSDAP, 1928.

1280 _____. *Die Rassengesetzgebung des Dritten Reiches.* Munich: Zentralverlag der NSDAP, 1934.

1281 _____, and Arthur Gütt. *Nordisches Gedankengut im Dritten Reich.* Munich: J. F. Lehmanns Verlag, 1936.

1282 Pfundtner, Hans. *Dr. Wilhelm Frick und sein Ministerium.* Munich: Zentralverlag der NSDAP, 1937.

1283 Radbruch, Gustav. "Des Reichsjustizministeriums Ruhm und Ende: Zum Nürnberger Juristen-Prozess," *Süddeutsche Juristenzeitung* 3 (February 1948):57–64.

1284 Strauss, Walter. "Das Reichsministerium des Innern und die Judengesetzgebung," *Vierteljahrshefte für Zeitgeschichte* 9 (July 1961): 262–313.

/Hans Fritzsche/

1285 Baird, Jay W. *The Mythical World of Nazi Propaganda.* London: Oxford University Press, 1975.

1286 Boelcke, Willi A. *Kriegspropaganda, 1939–1941.* Stuttgart, n.d.

1287 Bramsted, Ernest K. *Goebbels and National Socialist Propaganda, 1925–1945.* East Lansing: Michigan State University Press, 1965.

1288 Deutsche, Welle, ed. *Worschlacht im Äther: Der deutsche Auslandsrundfunk im Zweiten Weltkrieg.* Cologne: Haude und Spener, 1971.

1289 Fritzsche, Hans. *Krieg den Kriegshetzern.* Berlin: Brunner Verlag Willi Bischoff, 1940.

1290 ———. *The Sword in the Scales: As Told to Hildegard Springen.* Translated by Diana Pyke and Heinrich Fraenkel. London: A. Wingate, 1953.

1291 ———. *Zeugen gegen England.* Düsseldorf: Völkischer Verlag, 1941.

1292 Kris, Ernst; Hans Speier; et al. *German Radio Propaganda: Report on Home Broadcasts during the War.* London: Oxford University Press, 1944.

1293 Pohle, Heinz. *Der Rundfunk als Instrument der Politik: Zur Geschichte des deutschen Rundfunks von 1923–1938.* Hamburg: Verlag Hans Bredow- Inst., 1955.

1294 Scheel, Klaus. *Krieg über Ätherwellen: NS-Rundfunk and Monopole 1933–1945.* Berlin: Deutscher Verlag der Wissenschaften, 1970.

1295 Springer, Hildegard. *Es sprach Hans Fritzsche: Nach Gesprächen, Briefen und Dokumenten.* Stuttgart: Thiele-Verlag, 1949.

1296 ———, ed. *Das Schwert auf der Waage: Hans Fritzsche über Nürnberg.* Heidelberg: Vowinckel, 1953.

1297 Sündermann, Helmut. *Tagesparolen: Deutsche Presseanweisungen 1939–1945: Hitlers Propaganda und Kriegsführung.* Leoni am Starnberger See: Druffel, 1973.

1298 Zeman, Z. A. B. *Nazi Propaganda.* London: Oxford University Press, 1964.

/Walther Funk/

1299 Funk, Walther. *Grundsätze der deutschen Aussenhandelspolitik und das Problem der internationalen Verschuldung.* Berlin: Junker und Dünnhaupt Verlag, 1938.

1300 ———. *Das wirtschaftliche Gesicht des neuen Europas.* Berlin, 1942.

1301 ———. *Wirtschaftsordnung gegen Währungsmechanismus.* Königsberg, 1944.

1302 ———. *Wirtschaftsordnung im neuen Europa.* Vienna: Südost-Echo Verlagsgesellschaft, 1941.

1303 Oestreich, Paul. *Walther Funk: Ein Leben für die Wirtschaft.* Munich: Zentralverlag der NSDAP, 1940.

/Robert Ley/

1304 *Hitlers Stabsleiter der P.O., Dr. Ley: der Führer deutschen Arbeitsfront.* Berlin: Deutsche Kulturwacht, 1934.

1305 Kiehl, Walter. *Mann an der Fahne: Kameraden erzählen von Dr. Ley.* Munich: Zentralverlag der NSDAP, 1938.

1306 Ley, Robert. *Deutschland ist schöner geworden, herausgegeben von Hans Dauer und Walter Kiehl.* Berlin: Verlag der Deutschen Arbeitsfront, 1938.

1307 ———. *Die grosse Stunde: Das deutsche Volk in totalen Kreigseinstaz: Reden und Aufsätze aus den Jahren 1941–1943.* Munich: Zentralverlag der NSDAP, 1943.

1308 ———. *Soldaten der Arbeit.* Munich: Zentralverlag der NSDAP, 1940.

1309 ———. *Unser Socialismus-der Hass der Welt.* Berlin: Verlag der Deutschen Arbeitsfront, 1940.

1310 "Ley: Workers' Friend," *Newsweek* 25 (May 28, 1945):64.

/Constantin Freiherr von Neurath/

1311 Duff, Shiela Grant. *A German Protectorate: The Czechs under Nazi Rule.* London: Macmillan, 1942.

1312 Heineman, John L. "Constantin Freiherr von Neurath as Foreign Minister, 1932–1935." Ph.D. dissertation, Cornell University, 1965.

1313 ———. "Constantin von Neurath and German Policy at the London Economic Conference of 1933: Backgrounds to the Resignation of Alfred Hugenberg," *Journal of Modern History* 41 (June 1969):160–88.

1314 Mastny, Vojtech. *The Czechs under Nazi Rule: The Failure of National Resistance, 1939–1942.* New York: Columbia University Press, 1971.

/Franz von Papen/

1315 Bach, Jürgen A. *Franz von Papen in der Weimarer Republik: Aktivitäten in Politik und Puesse 1918–1932.* Düsseldorf: Droste Verlag, 1977.

1316 FitzGibbon, Constantine. *Denazification.* New York: Norton, 1969.

1317 Papen, Franz von. *Europa: Was nun?* Göttingen: Göttiger Verlagsanstalt, 1954.

1318 ———. *Vom Scheitern einer Demokratie, 1930–1933.* Mainz: v. Hase und Koehler Verlag, 1966.

1319 ———. *Der Wahrheit: Eine Gasse.* Munich: Paul List Verlag, 1952.

/Joachim von Ribbentrop/

1320 Forndran, Erhard; Frank Golczwewski; and Dieter Riesenberger; eds. *Nationalsozialistische Aussenpolitik: Determinanten internationaler Beziehungen in historischen Fallstudien.* Opladen: Westdeutscher Verlag, 1976.

1321 Funke, Manfred, ed. *Hitler, Deutschland und die Mächte: Materialen zur Aussenpolitik des Dritten Reiches.* Düsseldorf: Droste Verlag, 1976.

1322 Hillgruber, Andreas, ed. *Staatsmänner und Diplomaten bei Hitler: Vertrauliche Aufzeichnungen über Unterredungen mit Vertretern des Auslands.* 2 vols. Frankfurt am Main: Bernard und Graefe Verlag, 1967–1970.

1323 Jacobsen, Hans-Adolf. *Nationalsozialistische Aussenpolitik, 1933–1938.* Frankfurt am Main: Metzner, 1968.

1324 Michalka, Wolfgang. *Joachim von Ribbentrop und die deutsche Englandpolitik, 1933–1940.* Munich: Fink, 1976.

1325 Presseisen, Ernst L. *Germany and Japan: A Study in Totalitarian Diplomacy, 1933–1941.* The Hague: Nijhoff, 1958.

1326 Ribbentrop, Joachim von. *The Ribbentrop Memoirs.* Translated by Oliver Watson. London: Weidenfeld and Nicolson, 1954.

1327 Schwarz, Paul. *This Man Ribbentrop: His Life and Times.* New York: Julian Meissner, 1943.

1328 Seabury, Paul. "Ribbentrop and the German Foreign Office," *Political Science Quarterly* 66 (December 1951):532–55.

/Fritz Saukel/

1329 Didier, Friedrich. *Europa arbeitet in Deutschland: Sauckel mobilisiert die Leistungsreserven.* Berlin: Eher, 1943.

1330 Marrenbach, Otto. *Fundamente des Sieges, die Gesamtarbeit der deutschen Arbeitsfront von 1933 bis 1940.* Berlin: Verlag der Deutschen Arbeitsfront, 1940.

1331 Stamm, Kurt, ed. *Der Reichsarbeitsdienst: Reichsarbeitsdienstgesetz mit ergänzenden Bestimmungen und Erläuterungen.* 2d ed. Berlin: Verlag für Recht und Verwaltung, 1937.

/Hjalmar Schacht/

1332 Beck, Earl R. *Verdict on Schacht: A Study in the Problem of Political "Guilt."* Tallahassee: Florida State University Press, 1955.

1333 Maier, K. *Ist Schacht ein Verbrecher?* Reutlingen: Verlag die Zukunft, 1948.

1334 Reuter, Franz. *Schacht.* Stuttgart: Deutsche Verlags-Anstalt, 1937.

1335 Schacht, Hjalmar. *Abrechnung mit Hitler.* Hamburg: Rowohlt Verlag, 1948.

1336 ———. *Das Ende der Reparation.* Oldenburg: Gerhard Stalling, 1931.

1337 ———. *1933: Wie eine Demokratie stirbt.* Düsseldorf: Econ-Verlag, 1968.

1338 ———. *Sechs-und-siebzig Jahre meines Lebens.* Bad Worishofen: Kindler und Schiermeyer Verlag, 1953.

/Arthur Seyss-Inquart/

1339 Seyss-Inquart, Arthur. *Vier Jahre in den Niederlanden: Gesammelte Reden.* Amsterdam: Volk und Reich, 1944.

/Albert Speer/

1340 Janssen, Gregor. *Das Ministerium Speer: Deutschlands Rüstung im Krieg.* 2d ed. Berlin: Ullstein, 1969.

1341 Milward, Alan S. *The Fascist Economy in Norway.* Oxford: Clarendon Press, 1972.

1342 ———. *The German Economy at War.* London: Athlone Press, 1965.

1343 Speer, Albert. *Inside the Third Reich.* Translated by Richard and Clara Winston. New York: Macmillan, 1970.

1344 ———. *Spandau: The Secret Diaries.* Translated by Richard and Clara Winston. New York: Macmillan, 1976.

1345 ———, ed. *Neue deutsche Baukunst.* Berlin: Volk und Reich, 1940.

Nazi Party Defendants

1346 Bracher, Karl Dietrich. *The German Dictatorship: The Origins, Structure and Effects of National Socialism.* Translated by Jean Steinberg. New York: Praeger, 1970.

1347 *Organisationsbuch der NSDAP.* Munich: Zentralverlag der NSDAP, 1937.

1348 Orlow, Dietrich. *The History of the Nazi Party.* 2 vols. Pittsburgh: University of Pittsburgh Press, 1969–1973.

1349 Quinnett, Robert L. "Hitler's Political Officers: The National Socialist Leadership." Ph.D. dissertation, University of Oklahoma, 1973.

/Martin Bormann/

1350 Besymenski, Lew. *Die letzten Notizen von Martin Bormann: Ein Dokument und sein Verfasser.* Stuttgart: Deutsche Verlags-Anstalt, 1974.

1351 Lang, Jochen von. *Der Sekretär: Martin Bormann: Der Mann der Hitler beherrschte.* Stuttgart: Deutsche Verlags-Anstalt, 1977.

1352 Stevenson, William. *The Bormann Brotherhood.* New York: Harcourt Brace Jovanovich, 1973.

1353 Trevor-Roper, Hugh R., ed. *The Bormann Letters.* London: Weidenfeld and Nicolson, 1954.

1354 ———. "Martin Bormann," *Der Monat* 6 (May 1954):168–76.

1355 Wulf, Josef. *Martin Bormann, Hitlers Schatten.* Gütersloh: S. Mohn, 1962.

/Rudolf Hess/

1356 Bird, Eugege K. *Prisoner No. 7: Rudolf Hess.* New York: Viking Press, 1974.

1357 Brissaud, André. "Hess et les magiciens," *Miroir de L'Histoire* 258 (June 1971):89–100.

1358 Hess, Ilse, comp. *England-Nürnberg-Spandau: Ein Schicksal in Briefen.* Leoni am Starnberger See: Druffel, 1952.

1359 ———. *Gefangener des Friedens: Neue Briefe aus Spandau.* Leoni am Starnberger See: Druffel, 1965.

1360   Hutton, Bernard J. *Rudolf Hess: The Man and His Mission.* New York: Macmillan, 1971.

1361   Jacobsen, Hans-Adolf, ed. *Karl Haushofer: Leben und Werk.* 2 vols. Boppard am Rhein: Harald Boldt Verlag, 1978.

1362   Leasor, Thomas J. *Uninvited Envoy.* New York: McGraw-Hill, 1962.

1363   Manvell, Roger, and Heinrich Fraenkel. *Hess: A Biography.* New York: Drake Publishers, 1973.

1364   Rees, J. R., ed. *The Case of Rudolf Hess: A Problem in Diagnosis and Forensic Psychiatry.* London: William Heinemann, 1947.

/Alfred Rosenberg/

1365   Bäumler, Alfred. *Alfred Rosenberg und der Mythus des 20. Jahrhunderts.* Munich: Hoheneichen-Verlag, 1943.

1366   Cecil, Robert. *The Myth of the Master Race: Alfred Rosenberg and Nazi Ideology.* London: B. T. Batsford, 1972.

1367   Hart, S. T. *Alfred Rosenberg.* Munich: J. F. Lehmanns Verlag, 1933.

1368   Lang, Serge, and Ernst von Schenck, eds. *Porträt eines Menschheitsverbrechers: Nach den hinterlassenen Memoiren des ehemaligen Reichministers Alfred Rosenberg.* St. Gallen: Zollokofer, 1947.

1369   Rosenberg, Alfred. *Der Mythus des 20. Jahrhunderts.* Munich: Hoheneichen-Verlag, 1930.

1370   _____. *Die Protokolle der Weisen von Zion und Die Jüdische Weltpolitik.* Munich: Hoheneichen-Verlag, 1923.

1371   _____. *Sammelheft ausgewählter Vorträge und Reden für die Schulung in nationalpolitischer Zielsetzung.* Berlin: Zentralverlag der NSDAP, 1939.

1372   _____. *Die Spur der Juden im Wandel der Zeiten.* Munich: Volksverlag, 1920.

1373   _____. *Der Staatsfeindliche Zionismus.* Munich: Zentralverlag der NSDAP, 1938.

1374   _____. *Unmoral und Talmud.* Munich: Volksverlag, 1920.

1375   Seraphim, Hans-Günther. *Das politische Tagebuch Alfred Rosenbergs 1934–35 und 1939–40.* Göttingen: Musterschmidt-Verlag, 1956.

/Baldur von Schirach/

1376   Herzog, Robert. *Besatzungsverwaltung in den besetzten Ostgebieten, Abteilung Jugend.* Tübingen: Institut für Besatzungsfragen, 1960.

1377 Klönne, Arno. *Hitlerjugend: Die Jugend und ihre Organisation im Dritten Reich.* Hanover: Norddeutsche Verlagsanstalt O. Goedel, 1955.

1378 Klose, Werner. *Generation im Gleichschritt.* Oldenburg: Gerhard Stalling, 1964.

1379 Koch, H. W. *The Hitler Youth: Origins and Development, 1922–45.* New York: Stein and Day, 1976.

1380 Laqueur, Walter. *Die deutsche Jugendbewegung.* Cologne: Wissenschaft und Politik, 1962.

1381 Priepke, Manfred. *Die evangelische Jugend im Dritten Reich, 1933–1936.* Hanover: Norddeutsche Verlagsanstalt O. Goedel, 1960.

1382 Raabe, Felix. *Die bündische Jugend.* Stuttgart: Brentano Verlag, 1961.

1383 Schirach, Baldur von. *Die Feier der neuen Front.* Munich: Volksverlag, n.d.

1384 ———. *Die Hitlerjugend–Idee und Gestalt.* Berlin, 1934.

1385 ———. *HJ im Dienst.* Berlin: Bernard und Graefe Verlag, 1940.

1386 ———. *Ich glaubte an Hitler.* Hambug: Mosaik Verlag, 1967.

1387 ———. *Das Jugendwohnheim.* N.p.: Stubenrauch Verlagsbuchhandlung, 1943.

1388 ———. *Kriminalität und Gefahrdung der Jugend.* Berlin, 1941.

1389 ———. *Das Kulturprogramm: Rede im Wiener Burgtheater, April 6, 1941.* Vienna: Franz Eher Verlag Zweigniederlassung, c. 1941.

1390 ———. *Wille und Macht: Rede, Juli 1, 1938.* Munich: Zentralverlag der NSDAP, 1939.

1391 Schirach, Henriette von. *The Price of Glory.* Translated and adapted by Willi Frischauer. London: Frederich Muller, 1960.

1392 Schirach, Max von. *Geschichte der Familie von Schirach.* Berlin: Walter de Gruyter Verlag, 1939.

/Julius Streicher/

1393 Bein, Alexander. "Der moderne Antisemitismus und seine Bedeutung für die Judenfrage," *Vierteljahrshefte für Zeitgeschichte* 6 (October 1958):340–60.

1394 Bondy, Louis W. *Racketeers of Hatred: Julius Streicher and the Jew-Baiters' International.* London: N. Wolsey, 1946.

ALLIED POWERS PERSONALITIES

Judges

1395   Smith, Bradley F. *Reaching Judgment at Nuremberg.* New York: Basic Books, 1976.

/Norman Birkett (Baron Birkett of Ulverston)/

1396   Bardens, Dennis. *Lord Justice Birkett.* London: R. Hale, 1962.

1397   Birkett, Norman. "International Legal Theories Evolved at Nuremberg," *International Affairs* 23 (July 1947):317–25.

1398   Bowker, Archibald Edgar. *Behind the Bar.* London: Staples Press, 1948.

1399   Hyde, H. Montgomery. *Lord Justice: The Life and Times of Lord Birkett of Ulverston.* New York: Random House, 1965.

1400   "Right Honorable Sir Norman Birkett," *Law Journal* 107 (January 18, 1957):107.

/Francis Biddle/

1401   Biddle, Francis B. *In Brief Authority.* Garden City, N.Y.: Doubleday, 1962.

1402   ———. "Nuremberg: The Fall of the Supermen," *American Heritage* 13 (August 1962):65–76.

1403   ———. "The Nuremberg Trial," *Virginia Law Review* 33 (November 1947):679–96.

1404   ———. "The Nürnberg Trial," *Proceeding of the American Philosophical Society* 91 (1947):294–302.

1405   ———. "Le procès de Nuremberg," *Revue Internationale de Droit Pénal* 19 (1948):1–19.

/Henri F. A. Donnedieu de Vabres/

1406   Donnedieu de Vabres, Henri F. A. "Le jugement de Nuremberg et le principe de légalité des délits et des peines," *Revue de Droit Pénal et de Criminologie* 27 (July 1947):813–33.

1407   ———. "Le procès de Nuremberg," *Revue de Science Criminelle et de Droit Pénal Comparé* 2 (1947):171–83.

1408   ———. *Le procès de Nuremberg, cours de doctorat professé a la Faculté de droit de Paris.* Paris: Éditions Domat Montchrestien, 1947.

1409 ———. "Le procès de Nuremberg (Exposé fait le 27 février 1947 à la Conférence du Jeune Barreau)," *Revue de Droit Pénal et de Criminologie* 27 (1946–1947):480–90.

1410 ———. "Le procès de Nuremberg devant les principes modernes du droit pénal international," *Recueil des Cours de l'Académie de Droit International de la Haye* 70 (1947):477–582.

1411 ———. *Le procès de Nuremberg: Le statut du Tribunal Militaire International, les débats, les chefs d'accusation, le jugement.* Paris: Éditions Domat Montchrestien, 1947.

/Lord Justice Lawrence (Baron Oaksey)/

1412 Lawrence, Lord Justice G. "The Nuremberg Trial," *International Affairs* 23 (April 1947):151–59.

1413 ———. *The Nuremberg Trials and the Process of International Law.* Birmingham: Holdsworth Club of the University of Birmingham, 1947.

/John J. Parker/

1414 "John J. Parker: Senior Circuit Judge—Fourth Circuit," *American Bar Association Journal* 32 (December 1946):856–59, 901–03.

1415 Parker, John J. "The International Trial at Nuremberg: Giving Vitality to International Law," *American Bar Association Journal* 37 (July 1951):493–96, 549–55.

1416 ———. "The Nuremberg Trial," *Journal of the American Judicature Society* 30, no. 4 (December 1946):109–15.

1417 ———. "The Nuremberg Trial," *Kentucky State Bar Journal* 11 (June 1947):157–65, 185.

1418 Warren, Earl. "John J. Parker," *New York University Law Review* 33 (May 1958):649.

1419 Watkins, H. E. "A Great Judge and a Great American: Chief Judge John J. Parker," *American Bar Association Journal* 44 (May 1958):448.

Prosecution

/F. E. De Menthon/

1420 De Menthon, F. E. *Frankreich verlangt Gerechtigkeit im Namen der Menschheit.* Neustadt: Imprimerie Nationale, 1946.

1421 ———. *Le procès de Nuremberg, l'accusation française.* Paris: Office Français d'Information, 1946.

1422 ———. *Le procès de Nuremberg, son importance juridique et politique Conférence prononcée le 8 mars 1946.* Paris: Éditions du Mail, 1946.

/Robert H. Jackson/

1423 Aronéanu, Eugène. "Le Juge Jackson et la justice pénale internationale," *Revue de Droit International (Sottile-Geneva)* 32 (October–December 1954):361–72.

1424 Bishop, William W., Jr. "Robert H. Jackson—Obituary," *American Journal of International Law* 49 (January 1955):44–50.

1425 Dean, Gordon. "Mr. Justice Jackson: His Contribution at Nuremberg," *American Bar Association Journal* 41 (October 1955):912–15.

1426 Fairman, Charles. "Robert H. Jackson: 1892–1954—Associate Justice of the Supreme Court," *Columbia Law Review* 55 (April 1955): 445–87.

1427 Gerhart, Eugene C. *America's Advocate: Robert H. Jackson.* Indianapolis: Bobbs-Merrill, 1958.

1428 Jackson, Robert H. *The Case against the Nazi War Criminals and Other Documents.* New York: Knopf, 1946.

1429 ———. "A Country Lawyer at an International Court," *Virginia State Bar Association Proceedings* 58 (1947):190–200.

1430 ———. "The Nuremberg Trial: Civilizations Chief Salvage from World War II," *Vital Speeches* 13 (December 1, 1946):114–17.

1431 ———. "Nuremberg Trial of the Major Nazi Leaders," *New York State Bar Association Bulletin* 70 (1947):147–58.

1432 ———. "Nürnberg," *Common Cause* 3 (1950):285–94.

1433 ———. *The Nürnberg Case, as Presented by Robert H. Jackson.* New York: Knopf, 1947.

1434 ———. "The Nürnberg Trial Becomes an Historic Precedent," *Temple Law Quarterly* 20 (December 1946):167.

1435 ———. "The Significance of the Nuremberg Trials to the Armed Forces," *Military Affairs* 10 (Winter 1946):3–15.

1436 ———. "The Trials of War Criminals: An Experiment in International Legal Understanding," *American Bar Association Journal* 32 (June 1946):319–21.

United States Military Tribunals, Nuremberg, 1946–1949. (Control Council Trials)

PRIMARY EVIDENTIARY DOCUMENTS

1437 IMT. *Trials of War Criminals before the Nuremberg Military Tribunals under Control Council Law No. 10.* 15 vols. Washington, D.C.: GPO, 1949–1950.

1438 United Nations War Crimes Commission. *Law Reports of Trials of War Criminals.* 15 vols. London: HMSO, 1947–1949.

INDEXES

English

1439 Arndt, Karl, comp. *Alphabetical Index of All Witnesses and Defense Counsel Heard in the Twelve Nürnberg War Crimes Trials with Pages of the Official Transcripts of the Proceedings.* Bremen, 1949.

German

1440 *Indices zu den zwölf Nürnberger U.S.-Militärgerichtsprozessen.* 2 vols. Göttingen: Instituts für Völkerrecht der Universität Göttingen, 1950–1956.

OFFICIAL DOCUMENTS: GENERAL

1441 Central Registry of War Criminals and Security Suspects, Berlin. *Consolidated Wanted Lists.* 2 vols. and supplement. Berlin: U.S. Army, Allied Control Authority, 1947.

1442 ———. *Detention List.* 11 vols. Berlin: U.S. Army, Berlin Document Center, 1946–1948.

1443 Office of Military Government, United States (OMGUS). Adjutant General. *Trial of the Members of Criminals Organizations.* Berlin: OMGUS, 1947.

1444 United Nations War Crimes Commission. *List of War Criminals.* 80 vols. London: United Nations War Crimes Commission, 1944–1948.

1445 United States, Department of the Army. *Final Report to the Secretary of the Army on the Nuernberg War Crimes Trials under Control Council Law No. 10,* by Telford Taylor. Washington, D.C.: GPO, 1949.

OFFICIAL MICROFILM PUBLICATIONS

United States National Archives: World War II War Crimes Records, Record Group 238

/Records of the Twelve Cases Tried by U.S. Tribunals at Nuremberg and Assembled by the Court Archives of the Office of the Secretary General of Military Tribunals, 1946–1949/

1446 *United States of America v. Karl Brandt, et al. (Case 1), October 25, 1946–August 20, 1947.* M887. 46 rolls.

1447 *United States of America v. Erhard Milch (Case 2), November 13, 1946–April 17, 1947.* M888. 13 rolls.

1448 *United States of America v. Josef Altstoetter, et al. (Case 3), January 4, 1947–December 4, 1947.* M889. 53 rolls.

1449 *United States of America v. Oswald Pohl, et al. (Case 4), January 13, 1947–November 3, 1947.* M890. 38 rolls.

1450 *United States of America v. Friedrich Flick, et al. (Case 5), February 8, 1947–December 22, 1947.* M891. 42 rolls.

1451 *United States of America v. Carl Krauch, et al. (Case 6), May 3, 1947–July 30, 1948.* M892 (in progress).

1452 *United States of America v. Wilhelm List, et al. (Case 7), May 10, 1947–February 19, 1948.* M893. 48 rolls.

1453 *United States of America v. Ulrich Greifelt, et al. (Case 8), July 1, 1947–March 10, 1948.* M894. 38 rolls.

1454 *United States of America v. Otto Ohlendorf, et al. (Case 9), July 3, 1947–April 10, 1948.* M895. 38 rolls.

1455 *United States of America v. Alfried Felix Alwyn Krupp von Bohlen und Halbach, et al. (Case 10), August 16, 1947–July 31, 1948.* M896 (in progress).

1456 *United States of America v. Ernst von Weizsaecker, et al. (Case 11), November 4, 1947–April 13, 1949.* M897 (in progress).

1457 *United States of America v. Wilhelm von Leeb, et al. (Case 12), November 28, 1947–October 28, 1948.* M898 (in progress).

/Popular Case Name Designations/

Case I: Medical Case
Case II: Milch Case
Case III: Justice Case
Case IV: Pohl Case
Case V: Flick Case
Case VI: I. G. Farben Case
Case VII: Hostage Case
Case VIII: RuSHA Case
Case IX: Einsatzgruppen Case
Case X: Krupp Case
Case XI: Ministries Case
Case XII: High Command Case

GENERAL

1458 Arndt, Adolf. "Das Befreiungsgesetz ist kein Strafgesetz," *Süddeutsche Juristenzeitung* 3 (February 1948):110.

1459 Bardèche, Maurice. *Nuremberg II: Ou, les faux monnayeurs.* Paris: Les sept couleurs, 1950.

1460 Behling, Kurt. "Die Schuldansprüche im Nürnberger Juristenurteil vom 4./5. Dezember 1947," *Archiv des Völkerrechts* 2 (August 1950): 412–27.

1461 Benjamin, Hilde. "Die Interzonentagung der Juristen der VVN in Schönberg vom 20. bis 22. März 1948," *Neue Justiz* 2 (March 1948):56–58.

1462 Boissier, Pierre. "La Répression des 'petits' crimes de guerre," *Revue Internationale de Droit Pénal* 19 (1948):293–309.

1463 Boumal, J. "Les Jugements du Tribunal Militaire Américain de Nuremberg," *Revue de Droit Pénal et de Criminologie* 30 (May 1950): 844–61.

1464 Brooks, Willis Montford."Precedent for the American War Crimes Trials." M.A. thesis, University of California, Los Angeles, 1947.

1465 Citron, Curt. "Das Kontrollratsgesetz no. 10," *Gegenwart* 2 (1947): 23–24.

1466 Coning, Helmut. "Das Grundrecht der Menschenwürde der strafrechtliche Schutz der Menschlichkeit, und das Persönlichkeitsrecht des bürgerlichen Rechts," *Süddeutsche Juristenzeitung* 2 (December 1947): 641–45.

1467 "Escape Stories from Germany," *Newsweek* 31 (February 16, 1948): 38.

1468 Guski, Karl. "Rechtsfragen zum Befehl Nr. 201," *Neue Justiz* 1 (August–September 1947):172–78.

1469 Herbert, Paul M. "Nürnberg Subsequent Trials," *Insurance Counsel Journal* 16 (July 1949):226–32.

1470 Hodenberg, Hodo von. "Zur Anwendung des Kontrollratsgesetzes Nr. 10 durch deutsche Gerichte," *Süddeutsche Juristenzeitung* 2 [Special issue] (March 1947):113–24.

1471 Katzenberger, K. "Das Korps der politischen Leiter im Urteil von Nürnberg," *Neue Juristische Wochenschrift* 1 (July 1948):371–75.

1472 Kiesselbach, Wilhelm. "Zwei Probleme aus dem Gesetz Nr. 10 des Kontrollrats," *Monatsschrift für Deutsches Recht* 1 (1947):2–6.

1473 Kraus, Herbert. *Kontrollratsgesetz Nr. 10.* Hamburg: Rechts- und Staatswissenschaftlicher Verlag, 1947.

1474 Lange, Richard. "Das Kontrollratsgesetz Nr. 10 in Theorie und Praxis," *Deutsche Rechtszeitschrift* 3 (1948):185–93.

1475 ———. "Zum Denunziantenproblem," *Süddeutsche Juristenzeitung* 3 (June 1948):302–11.

1476 "Law No. 10: Punishment of Persons Guilty of War Crimes, Crimes against Peace and against Humanity," *Official Gazette of the Control Council for Germany* 3 (January 31, 1946):50–55.

1477 Logan, Andy. "Letter from Nuremberg," *New Yorker* 23 (December 27, 1947):40–47.

1478 Malézieux, R. "Le statut international des criminels de guerre," *Revue générale de Droit International Public* 49, no. 2 (1941–1945): 167–80.

1479 Melsheimer, Ernst. "Der Kampf der deutschen Justiz gegen die Naziverbrecher," *Neue Justiz* 2 (August 1948):126–31.

1480 Menzel, Eberhard. "Die Rechtsnatur der Spruchgerichte und des von ihn anzuwendenden Rechts," *Die Spruchgerichte* 3 (February-March 1949):39–44.

1481 Meyer, R. "Das Kontrollratsgesetz Nr. 10 in der Praxis der deutschen Strafgerichte," *Monatsschrift für Deutsches Recht* 1 (1947): 110–12.

1482 "Military Tribunals—Appointment of Judges at Nuremberg," *American Bar Association Journal* 33 (September 1947):896–97.

1483 Mittelbach, Hans. "Das Spruchgerichtsverfahren im Lichte der Urteile des amerikanischen Militärgerichtshofs Nr. II und III," *Die Spruchgerichte* 2 (1948):108–12.

1484 Mosler, Hermann. "Die Kriegshandlung in Rechtswidrigen Kriege," *Jahrbuch für Internationales und Ausländisches Öffentliches Recht* 1 (1948):335–57.

1485 Musmanno, Michael A. *In zehn Tagen kommt der Tod.* Munich: Droemer, 1950.

1486 "Nuremberg Trials Go On," *New York Times Magazine* (September 28, 1947):12–13.

1487 "A Prosecutors' Memorandum in a War Crimes Trial," *New Jersey Law Journal* 7 (April 8, 1948):129, 131, 133, 136.

1488 Schönke, A. "Grundsätzliche Strafmass im Spruchgerichtsverfahren," *Die Spruchgerichte* 2 (March 1948):65–66.

1489 Schulze, Hans Joachim. *Fragen zum "Allgemeinen Teil" des Kontrollratsgesetzes Nr. 10.* Munich, 1960.

1490 Sottile, Antoine. "Un peu plus de justice, S.V.P.! (À propos de certains verdicts et acquittements prononcés par les tribunaux militaires internationaux)," *Revue de Droit International (Sottile-Geneva)* 26 (October-December 1948):372–85.

1491 Thiele-Fredersdorf, Herbert. "Das Urteil des Militärgerichtshofes No. III in Nürnberger Juristen-Prozess," *Neue Juristische Wochenschrift* 1 (1948):112–26.

1492 Weber, Hellmuth von. "Der Einfluss der Militärstrafgerichtsbarkeit des Besatzungsmacht auf die deutsche Strafgerichtsbarkeit," *Süddeutsche Juristenzeitung* 2 (February 1947):65–70.

1493 ———. "Zur Auswirkung der Gesetzgebung der Besatzungsmächte auf das deutsche Strafgesetzbuch," *Süddeutsche Juristenzeitung* 1 (November-December 1946):238–40.

1494 Werner Wolfhart. "Der Grundsatz 'nullem crimen, nulla poena sine lege' und die Anwendung des Gesetzes nr. 10 des Allierten Kontrollrats durch deutsche Gerichte," *Die Spruchgerichte* 1 (1947):25–30.

1495 Wimmer, August. "Unmenschlichkeitsverbrechen und deutscherechtliche Straftat in einer Handlung," *Süddeutsche Juristenzeitung* 3 (May 1948):253–58.

1496 Winkelmann, Paul. "Aufgaben der Staatsanwälte und Gerichte in den Verfahren nach dem Befehl Nr. 201," *Neue Justiz* 1 (August-September 1947):169–72.

1497 Zeck, William A. "Nuremberg: Proceedings Subsequent to Goering, et al.," *North Carolina Law Review* 26 (June 1948):350–89.

THE TRIALS

Medical Cases

/Case I: *United States of America v. Karl Brandt, et al.*/

1498 Bader, Karl S. "Umschau—Zum Nürnberger Ärzteprozess," *Deutsche Rechtszeitschrift* 2 (1947):401–02.

1498a *German Medical War Crimes: A Summary of Information.* London: World Medical Association, 1948.

1499 Goldovsky, E., and K. Platonov. "The Crime of Nazi Doctors," *Voks Bulletin* 3–4 (1945):17–20.

1500 Goodman, Roger, ed. *The First German War Crimes Trial: Chief Judge Walter B. Beals' Desk Notebook of the Doctors' Trial, Held in Nuremberg, Germany, December 1946 to August 1947.* 2 vols. Salisbury, N.C.: R and D Books, 1976.

1501   Graham, Robert J., "The 'Right to Kill' in the Third Reich: Prelude to Genocide," *Catholic Historical Review* 62, no. 1 (January 1976):56–76.

1502   Graven, Jean. "Le procès des médecins nazis et les expériences pseudo-médicales: Esquisse d'une étude synthèse," *Annals de Droit International Médical* 8 (1962):11–75.

1503   Great Britain, Advisory Committee for the Investigation of German Medical War Crimes. *Scientific Results of German Medical War Crimes: Report of an Enquiry by a Committee under the Chairmanship of Lord Moran.* London: HMSO, 1949.

1504   "Herr Dr. Sadist: Twenty-three Nazi Doctors Arraigned in War Crimes Trial," *Newsweek* 28 (December 21, 1946):65.

1505   Inbona, J. M. "Le Procès de Medicins Allemands," *Revue Internationale* 3 (March-April 1947):242–46.

1506   "Indictment Case Number One—U.S. vs. Certain German Doctors," *Florida Law Journal* 21 (January 1947):15–22.

1507   Mant, A. K. "Medical War Crimes in Nazi Germany," *Saint Mary's Hospital Gazette* 27 (1961):1–6.

1508   Mitscherlich, Alexander, and Fred Mielke. *Das Diktat Menschenverachtung: Der Nürnberger Aertzeprozess und seine Quellen.* Heidelberg: Verlag Lambert Schneider, 1947.

1509   ———. *Doctors of Infamy: The Story of the Nazi Medical Crimes.* Translated by Heinz Norden. New York: H. Schuman, 1949.

1510   ———. *Wissenschaft ohne Menschlichkeit: Medizinische und eugenische Irrwege unter Diktatur, Burokratie und Krieg.* Heidelberg: Verlag Lambert Schneider, 1949.

1511   Smith, C. C. *Guide to the Documents That Were Admitted as Evidence for the Prosecution and Defense of the Nazi Doctors before the United States Military Tribunal at Nuremberg.* New York, 1955–1956.

Justice Case

/Case III: *United States of America v. Josef Altstoetter, et al.*/

1512   Boberach, Heinz, ed. *Richterbriefe: Dokumente zur Beeinflussung der deutschen Rechtsprechung 1942–1944.* Boppard am Rhein: Harald Boldt Verlag, 1975.

1513   Buchheit, Gert. *Richter in roter Robe: Freisler, Präsident des Gerichtshofes.* Munich: List, 1968.

1514 Figge, Robert. "Die Verantwortlichkeit des Richters," *Süddeutsche Juristenzeitung* 2 (March-April 1947):179–84.

1515 Haast, H. F. von. "A Second Nuremberg Trial: Judges Tried for Subservience to the Fuhrer," *New Zealand Law Journal* 24 (March 23, 1948):67–68.

1516 Haensel, Carl. "Das Urteil im Nürnberger Juristenprozess," *Deutsche Rechtszeitschrift* 3 (February 1948):40–43.

1517 Johe, W. *Die gleichschaltete Justiz.* Frankfurt am Main: Europäische Verlagsanstalt, 1967.

1518 Kaul, Friedrich K. *Geschichte des Reichsgerichts: 1933–1945.* Berlin: Akademie Verlag, 1971.

1519 Kintner, E. W., ed. *The Justice Trial: Trial of Joseph Altstoetter and Fifteen Others.* London: William Hodge, 1948.

1520 Kirchheimer, Otto. "Criminal Law in National-Socialist Germany," *Studies in Philosophy and Social Science* 8 (1940):444–63.

1521 Kramer, G. *The Influence of National Socialism on the Courts of Justice and the Police in the Third Reich.* London: Weidenfeld and Nicolson, 1955.

1522 La Follette, Charles M. "Justice Case at Nuremberg," *Information Bulletin* [Office of the U.S. High Commissioner for Germany] 138 (June 29, 1948):9–12; 139 (July 13, 1948):11–15; 140 (July 27, 1948):15–20.

1523 Melsheimer, Ernst. "Der Kampf der deutschen Justiz gegen die Naziverbrecher," *Neue Justiz* 2 (August 1948):126–31.

1524 Radbruch, Gustav. "Des Reichsjustizministeriums Ruhm und Ende: Zum Nürnberger Juristen-Prozess," *Süddeutsche Juristenzeitung* 3 (February 1948):57–64.

1525 Schorn, Hubert. *Der Richter im Dritten Reich.* Frankfurt am Main: Klostermann Verlag, 1959.

1526 Staff, Ilse. *Justiz im Dritten Reich.* Frankfurt am Main: Fischer-Bücherei, 1964.

1527 Sweet, William. "The Volksgerichtshof, 1934–1945," *Journal of Modern History* 46 (1974):314–29.

1528 Weinkauff, Hermann, et al. *Die deutsche Justiz und der Nationalsozialismus.* 3 vols. Stuttgart: Deutsche Verlags-Anstalt, 1968–1974.

1529 Willig, Kenneth C. H. "The Theory and Administration of Justice in the Third Reich." Ph.D. dissertation, University of Pennsylvania, 1975.

Ethnological (Nazi Race Policy) Cases

/Case IV: *United States of America v. Oswald Pohl, et al.*/

1530 Aronson, Shlomo. *Reinhard Heydrich und die Frühgeschichte von Gestapo und SD.* Stuttgart: Deutsche Verlags-Anstalt, 1971.

1531 Beyer, Alfred. "Zum Tatbestand des Organisationsverbrechens unter Berücksichtigung der Urteils des amerikanischen M.T. gegen Pohl und andere, vom 3. November 1947," *Die Spruchgerichte* 2 (1948):104–08.

1532 Buchheim, Hans. "Die höheren SS-und Polizeiführer," *Vierteljahrshefte für Zeitgeschichte* 11 (October 1963):362–91.

1533 ———. "Die SS in der Verfassung des Dritten Reiches," *Vierteljahrshefte für Zeitgeschichte* 3 (April 1955):127–57.

1534 ———; Martin Broszat; Hans-Adolf Jacobsen; and Helmut Krans-nick. *Anatomy of the SS State.* Translated by Richard Barry, Marian Jackson, and Dorothy Lang. New York: Walker, 1968.

1535 Crankshaw, Edward. *The Gestapo, Instrument of Tyranny.* New York: Viking Press, 1956.

1536 Delarue, Jacques. *Geschichte der Gestapo.* Düsseldorf: Droste Verlag, 1964.

1537 Desroches, Alain. *La Gestapo: Atrocités et secrets de l'inquisition nazie.* Paris: Éditions de Vecchi, 1972.

1538 Höhne, Heinz. *The Order of the Death's Head: The Story of Hitler's SS.* Translated by Richard Barry. New York: Coward-McCann, 1970.

1539 Kempner, Robert M. W. "Murder by Government," *Journal of Criminal Law and Criminology* 38 (September-October 1947):235–38.

1540 Kogen, Eugen. *Der SS-Staat.* Munich: Verlag Karl Alber, 1949.

1541 Neave, Avery, M. S. "The Trial of the S.S. at Nuremberg," *Revue Internationale de Droit Pénal* 17 (1946):277–90.

1542 Reitlinger, Gerald. *The SS: Alibi of a Nation, 1922–1945.* New York: Viking Press, 1957.

1543 Schleanes, Karl A. *The Twisted Road to Auschwitz: Nazi Policy toward German Jews, 1933–1939.* Urbana: University of Illinois Press, 1970.

/Case VIII: *United States of America v. Ulrich Greifelt, et al.*/

1544 Haag, John. "National Socialism in Action: The RKFDV and the Alvensleben-Schönborn Estate Case," *Historian* 26 (February 1964): 224–66.

1545 Koehl, Robert L. *RKFDV: German Resettlement and Population Policy, 1939–1945.* Cambridge: Harvard University Press, 1957.

/Case IX: *United States of America v. Otto Ohlendorf, et al.*/

1546 Goldstein, Anatole, and Maximilian Hurwitz, ed. *Operation Murder.* New York: World Jewish Congress, Institute of Jewish Affairs, 1949.

1547 Kempner, Robert M. W. *SS im Kreuzverhör.* Munich: Rütten und Loening, 1964.

1548 Smith, Arthur L., Jr. "Life in Wartime Germany: Colonel Ohlendorf's Opinion Service," *Public Opinion Quarterly* 36 (Spring 1972):1–7.

1549 "Undesirables," *Time* 51 (April 19, 1948):31.

Economic Cases

/General/

1550 Beckenbach, Ralf. *Der Staat im Faschismus: Ökonomie und Politik im Deutschen Reich 1920–1945.* Berlin: Verlag für das Studium der Arbeiterbewegung, 1974.

1551 Bettelheim, Charles. *Die deutsche Wirtschaft unter dem Nationalsozialismus.* Munich: Trikout-Verlag, 1974.

1552 Billig, Joseph. *Les camps de concentration dans l'economie du Reich Hitlérien.* Paris: Presses universitaires de France, 1973.

1553 Carroll, Bernice A. *Design for Total War: Arms and Economies in the Third Reich.* The Hague: Mouton, 1968.

1554 Ečer, B. "Accomplices of Hitler: The Criminal Responsibility of the German Financial and Industrial Leaders According to the Soviet Criminal Law," *Labour Monthly* 27 (1945):146–50.

1555 Esenwein-Rothe, Ingeborg. *Die Wirtschaftsverbände von 1933 bis 1945.*Berlin: Duncker und Humboldt, 1965.

1556 Federeau, Fritz. *Der Zweite Weltkrieg: Seine Finanzierung in Deutschland.* Tübingen: Wunderlich, 1962.

1557 Hofer, Walter, ed. *Wissenschaft im totalen Staat.* Munich: Nymphenburger Verlag, 1964.

1558 Klein, Burton H. *Germany's Economic Preparation for War.* Cambridge: Harvard University Press, 1959.

1559 Palyi, Melchoir. "Economic Foundations of the German Totalitarian State," *American Journal of Sociology* 46 (1941):469–86.

1560   Radandt, Hans. *Kriegsverbrecherkonzern Mansfeld: Die Rolle des Mansfeld-Konzerns bei der Vorbereitung und während des zweiten Weltkriegs.* Berlin: Verlag Tribüne, 1957.

1561   Schweitzer, Arthur. *Big Business in the Third Reich.* Bloomington: Indiana University Press, 1964.

1562 _____. "Business Policy in a Dictatorship," *Business History Review* 38, no. 4 (1964):412–38.

1563   Simpson, Amos E. "The Struggle for the Control of the German Economy, 1936–37," *Journal of Modern History* 31 (March 1959):37–45.

1564   Stolper, Gustav. *German Economy, 1870–1940: Issues and Trends.* New York: Reynal and Hitchcock, 1940.

1565   Thomas, Georg. *Geschichte der deutschen Wehr- und Rüstungswirtschaft (1918–1943/45).* Edited by Wolfgang Birkenfeld. Boppard am Rhein: Harald Boldt Verlag, 1966.

1566   Thyssen, Fritz. *I Paid Hitler.* New York: Farrar and Rinehart, 1941.

1567   Veicopoulos, Nicolas. "Les responsabilités des industriels dans la préparation de la guerre," *Revue de Droit International (Sottile-Geneva)* 26 (January-March 1948):53–62.

1568   Warner, Adolphe J. "What Case against the German Bankers?" *Commercial and Financial Chronicle* 165 (January 2, 1947):4, 17.

/Case V: *United States of America v. Friedrich Flick, et al.*/

1569   DeWitt, David S. "Military Tribunals for Trial of War Criminals as International Courts [Flick v. Johnson]," *Michigan Law Review* 48 (April 1950):881–83.

1570   Drobisch, Klaus. "Flick und die Nazis," *Zeitschrift für Geschichtswissenschaft* 14, no. 3 (1966):378–97.

1571   Thielecke, K.-H., ed. *Fall 5: Urteil, Anklageplädoyer, Dokumente und Materialien des Flickprozesses (Mit einer Studie über die 'Arisierung' des Flick-Konzerns).* Berlin: Deutscher Verlag der Wissenschaften, 1965.

/Case VI: *United States of America v. Carl Krauch, et al.*/

1572   Ambruster, H. W. "Farben Nazis on Trial," *Nation* 166 (March 20, 1948):321–23.

1573 _____. "They Cheated the Gallows: I. G. Farben Officials," *Nation* 167 (August 14, 1948):176–78.

1574   Clark, D. "Fabulous Farben Empire Faces Trial," *New York Times Magazine* (August 10, 1947):12–13.

1575 "Disaster and Dishonor: Farben and Krupp Directors Sentenced," *Newsweek* 32 (August 9, 1948):27.

1576 Dix, Hellmuth. "Die Urteile in den Nürnberger Wirtschaftsprozessen," *Neue Juristische Wochenschrift* 2 (September 1, 1949):647–52.

1577 Du Bois, Josiah Ellis, with Edward Johnson. *The Devil's Chemists: Twenty-four Conspirators of the International Farben Cartel Who Manufacture Wars.* Boston: Beacon Press, 1952.

1578 "Farben Process," *Newsweek* 30 (September 8, 1947):32–35.

1579 Honig, F. "German Industrialists on Trial," *World Affairs* 3 (April 1949):175–86.

1580 "I. G.Farben: Charges of Fomenting Warfare," *Nation* 164 (May 17, 1947):558.

1581 "Murder Incorporated," *New Republic* 116 (May 12, 1947):6.

1582 Norden, Albert. "The History of the Mannesmann Concern," Translated by Elizabeth Hartmann. *Free World* 7 (1944):223–30.

1583 Radandt, Hans, ed. *Fall 6: Urteil, Dokumente und Materialien zum I G Farben Prozess.* Berlin: Deutscher Verlag der Wissenschaften, 1970.

1584 Sasuly, Richard. *I. G. Farben.* New York: Boni and Gaer, 1947.

1585 Thiele-Fredersdorf, Herbert. "Das Urteil im IG-Farbenprozess," *Neue Juristische Wochenschrift* 2 (1949):376–77.

1586 *Das Urteil im I. G.-Farben-Prozess: Der vollständige Wortlaut mit Dokumentenanhang.* Offenbach am Main: Bollwerk-Verlag, 1948.

/Case X: *United States of America v. Alfried Felix Alwyn Krupp von Bohlen und Halbach, et al.*/

1587 Engelmann, Bernt. *Krupp: Legenden und Wirklichkeit.* Munich: Schneekluth, 1969.

1588 Herold, G. W. "Peculiar Case of Alfred Krupp," *United Nations World* 7 (April 1953):44.

1589 Kaufman, J. W. "Krupp: What Price Expediency?" *New Republic* 124 (February 26, 1951):15–16.

1590 Manchester, William. *The Arms of Krupp, 1587–1968.* Boston: Little, Brown, 1968.

1591 Maschke, Hermann M. *Das Krupp-Urteil und das Problem der "Plünderung."* Göttingen: Musterschmidt Wissenschaftlicher Verlag, 1951.

1592 Mühlen, Norbert. *Die Krupps.* Frankfurt am Main: Scheffler, 1960.

1593 Taylor, Telford. "The Krupp Trial: Fact v. Fiction," *Columbia Law Review* 53 (February 1953):197–210; Kronstein, Heinrich. "In Reply to Mr. Taylor," *Columbia Law Review* 53 (February 1953):211–13.

1594 Wilmowsky, Tilo Freiherr von. *Warum werde Krupp verurteilt? Legende und Justizirrtum.* Düsseldorf: Econ-Verlag, 1962.

Military Cases

/Case II: *United States of America v. Erhard Milch*/

1595 Irving, David. *The Rise and Fall of the Luftwaffe: The Life of Field Marshall Erhard Milch.* New York: Little, Brown, 1974.

/Case VII: *United States of America v. Wilhelm List, et al.*/

1596 Fisch, Arnold G. "Field Marshal Wilhelm List and the Hostages Case at Nuremberg: An Historical Reassessment." Ph.D. dissertation, Pennsylvania State University, 1975.

1597 "Indefensibles Defense," *Time* 47 (March 18, 1946):29.

1598 Rendulic, Lothar. *Glasenbach, Nürnberg, Landsberg: Ein Soldatenschicksal nach dem Krieg.* Graz: L. Stocker, 1953.

1599 Sawicki, Georges. "Châtiment ou encouragement? (En marge du jugement contre Wilhelm List et al.)," *Revue de Droit International (Sottile-Geneva)* 26 (July-September 1948):240–56.

1600 Zöllner, M., and Kazimierz, eds. *Fall 7: Das Urteil im Geisselmordprozess: Gefällt am 19. Februar 1948 in Nürnberg vom Militärgerichthof V . . . (Mit einer Einleitung und einer Chronik über den Volksbefreiungskampf in Jugoslawien, Griechenland und Albanien).* Berlin: Deutscher Verlag der Wissenschaften, 1965.

/Case XII: *United States of America v. Wilhelm von Leeb, et al.*/

1601 Betz, Herman Dieter. *Das OKW und seine Haltung zum Landkriegsvölkerrecht im zweiten Weltkrieg.* Bamberg: Difo-Druck, 1970.

1602 Clark, Delbert. "Bubble, Bubble, Toil and Trouble," *Saturday Review of Literature* 35 (December 6, 1952):29, 38.

1603 Cyprian, Tadeusz. *Wehrmacht: Zbrodnia i Kara.* Warsaw: Wydawn. Ministerstwa Obrony Narodowej, 1971.

1604 Douglas, J. J. "High Command Case: A Study in Staff and Command Responsibility," *International Lawyer* 6, no. 4 (October 1972): 686–705.

1605 "Guilty and Not Guilty: Thirteen Top German Commanders," *Newsweek* 32 (November 8, 1948):27.

1606 Hobbs, Malcolm. "Nürnberg's Indecent Burial," *Nation* 169 (December 3, 1949):634–35.

1607 "Justice for Germans? Case against the Field Marshalls," *Newsweek* 32 (October 4, 1948):35.

Government Case

/Case XI: *United States of America v. Ernst von Weizsaecker, et al.*/

1608 Boveri, Margaret. *Der Diplomat vor Gericht.* Berlin: Minerva Verlag, 1948.

1609 Craig, Gordon, and Felix Gilbert, eds. *The Diplomats, 1919–1939.* Princeton: Princeton University Press, 1953.

1610 Dirksen, Herbert von. *Moscow, Tokyo, London: Twenty Years of German Foreign Policy.* Norman: University of Oklahoma Press, 1952.

1611 Frend, W. H. C. "Hitler and His Foreign Ministry, 1937–1939," *History* 42 (1957):118–29.

1612 Hill, Leonidas E. "The Wilhelmstrasse in the Nazi Era," *Political Science Quarterly* 82 (December 1967):546–70.

1613 ———, ed. *Die Weizsäcker-Papiere.* Berlin: Propyläen, 1974.

1614 Jones, E. "Case against Wilhelmstrasse," *London Calling* 446 (1948):8, 15.

1615 Kordt, Erich. *Nicht aus den Akten: Die Wilhelmstrasse in Frieden und Krieg: Begebungen, Eindrücke, 1928–1945.* Stuttgart: Union, 1950.

1616 Krosigk, Graf Lutz Schwerin von. *Es geschah in Deutschland.* Tübingen: Wunderlich, 1951.

1617 ———. *Staatsbankrott: Die Geschichte der Finanzpolitik des Deutschen Reiches von 1920 bis 1945, geschrieben vom letzten Reichsfinanzminister.* Göttingen: Musterschmidt-Verlag, 1974.

1618 "Last Judgments," *Newsweek* 33 (April 25, 1949):36, 38.

1619 Medicus, Franz A. *Das Reichsministerium des Innern: Geschichte und Aufbau.* Berlin: Junker und Dünnhaupt Verlag, 1940.

1620 Meissner, Otto. *Staatssekretär unter Ebert-Hindenburg-Hitler: Der Schicksalweg der deutschen Volks von 1918–1945, wie ich erlebte.* Hamburg: Hoffmann und Kampe, 1950.

1621 Mommsen, Hans. *Beamtentum im Dritten Reich.* Stuttgart: Deutsche Verlags-Anstalt, 1966.

1622   Norton, Henry K. "Foreign Office Organization," *Annals of the American Academy of Political and Social Science* 143 [Supplement] (May 1929).

1623   Peterson, Edward D. *The Limits of Hitler's Power.* Princeton: Princeton University Press, 1969.

1624   Poole, DeWitt C. "Light on Nazi Foreign Policy," *Foreign Affairs* 25 (October 1946):130–58.

1625   Röhl, J. C. G. "Higher Civil Service in Germany," *Journal of Contemporary History* 2, no. 3 (1967):101–21.

1626   Schmidt, Paul. *Hitler's Interpreter.* Edited by R. H. C. Steed. New York: Macmillan, 1951.

1627   Seabury, Paul. *The Wilhelmstrasse: A Study of German Diplomats under the Nazi Regime.* Berkeley: University of California Press, 1954.

1628   Smith, Arthur L., Jr. "Hitler's *Gau* Ausland," *Political Studies* 14, no. 1 (February 1966):90–95.

1629   Tillmann, H., and P. Kircheisen, eds. *Dokumente zum Wilhelmstrasseprozess mit Auszügen aus dem Urteil und der Anklageschrift.* Berlin: Deutscher Verlag der Wissenschaften, 1970.

1630   *Das Urteil im Wilhelmstrasse-Prozess: Der amtliche Wortlaut der Entscheidung mit Einführungen von Robert M. W. Kempner und Carl Haensel.* Munich: Alfons Bürger Verlag, 1950.

1631   Watt, D. C. "German Diplomats and Nazi Leaders," *Journal of Central European Affairs* 15 (1955):152.

1632   Weinberg, Gerhard L. *The Foreign Policy of Hitler's Germany: Diplomatic Revolution in Europe, 1933–36.* Chicago: University of Chicago Press, 1970.

1633   Weizsäcker, Ernst von. *Memoirs.* Translated by John Andrews. Chicago: Henry Regnery, 1951.

GERMAN COURT DECISIONS UNDER CONTROL LAW NO. 10

1634   Spruchgericht Bielefeld. "Urteil vom 11.9.1947–3 Sps Ls 1042/47," *Die Spruchgerichte* 1 (December 1947):88.

1635   Oberlandesgericht Braunschweig. "Beschluss vom 26.2.1947–Ss 7/47," *Monatsschrift für Deutsches Recht* 1 (April 1947):37–38.

1636   ———. "Beschluss vom 25.11.1947–Ws 30/47," *Monatsschrift für Deutsches Recht* 2 (April 1948):125.

1637 ———. "Beschluss vom 28/29.11.1947–Ss 46/47," *Süddeutsche Juristenzeitung* 3 (May 1948):268–70.

1638 Oberlandesgericht Dresden. "Urteil vom 21.3.1947–20.2/47," *Neue Justiz* 1 (April-May 1947):107–08.

1639 ———. "Urteil vom 18.4.1947–20.30/47," *Neue Justiz* 1 (April-May 1947):108.

1640 ———. "Urteil vom 16.5.1947–20.18/47," *Neue Justiz* 1 (June 1947):139–40.

1641 ———. "Urteil vom 16.5.1947–21.18/47," *Neue Justiz* 2 (January-February 1948):25–26.

1642 ———. "Urteil vom 23.5.1947–20.58/47," *Neue Justiz* 1 (June 1947):139.

1643 ———. "Urteil vom 16.7.1947–21 ERKs 146/48," *Neue Justiz* 2 (July-August 1948):171.

1644 ———. "Urteil vom 12.9.1947–20.188/47," *Neue Justiz* 1 (August-September 1947):195–96.

1645 ———. "Urteil vom 12.9.1947–20.182/47," *Neue Justiz* 1 (November-December 1947):257.

1646 ———. "Urteil vom 6.2.1948–21 ERKs 8/47," *Neue Justiz* 2 (March 1948):55–56.

1647 ———. "Urteil vom 13.2.1948–21 ERKs 39/47," *Neue Justiz* 2 (March 1948):56.

1648 ———. "Urteil vom 13.2.1948–21 ERKs 6/47," *Neue Justiz* 2 (April-May 1948):86–87.

1649 ———. "Urteil vom 2.3.1948–21 ERKs 30/48," *Neue Justiz* 2 (April-May 1948):87.

1650 ———. "Urteil vom 16.3.1948–21 ERKs 72/48," *Neue Justiz* 2 (April-May 1948):87–88.

1651 ———. "Urteil vom 11.5.1948–21 ERKs 112/48," *Neue Justiz* 2 (June 1948):115.

1652 ———. "Urteil vom 1.7.1948–ERKs 130/48," *Neue Justiz* 2 (July-August 1948):169–71.

1653 ———. "Urteil vom 25.5.1948–21 ERKs 121/48," *Neue Justiz* 2 (June 1948):115.

1654 Schwurgericht Dresden. "Urteil vom 7.7.1947–1 Ks 58/47," *Neue Justiz* 1 (August-September 1947):193–95.

1655 Oberlandesgericht Düsseldorf. "Urteil vom 14.11.1947–Ss 147/47," *Monatsschrift für Deutsches Recht* 2 (April 1948):123–25.

1656 Landgericht Freiburg. "Urteil vom 12.9.1947–1 Js 254/46," *Monatsschrift für Deutsches Recht* 2 (April 1948):126–27.

1657 Oberlandesgericht Gera. "Urteil vom 3.3.1948–1 ERKs 34/48," *Neue Justiz* 2 (June 1948):115–16.

1658 Landgericht Hagen, Strafkammer III. "Urteil vom 4.8.1947–11 K. Ls.2/47," *Monatsschrift für Deutsches Recht* 2 (March 1948):89–92.

1659 Oberlandesgericht Halle. "Urteil vom 16.4.1947–Ss 22/47," *Neue Justiz* 1 (July 1947):166.

1660 Oberlandesgericht Hamburg. "Urteil vom 18.6.1947–Ss 37/47 [Comment by Gerhard Erdsiek]," *Süddeutsche Juristenzeitung* 3 (January 1948): entire issue.

1661 Oberster Spruchgerichtshof Hamm, 2. Spruchsenat. "Beschluss vom 10.10.1947," *Die Spruchgerichte* 1 (December 1947):81.

1662 _____, 2. Spruchsenat. "Beschluss vom 21.10.1947 (Spruchgericht Bielefeld–2 Sp Ws 5/47)," *Die Spruchgerichte* 1 (December 1947):82.

1663 _____, 1. Spruchsenat. "Urteil vom 14.10.1947 (Spruchgericht Benefeld-Bomlitz–Sp Ss 14/47)," *Die Spruchgerichte* 1 (December 1947): 76.

1664 _____, 1. Spruchsenat. "Urteil vom 21.10.1947 (Spruchgericht Bergedorf–Sp Ss 23/47)," *Die Spruchgerichte* 1 (December 1947):86.

1665 _____, 1. Spruchsenat. "Urteil vom 21.10.1947 (Spruchgericht Stade–1 Sp Ss 21/47)," *Die Spruchgerichte* 1 (December 1947):84.

1666 _____, 2. Spruchsenat. "Urteil vom 21.10.1947 (Spruchgericht Stade–Sp Ss 18/47)," *Die Spruchgerichte* 1 (December 1947):79.

1667 _____, 1. Spruchsenat. "Urteil vom 28.10.1947 (Spruchgericht Recklingshausen–Sp Ss 20/47)," *Die Spruchgerichte* 1 (December 1947): 78.

1668 _____, 2. Spruchsenat. "Beschluss vom 30.10.1947–2 Sp Ws 11/47," *Die Spruchgerichte* 1 (December 1947):82.

1669 Oberlandesgericht Hamm. "Beschluss vom 29.11.1947–Ws 91/47," *Monatsschrift für Deutsches Recht* 2 (March 1948):94.

1670 Oberlandesgericht Hamm, 2. Strafsenat. "Beschluss vom 20.9. 1948–2 Ws 83/48," *Monatsschrift für Deutsches Recht* 3 (February 1949):121.

1671 Oberster Spruchgerichtshof Hamm, 2. Spruchsenat. "Beschluss vom 23.9.1947–2 Sp s1/47," *Die Spruchgerichte* 1 (December 1947):80.

1672 ———, 3. Spruchsenat. "Urteil vom 14.1.1948–3 Sp Ss 105/47," *Die Spruchgerichte* 2 (April 1948):114.

1673 Spruchgericht Hiddesen. "Urteil vom 27.8.1947–4 Sp Ls 12/47," *Die Spruchgerichte* 1 (September 1947):15.

1674 ———. "Urteil vom 7.10.1947–5 Sp Ls 134/47," *Die Spruchgerichte* 1 (December 1947):89.

1675 Oberlandesgericht Kiel. "Urteil vom 26.3.1947–Ss 27/47 [Comment by Adolf Arndt]," *Süddeutsche Juristenzeitung* 2 (June 1947): 330–37.

1676 ———. "Beschluss vom 3.10.1947–Ws 67/47," *Monatsschrift für Deutsches Recht* 1 (December 1947):307.

1677 Oberster Gerichtshof für die britische Zone, Köln. "Urteil vom 22.6.1948–St S 8/48," *Monatsschrift für Deutsches Recht* 2 (September 1948):303–04.

1678 Landesgericht Konstanz. "Urteil vom 28.2.1947–Kls 3/47 [Comment by Gustav Radbruch]" *Süddeutsche Juristenzeitung* 2 (June 1947): 343–45.

1679 ———, 2. Strafkammer. "Urteil vom 2.9.1947–KLS 22/47," *Monatsschrift für Deutsches Recht* 1 (December 1947):305–06.

1680 Oberlandesgericht Schwerin. "Urteil vom 14.7.1947–Ss 47/47," *Neue Justiz* 1 (July 1947):165–66.

1681 Landgericht Siegen. "Beschluss vfl. 8.5.1947–4 Js 80/46," *Monatsschrift für Deutsches Recht* 1 (September 1947):203.

1682 Oberlandesgericht Stuttgart, Nebensitz Karlsruhe, 1. Strafsenat. "Urteil vom 13.5.1948–Ss 33/48," *Monatsschrift für Deutsches Recht* 2 (August 1948): entire issue.

Subsequent Allied Proceedings, Germany, 1945–1949

GENERAL

1683 Cyprian, Tadeusz, ed. *Siedem Wyroków Najwyższego Trybunału Narodowego.* Poznań: Instytut Zachodni, 1962.

1684 "For Crimes against Humanity: Last Gang of Nazi War Criminals Tried and Sentenced," *Scholastic* 54 (April 27, 1949):10.

1685 "Finis," *Time* 53 (April 25, 1949):29.

1686 Gumkowski, Janusz, and T. Kulakowski. *Zbrodniarze hitlerowscy przed Najwyzszym Trybunalem Narodowym.* Warsaw: Wydawn. Prawnicze, 1967.

1687 Heinze, Kurt, comp. *Die Rechtsprechung der Nünberger Militärtribunale: Sammlung der Rechtsthesen der Urteile und gesonderten Urteilsbegründungen der dreizehn Nürnberger Prozesse.* Bonn: Girardet, 1952.

1688 Koessler, M. "International Law on Use of Enemy Uniforms as a Strategem and the Acquittal in the Skorzeny Case," *Missouri Law Review* 24 (1959):16–43.

1689 Muszkat, M., ed. *The Trial of Arthur Greiser.* London: William Hodge, 1948.

1690 "Resume Hanging of Germans Probably Innocent," *Christian Century* 66 (February 2, 1949):131.

1691 Winner, Percy. "Simply Murderers," *New Republic* 124 (February 19, 1951):8.

PRINCIPAL TRIALS

The "Peleus" Trial, Hamburg, 1945

1692 Cameron, John, ed. *Trial of Heinz Eck, August Hoffman, Walter Weisspfennig, Hans Richard Lenz and Wolfgang Schwender (The Peleus Trial).* London: William Hodge, 1948.

The "Hadmar" Trial, Wiesbaden, 1945

1693 Kintner, Earl W., ed. *The Hadmar Trial: Trial of Alfons Klein, Adolf Wahlmann, Heinrich Rouff.* London: William Hodge, 1949.

The "Dulag-Luft" Trial, Wuppertal, 1945

1694 Cuddon, Eric, ed. *Trial of Erich Killinger, Heinz Junge, Otto Boehringer, Heinrich Eberhardt, Gustev Baur-Schlichtegroll (The Dulag Luft Trial).* London: William Hodge, 1952.

The "Belsen" Trial, Lüneberg, 1945

1695 Bentwich, Norman. "The Belsen Trial," *Law Journal* 95 (November 24, 1945):394.

1696 Goderie, Jan. *De Berechting Oorlogsmisdadigers een Karakterschets uit het proces te Lueneburg.* Gonda: J. Mulder, 1946.

1697 Gordey, Michael. "Echoes from Auschwitz," *New Republic* 117 (December 22, 1947):14–15.

1698 Phillips, Raymond, ed. *Trial of Josef Kramer and Forty-Four Others: The Belsen Trial.* London: William Hodge, 1949.

The "Borkum Island" Trial, Ludwigsburg, 1946

1699 Hammerstein, Kurt Wentzel. *Landsberg, Henker des Rechts?* Wuppertal: Abendland-Verlag, 1952.

1700 Koessler, Maximilian. "Borkum Island Tragedy and Trial," *Journal of Criminal Law and Criminology* 47 (July–August 1956):183–96.

The "Velpke Baby Home" Trial, Brunswick, 1946

1701 Brand, George, ed. *The Velpke Baby Home Trial: Trial of Heinrich Gerike.* London: William Hodge, 1950.

The "Malmedy Massacre" Trial, Dachau, 1946

1702 Aschenauer, Rudolf. *Seven Years after the Malmedy Trial: An Unsolved Problem Endangering US Prestige in Europe.* Miesbach, 1953.

1703 _____. *Um Recht und Wahrheit im Malmedy-Fall: Eine Stellungnahme zum Bericht eines Untersuchungsausschusses des amerikanischen Senats in Sachen Malmedy-Prozess.* Nürnberg, 1950.

1704 Belgium, Commission des crimes de guerre, ministre de la justice. *Les crimes de guerre commis pendant la contre-offensive de von Runstedt dans les Ardennes, décembre 1944–janvier 1945.* Liège: Georges Thone, 1948.

1705 "Clemency: Malmedy Massacre," *Time* 53 (January 17, 1949):19.

1706 Doenecke, Justus D. "Protest over Malmedy: A Case of Clemency," *Peace and Change* 4, no. 2 (Spring 1977):28–33.

1707 Glazer, Nathan. "Method of Senator McCarthy: Malmedy Case," *Commentary* 15 (March 1953):244–56.

1708 Greil, Lothar. *Die Wahrheit über Malmedy.* 3d ed. Munich: Schild Verlag, 1958.

1709 Grevy, R. "La répression des Crimes de Guerre en droit belge," *Revue de Droit Pénal et de Criminologie* 28 (1947–1948):806–23.

1710 Heidenberger, Peter. *Der "common design" in der Rechtsprechung des Völkerrechts nach dem II. Weltkrieg.* N.p., 1949.

1711 "Hold Up Executions of Malmedy Germans," *Christian Century* 66 (March 30, 1949):389.

1712 United States, Congress, Senate. *Malmedy Massacre Investigation: Hearings before a Subcommittee of the Committee on Armed Services . . . Pursuant to S. Res. 42, Investigation of Action of Army with Respect to Trial of Persons Responsible for the Massacre of American Soldiers, Battle of the Bulge, Near Malmedy, Belgium, December 1944.* 81st Cong., 1st sess. 2 pts. Washington, D.C.: GPO, 1949.

1713 Utley, Freda. "Malmedy and McCarthy," *American Mercury* 79 (November 1954):53–58.

1714 Whiting, Charles. *Massacre at Malmédy.* New York: Stein and Day, 1971.

1715 Ziemssen, Dietrich. *The Malmédy-Trial: A Report Based on Documents and Personal Experiences.* Munich, 1952.

The Trial of General von Falkenhorst, Hamburg, 1946

1716 "Falkenhorst: The Alibi," *Newsweek* 25 (May 21, 1945):56.

1717 Stevens, E. H., ed. *Trial of Nikolaus von Falkenhorst, Formerly Generaloberst in the German Army.* London: William Hodge, 1949.

The "Sachsenhausen" Trial, Berlin, 1947

1718 "Poor Misguided People: Sachsenhausen's Jailers," *Time* 50 (November 10, 1947):30.

1719 Rodney, C. M. "The Trial of Sachsenhausen," *Central European Observer* 24 (1947):329–33.

1720 Sigl, Fritz, comp. *Todeslager Sachsenhausen: Ein Dokumentarbericht vom Sachsenhausen-Prozess.* Berlin: SWA-Verlag, 1948.

The "Dachau-Buchenwald" Trial, Landsberg, 1947

1721 Aschenauer, Rudolf. *Landsberg: Ein dokumentarischer Bericht von deutscher Seite.* Munich: Stachus-Verlag, 1951.

1722 "Case Closed: Nazi Criminals Hanged," *Time* 57 (June 18, 1951):38.

1723 "Death in the Sunshine," *Time* 49 (June 9, 1947):31.

The "Tillessen" Trial, Rastatt, 1947

1724 Arndt, Adolf. "Just Peace," *Süddeutsche Juristenzeitung* 3 (January 1948):1–14.

1725 ———. "Status and Development of Constitutional Law in Germany," *Annals of the American Academy of Political and Social Science* 140 (November 1948):1–9.

1726   "Tribunal général de la zone française d'occupation siegeant à Rastatt affaire Tillessen," *Journal Officiel du Commandement en Chef Française en Allemagne* 61 (March 26, 1947):606-36.

The "Stalag Luft III" Trial, 1948

1727   Elam, Henry, ed. *The Stalag Luft III Trial: Trial of Max Wielen and Seventeen Others.* London: William Hodge, 1948.

The "Zyklon B—Buchenwald" Trial, Dachau, 1947

1728   Barrington, J. H., ed. *The "Zyklon B" Trial: Trial of Bruno Tesch and Two Others.* London: William Hodge, 1948.

1729   Denson, William D., et al. *An Information Booklet on the Buchenwald Concentration Camp Case: The United States of America v. Josias Prince zu Waldeck et al., to Be Heard at Camp Dachau, Germany 11 April 1947.* Dachau, 1947.

1730   "Execution of Landsberg War Criminals," *Department of State Bulletin* 24 (June 18, 1951):988.

1731   "Guilty: Butchers of Buchenwald," *Life* 23 (August 25, 1947):39.

1732   Koessler, Maximilian. "The Ilse Koch Senate Investigation and Its Legal Problems with Observations on Double Jeopardy and *res judicata*," *Missouri Law Review* 23 (January 1958):1-23.

1733   United States, Office of High Commissioner for Germany. *Landsberg: A Documentary Report.* Frankfurt am Main, 1951.

1734   "Widow and Her Friends," *Time* 50 (August 25, 1947):24.

1735   *Wieder Hinrichtungen in Landsberg?* Munich: A. Girnth, 1951.

The Trial of Field Marshal von Manstein, Hamburg, 1949

1736   "Last Defendant," *Time* 54 (December 26, 1949):15.

1737   Leverhuehn, Paul. *Verteidigung Manstein.* Hamburg: H. H. Nölke, 1950.

1738   Manstein, Erich von. *Aus einem Soldetenleben 1887-1939.* Bonn: Athenäum, 1958.

1739   ———. *Verlorene Siege.* Bonn: Athenäum, 1955.

1740   Paget, Reginald Thomas. *Manstein: His Campaigns and His Trial.* London: Collins, 1951.

The "Natzweiler" Trial, Rastatt, 1947

1741 "Tribunal général du gouvernment militaire de la zone française d'occupation à Rastatt: Procès des camps de concentration Nazis de Natzweiler, camps de Schomberg, Schorzingen, Spaichingen, Erzingen, Dautmergen," *Journal Officiel du Commandement en Chef Français en Allemagne* 64 (April 15, 1947):653–66.

1742 Webb, Anthony M., ed. *Trial of Wolfgang Zeuss (The Natzweiler Trial).* London: William Hodge, 1949.

Subsequent National Trials, 1949–

GERMANY

Documents: General Compilations

1743 Germany (Federal Republic), Ministry of Justice. *Die Verfolgung nationalsozialistischer Straftaten im Gebiet der Bundesrepublik Deutschland seit 1945.* Bonn: Deutscher Bundesverlag, 1964.

1744 Germany (Democratic Republic), Supreme Court. *Strafsache gegen Haase u. a. (Organisation Gehlen).* Berlin: Zentralverlag, 1954.

1745 International Conference on Prosecution of Nazi Criminals, Moscow, 1969. *War Criminals Must Be Punished . . . : Main Documents.* Moscow: Novosti Press Agency Publishing House, 1969.

1746 Rüter-Ehlermann, Adelheid L., and C. F. Rüter, comps. *Justiz und Verbrechen: Sammlung deutscher Strafurteile wegen nationalsozialistischer Tötungsverbrechen 1945–1966.* 21 vols. Amsterdam: Associated Publishers, 1968.

1747 Van Dam, H. G., and R. Giordano, eds. *KZ-Verbrecher vor deutschen Gerichten: Dokumente aus den Prozessen gegen Sommer (KZ Buchenwald) Sorge, Schubert (KZ Sachsenhausen) Unkelbach (Ghetto in Czenstochau).* Frankfurt am Main: Europäische Verlagsanstalt, 1962.

1748 ———. *KZ-Verbrecher vor deutschen Gerichten: Einsatzkommando Tilsit, der Prozess zu Ulm.* Frankfurt am Main: Europäische Verlagsanstalt, 1966.

General

1749 Blessin, G., et al. *Bundes-Entschädigungsgesetze: Bundes-Ergänzungsgezetz zur Entschädigung für Opfer der nationalsozialistischen Verfolgung.* Munich: Beck, 1954.

1750 "Closing the Loophole: Undetected German War Criminals Immune from Future Prosecution," *Time* 94 (July 18, 1969):40.

1751 Dolle, Renate, and Horst Richter. "Die Anerkennung der Urteile gegen Kriegs– und Naziverbrecher muss notwendiger Bestandteil eines Friedensvertrages mit Deutschland sein!" *Staat und Recht* 8, no. 5 (May 1955):962–78.

1752 Dornberg, John. *Schizophrenic Germany.* New York: Macmillan, 1961.

1753 *Essays über Naziverbrechen, Simon Wiesenthal gewidmet.* Amsterdam: Wiesenthal Fonds, c. 1973.

1754 European Court of Human Rights. *Affaire "Wemhoff."* Strasbourg: Greffe de la Cour, Conseil de l'Europe, 1969.

1755 "From the Sentence against Concentration Camp Doctor Fischer Pronounced by the GDR Supreme Court on March 25, 1966," *Law and Legislation in the German Democratic Republic,* no. 2 (1966):51–63.

1756 Fuz, G. C. "Justice Denied: Shielding Nazi Murderers of Postal Employees in Danzig," *Nation* 205 (October 23, 1967):386.

1757 Gorzkowska, J.; J. Zakowska; and E. Zakowska. *Nazi Criminals before West German Courts.* Warsaw: Zachodnia Agencja Prasowa, 1965.

1758 Green, L. C. "Trials of Some Minor War Criminals," *Indian Law Review* 4 (1950):249–75.

1759 *Die Haltung der beiden deutschen Staaten zu den Nazi-und Kriegsverbrechen.* Berlin: Staatsverlag, 1965.

1760 "I Knew I Did Nothing: Former SS Officials Slottke, Zoepf and Harster," *Newsweek* 69 (February 6, 1967):58.

1761 "Judging the Judges: First Nazi Judge Ever Tried in a German Court, Convicted of War Crimes," *Time* 90 (July 14, 1967):30, 32.

1762 "Justice Denied: Trial Delays of Nazi War Criminals in West Germany," *Time* 100 (November 6, 1972):64–65.

1763 Klafowski, Alfons. *Ściganie zbridniarzy wojennych w Nièmiekiej Republice Federalnej w świetle prawa miedzynárodowego.* Poznań: Wydawn. Poznańskie, 1968.

1764 Kulka, Erich. *Soudcové, Žalobci, Obhájci: Process s Osětimskými Zločinci.* Prague: Svaboda, 1966.

1765 Kunz, Wolfgang. *Der Fall Marzabatto: Analyse eines Kriegsverbrecherprozesses.* Würzburg: Holzer, 1967.

1766   Langbein, Hermann. *Im Namen des deutschen Volkes: Zwischenbilanz der Prozesse wegen nationalsozialistischer Verbrechen.* Vienna: Europa Verlag, 1963.

1767   Lummert, G. *Die Strafverfahren gegen Deutsche im Ausland wegen "Kriegsverbrechens."* Hamburg: Christian, 1949.

1768   Martínez, José Agustín. *Los procesos penales de la postguerra: Documentos para la historia contemporánea.* Madrid: Ediciones y Publicaciones Españolas, 1955.

1769   Martini, Winfried. *Die NS-Prozesse im ost-westlichen Spannungsfeld.* Pfaftenhoten: Imgau-Verlag, 1969.

1770   "Penny a Head: Arrest of F. Stangl in Brazil," *Time* 89 (March 10, 1967):40.

1771   "Searching Out of Nazi War Criminals," *Time* 89 (March 31, 1967):98.

1772   "Semifinal Solution: West German Decision on Statute of Limitations," *Newsweek* 73 (May 5, 1969):44.

1773   Skorzeny, Otto. *Geheimkommando Skorzeny.* Hamburg: Hansa Verlag, 1950.

1774   "Sunday Kind of Hate: Village of Marzabotta Votes to Keep German War Criminal in Prison," *Newsweek* 70 (July 31, 1967):43.

1775   "Trapping No. 3: Arrest of Franz Paul Stagl," *Newsweek* 69 (March 13, 1967):63.

1776   Wilkens, E. *N.S.-Verbrechen, Strafjustiz, deutsche Selbstbesinnung.* Berlin: Lutherisches Verlagshaus Herbert Reuner, 1964.

1777   Wimmer, August. "Unmenschlichkeitsverbrechen und deutscherechtliche Straftat in einer Handlung," *Süddeutsche Juristenzeitung* 3 (May 1948):253–58.

1778   World Jewish Congress. Institute of Jewish Affairs. *The Prosecution of War Criminals since the End of the War: A Brief Survey.* New York: World Jewish Congress, 1961.

The Auschwitz Trial, Frankfurt Am Main, 1963–1965

1779   Bauer, F. *Krigsforbrydere for domstolen: Med forord af S. Auswitz.* Copenhagen: Westermann, 1945.

1780   Bonhoeffer, Emmi. *Auschwitz Trials: Letters from an Eyewitness.* Richmond: John Knox Press, 1967.

1781   Bulawko, H. *Le procès d'Auschwitz n'a pas eu lieu.* Paris: Presses du Temps Présent, 1965.

1782 Committee of Anti-Fascist Resistance Fighters in the German Democratic Republic, eds. *IG-Farben, Auschwitz, Mass Murder.* Berlin: 1964.

1783 *Frankfurtský Process: Reportáž z procesu s Draadvaceti Osvětimskými Zločinci.* Prague: Naše vojsko, 1964.

1784 Hirthe, G. "Zum Urteil im Auschwitz-Prozess," *Neue Justiz* 19 (1965):568–72.

1785 Höss, Rudolf. *Kommandant in Auschwitz: Autographische Aufzeichnungen von Rudolf Höss.* Stuttgart: Deutsche Verlags-Anstalt, 1958.

1786 Kakol, Kazimierz. *Sąd nierychliwy: Frankfurcki process oprawcóq z Oświeęima.* Warsaw: Książka i Wiedza, 1966.

1787 Kaul, Friedrich Karl. "About the Auschwitz Trials in Frankfurt/Main," *Law and Legislation in the German Democratic Republic,* no. 1 (1967):65–72.

1788 ———. *Auschwitz-Prozess, Frankfurt am Main.* Berlin: Komittee der Antifaschist, 1965.

1789 Langbein, Hermann, comp. *Der Auschwitz-Prozess: Eine Dokumentation.* 2 vols. Frankfurt am Main: Europäische Verlagsanstalt, 1965.

1790 Latersner, Hans. *Die andere Seite im Auschwitz-Prozess 1963/65: Reden eines Verteidigers: Mit einer einführenden Untersuchung über die Prozessführung.* Stuttgart: Seewald, 1966.

1791 "Looking Backward: Auschwitz," *Newsweek* 66 (November 8, 1965):53.

1792 Naumann, Bernd. *Auschwitz: A Report on the Proceedings against Robert Karl Ludwig Mulka and Others before the Court at Frankfurt.* Translated by Jean Steinberg. New York: Praeger, 1966.

1793 "Notes and Comments: Sentence of Auschwitz Pharmacist and His Comrades," *New Yorker* 41 (September 11, 1965):41.

The Trial of Hans Globke, Berlin, 1963

1794 Boulier, Jean, et al. *Der Prozess gegen Dr. Hans Globke (8–23.7. 1963).* Berlin, 1963.

1795 *Excerpts From the Protocol of the Trial Held against Bonn State Secretary Hans Globke before the First Criminal Senate of the Supreme Court of the German Democratic Republic from July 8th to 23rd 1963, in Berlin.* Berlin: Press Centre Globke Trial, 1963.

1796 "Urteil des Obersten Gerichts der DDR gegen Dr. H. Globke," *Neue Justiz* 17 (1963):449–512.

The Oberwalde Asylum Case, Brunswick, 1965

1797 "Murder by Marmalade: Trial of Former Nurses at the Oberwalde Insane Asylum in Brandenburg," *Time* 85 (March 19, 1965):35.

The Trial of Fritz von Hahn, Bonn, 1968

1798 "Innocents: K. Kiesinger Testimony at the Fritz Gebhard von Hahn Trial," *Nation* 207 (July 22, 1968):36.

1799 "Witness for the Defense: Kiesinger in Bonn Courtroom," *Time* 92 (July 12, 1968):24.

The Case of Bishop Defregger, 1969

1800 "Bishop Defregger Case," *America* 121 (August 2, 1969):52; *America* 121 (August 30, 1969):107.

1801 "Bishop Who Was a Major," *Time* 94 (July 18, 1969):63–64.

1802 Cook, P. S. "Bishop's Burden: M. Defregger and the Filetto di Camarda Massacre," *Newsweek* 74 (August 18, 1969):56–57.

1803 "Under the Circumstances: M. Defregger Suspected Accomplice to Italian Atrocity," *Newsweek* 74 (July 12, 1969):40.

AUSTRIA

1804 Friedmann, T. *Schupo-Kriegsverbrecher in Kolomea vor dem Wiener Volksgericht: Dokumentensammlung.* Haifa: Verband der ehemaligen Einwohner von Kolomea in Israel, 1957.

1805 *Der Hochverratsprozess gegen Dr. Guido Schmidt vor dem Wiener Volksgericht: Die gerichtliche Protokolle mit den Zeugenaussagen, unveröffentlichen Dokumenten, sämtlichen Geheimbriefen und Geheimakten.* Vienna: Österreichische Staatsdruckerei, 1947.

1806 Höss, Rudolf. *J'ai tué seulement 2.500.000 personnes: Le procès de Rudolf Hoess commendant d'Auschwitz (Varsavie 11 Mars–2 Avril 1947).* Paris: Edition de l'Amicale des Déportés d'Auschwitz, n.d.

1807 "Das österreichische Kriegsverbrechergesetz 1947," *Die Spruchgerichte* 2 (1948):349–50.

1808 Szecsi, M., and K. Stadler. *Die NS-Justiz in Österriech und ihre Opfer.* Vienna: Herold, 1962.

BELGIUM

1809 Ardenne, R. [pseud.] *German Exploitation of Belgium.* Washington, D.C.: Brookings Institution, 1942.

1810 Bergmeier, Th. "Die Bandenanklage im belgischen Kriegsverbrechprozess," *Neue Juristische Wochenschrift* 3 (1950):252–53.

1811 Bley, C. "Falkenhausen vor den Richtern," *Frankfurter Hefte* 6 (March 1951):159–68.

1812 Dautricourt, J. Y. "Nature et compétence 'De lege ferenda' de la jurisprudence belge pour la répression des crimes de guerre," *Revue de Droit Pénal Militaire et de Droit de la Guerre* 5 (1966):63–82.

1813 ———. "La Répression de l'Incivisme en Belgique," *Revue International de Droit Pénal* 17 (1946):133–54.

1814 Fox, Grace E. *Civil Rights in German Occupied Belgium and Northern France.* Chicago: American Bar Association, Junior Bar Conference, 1941.

1815 Goris, Jan Albert. *Belgium in Bondage.* New York: L. B. Fischer, 1943.

1816 Quintano Ripollés, Antonio. "El proceso de von Falkenhausen ante el consejo de guerra de Bruselas," *Revista Española de Derecho Internacional* 4 (1951):161–64.

1817 Rigaux, M., and P. E. Trousse. "La qualification des crimes de guerre en droit pénal belge," *Journal des Tribunaux* 63 (1948):229–32.

1818 Sluzny, M. "La loi de 20 juin 1947 relative à la compétence des juridictions militaires en matière de crimes de guerre," *Journal des Tribunaux* 62 (1947):413–15.

1819 Volkmann, Kurt. "Kriegsverbrechenverfahren in Belgien," *Neue Juristische Wochenschrift* 2 (1949):455–56.

1820 Wauters, A. "La répression des crimes de guerre en Belgique," *Revue de Droit Pénal et de Criminologie* 27 (1946–1947):431–35.

1821 Willequet, J. "Le procès Falkenhausen," *Revue d'Histoire de la Deuxième Guerre Mondiale* 1 (1951):59–65.

1822 Wolf, Jules. *Le procès de Breendouk.* Brussels: Larcier, 1973.

1823 ———. "La question des crimes de guerre en Belgique," *Journal des Tribunaux* 61 (1946):513–17.

CANADA

1824 MacDonald, B. J. S. *The Trial of Kurt Meyer.* Toronto: Clarke, Irwin, 1954.

CZECHOSLOVAKIA

1825 Czechoslovakia, Ministry of Information. *Ceský narod soudí K. H. Franks.* Prague: Ministry of Information, 1947.

1826   Daxner, Igor. *Ludáctvo pred Národnýn Súdom, 1945–1947.* Bratislava: Vydavateľstvo Slovneskej Akadémie Vied, 1961.

1827   *Justiz im Dienste der Vergeltung: Erlebnisberichte und Dokumente über die Rechtsprechung der tschechoslowakischen ausserordentlichen Volksgerichte gegen Deutsche (1945–48).* Munich: C. Wolf, 1962.

1828   Kulka, Erich. *Tu sa koncin stopy SS . . .* Bratislava: Vydavateľstvo politickej literatúry, 1965.

1829   *Verbrecher in Richterroben: Dokumente über die verbrecherische Tätigkeit von 230 nazistischen Richtern und Staatsanwälten auf dem okkupierten Gebiet der Tschecholowakischen Republik, die gegenwärtig in der west-deutschen Justiz dienen.* Prague: Orbis, 1960.

DENMARK

1830   Best-Sagen: *Kobenhavns byrets, Østre landsrets og Højesterets domme.* Copenhagen: G. E. C. Gad, 1950.

1831   Thomsen, Erich. *Deutsche Besatzungspolitik in Dänemark 1940–1945.* Düsseldorf: Bertelsmann Universitätsverlag, 1971.

FINLAND

1832   Kaila, Toivo Torsten. *Sotaansyyllisemme säätytalossa.* Helsinki: Söderström, 1946.

1833   Kuusinen, O. "The Trial of the Finnish War Criminals," *USSR Embassy Information Bulletin* 6, no. 18 (1945):146–50.

1834   Procopé, Hjalmar J. *Sowjetjustiz über Finnland: Prozessakten aus dem Verfahren gegen die Kriegsverantwortlichen in Finnland.* Zurich: Thomas Verlag, 1947.

1835   Soini, Yrjö. *Kuin Pietari hiilivalkealla: Sotasyyllisyysasian vaiheet, 1944–1949.* 2d ed. Helsinki: Otava, 1956.

1836   Sotasyyllisoikeudenkäynnin asiakirjoja. Helsinki: Suomalaisen Kirjallisuuden Seuvan Kirjapaino, 1945.

1837   Starkenberg, Olof. *Kriegsansvarighetsprocessen i Finland.* Stockholm: Utrikespolitiska institutet, 1946.

FRANCE

1838   Aujol, J. L. *Le procès Benoist-Méchin (29 mai–6 juin 1947).* Paris: Éditions Albin Michel, 1948.

1839   Boulier, Jean. *Les juges nazis l'appareil d'État de la République fédérale allemande.* Brussels: Éditions de l'Association internationale des juristes démocrates, 1962.

1840 Chaudet, H. *Le procès Maurras.* Lyon: Éditions de Savoie, 1945.

1841 Doblhoff, Lily. "Traitor or Patriot? Abetz Trial in France," *Commonweal* 50 (August 19, 1949):461–62.

1842 Donnedieu de Vabres, Henri. *Traité de droit criminel et de législation pénale comparée.* 3d ed. Paris: Recueil Sirey, 1947.

1843 Eisele, A. "Réflexions sur les procès des criminels de guerre en France," *Revue de Droit Pénal et de Criminologie* 31 (December 1950): 305–17.

1844 Jaffré, Yves Frédéric. *Les Tribunaux D'Exception, 1940–1962.* Paris: Nouvelles Éditions Latines, 1963.

1845 Jescheck, H.-H. "Kriegsverbrecherprozesse gegen deutsche Kriegsgefangene in Frankreich (Ordonnance vom 28.8.1944)," *Süddeutsche Juristenzeitung* 4 (1949):107–16.

1846 Julien, M. *La Loi du 15 septembre 1948 sur les crimes de guerre.* Paris: Institut de Criminologie, 1952.

1847 Luther, Hans. "Zu den gegenwärtigen Kriegsverbrecherprozessen in Frankreich," *Neue Juristische Wochenschrift* 7 (1954):376–77.

1848 Meyrowitz, Henri. "Ein französisches Gutachten zu den Kriegsverbrecherprozessen in Frankreich," *Deutsche Rechtszeitschrift* 5 (1950): 403–05.

1849 Mezger, Ernst. "Französische Gesetze und Rechtsprechung über das Schicksal von Verträgen zwischen Franzosen und Deutschen aus der Zeit der deutschen Besatzung, 1940–1945," *Nachrichten der Studiengesellschaft für privatrechtliche Auslandsinteressen* 9 (1950):5–8.

1850 ———. "Schutz der Genfer Konvention für deutsche Kriegsgefangene unter Anklage wegen Kriegsverbrechens in Frankreich," *Süddeutsche Juristenzeitung* 6 (1951):332–333.

1851 Morellet, Charles. *Saint-Louis: Ou, La Justice sous les Chaînes, 1944: Avant propos de Camille Chautemps.* Paris: Éditions de L'Ermite, 1949.

1852 Patin, M. "La France et le jugement des crimes de guerre," *Revue de Science Criminelle et de Droit Pénal Comparé* 6 (1951):393–405.

1853 Rey, Francis. "Violations du droit international commises par les allemands en France dans la guerre de 1939," *Revue Générale de Droit International Public* 49, no. 2 (1941–1945):1–127.

1854 Servus Juris [pseud.]. *Lettre ouverte à Messieurs les Présidents des cours de justice.* Paris: A. Bonne, 1948.

1855   Tribunal Militaire Permanent de Paris. *Dossiers des pièces de la procédure suivie contre le Général von Stülpnagel, otto et autres, inculpés d'assassinàtes complicité d'assassinàtes, pillage jugement no 556/1870 du 31 mai 1949.* Paris: Tribunal Militaire Permanent de Paris, 1949.

The Oradour-sur-Glane Massacre Trial, 1953

1856   Gleischläger, Robert. "Der Prozess Frankreichs: Die Kriegsverbrecher von Oradour," *Juristische Blätter* 75 (1953):653–54.

1857   Jescheck, Hans-Heinrich. "Zum Oradour-Prozess," *Süddeutsche Juristenzeitung* 8 (March 5, 1953):156–57.

1858   Maunoir, Jean-Pierre. "Le procès d'Oradour," *Revue de Droit International (Sottile-Geneva)* 31 (April-June 1953):181–86.

1859   Mouret, G. *Oradour, le crime, le procès.* Paris: Plon, 1958.

1860   Pauchou, Guy, and Pierre Masfrand. *Oradour-sur-Glane: Vision d'épouvante.* Limoges: Charles-Lavauzelle et Cie, 1966.

1861   Stitzer, K. *Mordprozess Oradour nach Prozessberichten der "Humanité."* Berlin: Dietz Verlag, 1954.

HUNGARY

1862   Pinter, István, and Lászlo Szabó, eds. *Criminals at Large.* Budapest: Pannonia, 1961.

1863   Radványi, Deszö. *Idézés Bunügyben: Tanúnak Megidézve az olvaśot.* Budapest: Kossuth Könyvkiadó, 1967.

1864   Szalai, Sándor. *Jugements du Peuple contre les Criminels de Guerre Hongrois.* Budapest: Édition "Athenaeum," 1946.

1865   Van Garse, Y. *Hungarian Literature on War Crimes and Crimes against Humanity.* St. Niklaas: Information Retrieval System, 1970.

ITALY

1866   Belardinelli, E. "Crimini di guerra: La relativa giurisdizione ed i procedimenti in Italia," *La Giustizia Penale* 56, pt. 1 (1951):188.

1867   Borrini, Carlo. *Criminali di guerra italiani.* Milan: IDOS, 1968.

1868   Rossi, M. "Liberation Betrayed: Italian War Criminals," *Nation* 168 (March 26, 1949):355–56.

1869   Smyth, Howard McGraw. *Secrets of the Fascist Era: How Uncle Sam Obtained Some of the Top-Level Documents of Mussolini's Period.* Carbondale: Southern Illinois University Press, 1975.

The Siena Trial, 1947–1948

1870 Associazione nazionale partigiani d'Italia. *Criminali all sbarra: Il processo di Montemaggio.* Siena: La Poligrafica, 1948.

The Trial of Herbert Kappler, Rome, 1948

1871 "The Missing Cancer Patient: Springing a Nazi War Criminal with Suitcase and Chivalry," *Time* 110 (August 29, 1977):42–43.

1872 Tribunale Militara Territoriale, Rome. *Sentenza nella causa contro . . . Data 20.7.1948.* Library of Congress Microfilm, Law–97.

The Trial of Field Marshal Albert Kesselring, 1948

1873 Kesselring, Albert. *Kesselring: A Soldier's Record.* Translated by Lynton Hudson. New York: Morrow, 1953.

1874 "Kesselring: Soft Soap," *Newsweek* 25 (May 21, 1945):56.

1875 Scotland, A. P. *The Kesselring Case Being a Representation of the Trial in Venice, Italy, Spring 1947.* Bonn: Köllen, 1952.

1876 Wheeler-Bennett, John W. *Trial of Field-Marshall Kesselring.* London: William Hodge, 1948.

NETHERLANDS

1877 Friedman-Van Der Heide, Reine. *Drie Processen.* Amsterdam: N.V. Amsterdamsche Boeken Courantmij, 1946.

1878 Goderie, Jan. *De Berschting van Oorlogsmisdadigers: Een karkaklerschets uit het process te Lueneburg, door den Nederlandschen oorlogscorrespandent, Jan Goderie.* Gonda: J. Mulder, 1946.

1879 Kempner, Robert M. W. *Edith Stein und Anne Frank: Zwei von Hunderttausend.* Freiburg: Herder-Bücherei, 1968.

1880 Maass, Walter B. *The Netherlands at War.* London: Abelard-Schumann, 1970.

1881 Menzel, Eberhard. "Die ausländische Kriegsverbrechergesetzgebung (Polen, Norwegen, Niederlande), *Archiv des öffentlichen Rechts* 75 (1949):424–52.

1882 Mouton, Martinus Willem. *Oorlogsmisdrijven en het internationale recht.* The Hague: A. A. M. Stols, 1947.

1883 _____. "War Crimes and International Law: The Netherlands' Share in the Detection and Punishment of War Criminals," *Grotius Annuaire International* (1940–1946):38–62.

1884   N.K.C.A. in 't Veld, ed. *De SS en Nederland: Documenten uit SS-Archieven, 1935–1945.* 2 vols. The Hague: Nijhoff, 1976.

1885   *Processen . . . Max Blokzijl.* Amsterdam: Uitgerverij Buyten en Schipperheyn, 1947.

1886   Rijkinstituut voor Oorlogsdocumentatic. *Het Process Christiansen.* The Hague: Nijhoff, 1950.

1887   ———. *Het Process Mussert.* The Hague: Nijhoff, 1948.

1888   ———. *Het Process Rauter.* The Hague: Nijhoff, 1952.

1889   Warmbrunn, Werner. *The Dutch under German Occupation, 1940–1945.* Stanford: Stanford University Press, 1963.

1890   "White-Gloved Killers: Attempt to Avenge Dutch Jewry," *Newsweek* 69 (January 30, 1967):48.

NORWAY

1891   Menzel, Eberhard. "Die ausländische Kriegsverbrechergesetzgebung (Polen, Norwegen, Niederlande)," *Archiv des Öffentlichen Rechts* 75 (1949):424–52.

POLAND

1892   Central Committee for the Investigation of German Crimes in Poland. *German Crimes in Poland.* Warsaw, 1947.

1893   Cyprian, Tadeusz. *Głos ma prokurator. . . .* Warsaw: Iskry, 1966.

1894   Gumkowski, Janusz, and T. Kulakowski. *Zbrodniarze hitlerowscy przed Najwyzszym Trybunałem Narodowym.* Warsaw: Wydawn. Prawnicze, 1967.

1895   Kubicki, L. *Zbrodnie wojenne w swietle prawa polskiego.* Warsaw: Panstwowe Wydawn. Naukowe, 1963.

1896   Menzel, Eberhard. "Die ausländische Kriegsverbrechergesetzgebung (Polen, Norwegen, Niederlande)," *Archiv des Öffentlichen Rechts* 75 (1949):424–52.

1897   Muszkat, M. *Polish Charges against War Criminals* [Submitted to the United Nations War Crimes Commission]. Varsovie, 1948.

1898   Orlovskii, S., and R. Ostrovich. *Erich Koch pered polskim sudom.* Moscow: Izd-vo Mezdunarodnych, 1961.

1899   Sawicki, J. "Law and the Demands of Justice," *Poland of Today* 2 (1947):4–7, 14.

1900 Siekanowicz, Peter, comp. *Legal Sources and Bibliography of Poland.* Library of Congress, Mid-European Law Project. New York: Praeger, 1964.

The Trial of Amon Leopold Goeth (The Treblinka Trial), Krakow, 1947

1901 *Process Iudobójey Amona Leopolda Goetha przed Najwyzszym Trybunałem Narodowym.* Warsaw: Centralna Żydowska Komisja Historyczm w Polsce, 1947.

RUMANIA

1902 United States Office of Strategic Services (OSS). *The First War Criminal Trial in Rumania.* Research and Analysis Branch no. 2957.2. Washington, D.C., 1945.

1903 ————. *Progress of Epuration under the Groza Government of Rumania.* Research and Analysis Branch no. 2957.1. Washington, D.C., 1945.

SOVIET UNION (USSR)

1904 Frey, G. "Das Strafverfahren gegen deutsche Kriegsgefangene in der Sowjetunion," *Osteuropa-Recht* 1 (1955):31–37.

1905 "Legal Proceedings on the War Crimes of German Fascist-Usurpers in the Crimea and the Kuban," *Soviet Press Translations* 3 (1948):89–91.

1906 Maurach, Reinhart. *Die Kriegsverbrecherprozesse gegen deutsche Gefangene in der Sowjetunion.* Hamburg: Arbeitsgemeinschaft vom Roten Kreuz in Deutschland, 1950.

1907 Nikitin, M. N., and P. I. Vagin. *The Crimes of the German Fascists in the Leningrad Region: Materials and Documents.* London: Hutchinson, 1946.

1908 *Prozess in der Strafsache gegen die faschistischen deutschen Okkupanten und ihre Helfershelfer wegen ihre Bestialitäten im Gebiet der Stadt Krasnoder und des Krasnodarer Gans während der zeitweiligen Besatzung dieses Gebietes: Verhandelt am 14–17 juli 1943.* Moscow: Verlag für fremdsprachige Literatur, 1943.

The Trial of Reinhard Retzlaff, et al. (The Kharkov Trial), Kharkov, 1943

1909 *Deutsche Greuel in Russland: Gerichtstag in Charkow.* Vienna: Stern-Verlag, n.d.

1910 Ečer, B. *The Lessons of the Kharkov Trial.* London: Russia Today Society, 1944.

1911 Lauterbach, Richard E. "How the Russians Try Nazi Criminals: Kharkov Trial," *Harper's* 190 (June 1945):658–64.

1912 *The People's Verdict: A Full Report of the Proceedings at the Krasvrodar and Kharkov German Atrocity Trials.* London: Hutchinson, 1944.

1913 *The Trial in the Case of the Activities Committed by the German Fascist Invaders in the City of Kharkov and in the Kharkov Region, December 15–18, 1943.* Moscow: Foreign Languages Publishing House, 1944.

The Trial of Otozo Yamada, et al. (The Khabarovsk Trial), Khabarovsk, 1949 (*See* under Subsidiary Proceedings, the Far East, 1945–1949)

YUGOSLAVIA

1914 Cassius [Michael Foot]. *The Trial of Mussolini: Being a Verbatim Report of the First Great War Crimes Trial Held in London Sometime in 1944 or 1945.* London: V. Gollancz, 1943.

1915 Krzisnik, A. "Kocevski proces njegov zgodovinski okvir in pomen," *Pravnik* (1963):378–95.

International Military Tribunal, Far East, Tokyo, 1946–1948

PRIMARY EVIDENTIARY DOCUMENTS

English Editions

1916 *Affidavit of Hideki Tojo, Individual Defense.* Defense doc. no. 3000. Tokyo: IMTFE, 1947.

1917 IMTFE. *Judgment of the International Military Tribunal for the Far East.* Tokyo: IMTFE, 1948.

1918 _____. *Tokyo War Crimes Trials: Documents, Exhibits for the Defense.* Defense doc. nos. 1–3088 [January 27, 1947–February 10, 1948]. 23 vols. Tokyo: IMTFE, 1948.

1919 _____. *Tokyo War Crimes Trials: Documents, Exhibits for the Prosecution.* Exhibit nos. 1–2282 [May 4, 1946–January 24, 1947]. 22 vols. Tokyo: IMFTE, 1947.

1920 _____. *Tokyo War Crimes Trials: Proceedings (818 Sessions [May 3, 1946–April 16, 1948]).* Tokyo: IMTFE, 1948.

1921 SCAP, IPS. *Analysis of Documentary Evidence.* IPS doc. no. 0012. 27 vols. Tokyo: IMTFE, 1947.

1922 _____. *Chronological Summary* [*of Evidence*]. IPS doc. no. 0001. Tokyo: IMTFE, 1947.

1923 _____. *Decision of Imperial Conferences, Cabinet Meetings, and Other Conferences and Meetings Which Appear in the Prosecution's Evidence.* IPS doc. no. 0004. Tokyo: IMTFE, 1947.

1924 _____. *Tokyo War Crimes Trials, Japanese Cabinet Officials, 1927–1945.* Tokyo: IMTFE, c. 1947.

Japanese Editions

1925 IMTFE. *Kyokutō Kokusai Gunji Saiban Kohan sok kiroku.* 10 vols. Tokyo, 1946–1948.

1926 Pal, Radhabinod. *Nihon muzairon.* Tokyo: Nihonshobo, 1952.

OFFICIAL DOCUMENTS: GENERAL

1927 Bernard, Henri. *Memorandum: Dissenting Opinion.* Tokyo: IMTFE, 1948.

1928 Jaranilla, Delfin. *Separate Opinion Concurring: The Majority Judgment.* Tokyo: IMTFE, 1948.

1929 Pal, Radhabinod. *International Military Tribunal for the Far East: Dissentient Judgment.* Calcutta: Sanyal, 1953.

1930 Röling, Bernard V. A. *Opinion of Mr. Justice Röling, Member for the Netherlands.* Tokyo: IMTFE, 1948.

1931 SCAP. *International Military Tribunal for the Far East, Established at Tokyo, January 19, 1946.* State Department Pub. no. 2765. Washington, D.C.: GPO, 1947.

1932 "Trial of Far Eastern War Criminals, Special Proclamation: Establishment of an International Military for the Far East, Charter of the Tribunal," *Department of State Bulletin* 14 (1946):361–64, 890–907.

1933 United Nations War Crimes Commission. *Charges by the European and the United States Governments against German, Italian and Japanese War Criminals.* 41 vols. London: HMSO, 1944–1947.

1934 United States, Army Forces, Pacific. *Regulations Governing the Trial of War Criminals* [in the Pacific and China Theaters: September 24, 1945–December 27, 1946]. N.p.: U.S. Army Forces, Pacific, 1945–1946.

1935 United States, Department of State. *The Far Eastern Commission: Second Report by the Secretary General.* State Department Pub. no. 3420. Washington, D.C., 1949.

1936 _____. *Foreign Relations of the United States, 1946: Diplomatic Papers.* 11 vols. Vol. 8: *The Far East.* Washington, D.C.: GPO, 1969–1972.

1937 _____. *Papers Relating to the Foreign Relations of the United States: Japan, 1931–1941.* 2 vols. Washington, D.C.: GPO, 1943.

1938 _____. *Peace and War, United States Foreign Policy, 1931–1941.* State Department Pub. no. 1983. Washington, D.C.: GPO, 1943.

1939 _____. *Trial of Japanese War Criminals: Documents: 1. Opening Statement by Joseph B. Keenan. 2. Charter of the International Military Tribunal for the Far East. 3. Indictment.* State Department Pub. no. 2613. Washington, D.C.: GPO, 1946.

DOCUMENTS COLLECTIONS: UNOFFICIAL

1940 Kukche Munje Yon'guhoe. *Kuktong kukche kunsa cheap'ah.* Tokyo, 1949.

1941 Takayanagi, Kenzo. *The Tokio Trials and International Law: Answer to the Prosecutor's Arguments on International Law Delivered at the International Military Tribunal for the Far East on 3 and 4 March 1948.* Tokyo: Yuhikaku, 1948.

OFFICIAL MICROFILM PUBLICATIONS

1942 IMTFE. *Prosecution Documents Which Were Either Not Offered or Were Rejected.* Library of Congress Microfilm, Law–133.

1943 _____. *Record of Proceedings, 1946–1948.* 36 reels. Library of Congress Microfilm, 1964.

1944 _____. *Rejected Defense Documents.* Library of Congress Microfilm, Law–128.

1945 _____. *Transcript of Proceedings: 7 January and 1 October, 1947.* Library of Congress Microfilm, Law–134.

GUIDES AND BIBLIOGRAPHIES

1946 Brown, Delmer M. "Instruction and Research: Recent Japanese Political and Historical Materials," *American Political Science Review* 43 (October 1949):1010–17.

1947 Cho, Sung Yoon. "The Tokyo War Crimes Trial," *Quarterly Journal of the Library of Congress* 24, no. 4 (October 1967):309–18.

1948 Dull, Paul S., and Michael Takaaki Umemura. *The Tokyo Trials: A Functional Index to the Proceedings of the International Military Tribunal for the Far East.* Center for Japanese Studies, Occasional Paper 6. Ann Arbor: University of Michigan Press, 1957.

1949 IMTFE. Language Arbitration Board. *Index of Language Corrections Affecting Documents Admitted into Evidence and the Court Records of the International Military Tribunal for the Far East.* Tokyo, 1948.

1950 Kirchman, Charles V., and Garry D. Ryan, comps. *Preliminary Inventory of the Textual Records of the International Military Tribunal for the Far East.* Washington, D.C.: National Archives and Record Service NM 62, 1965.

1951 Mori, Kyōzō. *Kyokutō Kokusai Gunji Saiban kiroku mokuroku oyobi.* Tokyo, 1953.

1952 Morley, James W. "Check List of Seized Japanese Records in the National Archives," *Far Eastern Quarterly* 9, no. 3 (May 1950):306–33.

1953 SCAP, IPS. *General Index of the Record of the Defense Case.* IPS doc. no. 0008. Tokyo: IMTFE, 1947.

1954 _____. *General Index of the Record of the Prosecution's Case.* IPS doc. no. 0005. Tokyo: IMTFE, 1947.

1955 _____. *Narrative Summary of the Record.* Tokyo: IMTFE, 1947.

1956 _____. *Tokyo War Crimes Trials: Addendum to Revised Index of Documents.* Tokyo: IMTFE, 1947.

1957 _____. *Tokyo War Crimes Trials, Documents, Exhibits for the Defense: Index.* Exhibit nos. 2283–3915 [February 26, 1947–April 16, 1948]. Tokyo: IMTFE, 1947–1948.

1958 _____. *Tokyo War Crimes Trials, Documents, Exhibits for the Prosecution: Index.* [May 4, 1946–January 24, 1947]. Tokyo: IMTFE, 1946–1947.

1959 _____. *Tokyo War Crimes Trials, Index of Documents Not Specifically Linked to One or More of the Defendants.* Tokyo: IMTFE, 1947.

1960 _____. *Tokyo War Crimes Trials, Index of Witnesses.* Tokyo: IMTFE, 1948.

1961 _____. *Tokyo War Crimes Trials, Index to Documents (by Phrase and Subject).* Tokyo: IMTFE, 1947.

1962 _____. *Tokyo War Crimes Trials, Numerical List of IPS Documents Introduced as Court Exhibits.* Tokyo: IMTFE, 1947.

1963 _____. *Tokyo War Crimes Trials, Revised Index of Documents by Defendants.* Tokyo: IMTFE, 1947.

1964 Tōkyō Daigaku, Shakai Kagaku Kenkyūjo, Tokutei Kenkyū Nihon Kindaika Kenkyū Soshiki. *Kyokutō Kokusai Gunji Saiban kiroku, mokuroku.* 1 vol. to date. Tokyo, 1971.

1965 Uyehara, Cecil H., comp. *Checklist of Archives in the Japanese Ministry of Foreign Affairs, Tokyo, Japan, 1868–1945: Microfilmed for the Library of Congress, 1949–1951.* Washington, D.C.: Library of Congress, Photoduplication Service, 1954.

1966 Webb, Herschel, with the assistance of Marleigh Ryan. *Research in Japanese Sources: A Guide.* New York: Columbia University Press, 1965.

1967 Young, John, comp. *Checklist of Microfilm Reproductions of Selected Archives of the Japanese Army, Navy, and Other Government Agencies, 1868–1945.* Washington, D.C.: Georgetown University Press, 1959.

JAPANESE LAW AND GOVERNMENT

1968 Akita, George. *Foundations of Constitutional Government in Japan, 1868–1900.* Cambridge: Harvard University Press, 1967.

1969 Colegrove, Kenneth W. "The Japanese Cabinet," *American Political Science Review* 30 (1936):903–23.

1970 _____. "The Treaty Making Power in Japan," *American Journal of International Law* 25 (1931):270–97.

1971 Earl, David Magarey. *Emperor and Nation in Japan.* Seattle: University of Washington Press, 1964.

1972 Mehren, Arthur Taylor von, ed. *Law in Japan: The Legal Order in a Changing Society.* Cambridge: Harvard University Press, 1963.

1973 Minear, Richard. *Japanese Tradition and Western Law.* Cambridge: Harvard University Press, 1970.

1974 Mitchell, Richard H. *Thought Control in Prewar Japan.* Ithaca: Cornell University Press, 1976.

1975 Nakano, Tomio. *The Ordinance Power of the Japanese Emperor.* Baltimore: Johns Hopkins Press, 1923.

1976 Reischauer, Edwin O. *Japan, Past and Present.* New York: Knopf, 1954.

1977 Reischauer, Karl Robert. *Japan Government-Politics.* New York: Nelson, 1939.

1978 Titus, David Anson. *Palace and Politics in Prewar Japan.* New York: Columbia University Press, 1974.

1979 Tsunoda, R.; W. T. de Bary; and D. Keene. *Sources of the Japanese Tradition.* New York: Columbia University Press, 1958.

THE TRIAL: GENERAL

1980 Allen, Lafe Franklin. "Japan's Militarists Face the Music," *American Foreign Service Journal* 24 (August 1947):14–17, 41–44.

1981 ———. "Judgment Day in Tokyo," *Military Government Journal* 2 (Fall 1949):7–8, 12.

1982 "Apprehension, Trial, and Punishment of War Criminals in the Far East," *Department of State Bulletin* 16 (May 4, 1947):804–06.

1983 Asahi Shimbun Hōtei Kishadan. *Tokyō saiban.* 8 vols. Tokyo: Niyūsusha, 1947–1949.

1984 ———. *Tokyo saiban.* 3 vols. Tokyo: Asahi, 1962.

1985 Australia, Department of External Affairs. "War Crimes," *Current Notes on International Affairs* 16 (October-November 1945):217–20.

1986 Basu, K. K. "Tokio Trials," *Indian Law Review* 3 (1949):25–30.

1987 Blankeney, Ben Bruce. "International Military Tribunal, Argument for Motions to Dismiss," *American Bar Association Journal* 32 (August 1946):475–77, 523.

1988 Blewett, George F. "Victor's Injustice: The Tokyo War Crimes Trial," *American Perspective* 4, no. 3 (Summer 1950):282–92.

1989 Boudkevitch, S. L. "Tirée du procès des grands criminels de guerre de Tokyo," *La Vie Internationale* 9 (1968):126–30; 11 (1968):128–36.

1990 Brines, Russell. *MacArthur's Japan.* Philadelphia: Lippincott, 1948.

1991 "Bring the War Criminals to Justice," *New Times* 6 (February 8, 1950):3–5.

1992 Brown, Brenden F. "Red China, the Tokyo Trial, and Aggressive War," *Louisiana Bar Journal* 3 (January 1956):145–59.

1993 Comyns-Carr, A. S. "The Judgment of the International Military Tribunal for the Far East," *Transactions of the Grotius Society* 34 (1948): 141–51.

1994 ———. "The Tokyo War Crimes Trial," *Far Eastern Quarterly* 18 (May 18, 1949):109–14.

1995   Fixel, Rowland Wells. *Trial of Japan's War Lords.* N.p., 1959.

1996   "For God's Sake! Japanese War Criminals," *Time* 51 (February 16, 1948):31.

1997   "For Posterity," *Time* 52 (December 20, 1948):25–26.

1998   "General Douglas MacArthur's Review of the War Crimes Sentences Issued on November 24, 1948," *Contemporary Japan* 17 (July-December 1948):433–34.

1999   Golunsky, S. "The Trial of the Japanese War Criminals," *New Times* 18 (May 1, 1947):6–10.

2000   "Greatest Trial in Tokyo," *Time* 51 (January 5, 1948):24–25.

2001   Hanayama, Shinshō. *Heiwa no hakken.* Tokyo, 1970.

2002   Hattori, Takushiro. *Dai Toa Senso Zenshi.* Tokyo: Masu Publishing, 1953.

2003   "Have We Lost the Peace? Japanese Convicted in War Crime Trials," *Christian Century* 66 (July 13, 1949):383–89.

2004   Hayashi, Itsurō, ed. *Haija.* Tokyo, 1960.

2005   Hessel, E. A. "Let the Judges Do the Hanging! Japanese Awaiting Trial," *Christian Century* 66 (August 24, 1949):984–86.

2006   "Hidoi!" *Time* 52 (November 22, 1948):31–32.

2007   Horowitz, Solis. "The Tokyo Trial," *International Conciliation* 465 (November 1950):473–584.

2008   Hyder, E. M., Jr. "The Tokyo Trial," *Texas Bar Journal* 10 (April 1947):136–37, 166–67.

2009   "The International Military Tribunal for the Far East," *Current Notes on International Affairs* 19 (May 1948):231–41.

2010   "International Military Tribunal for the Far East," *International Organization* 1 (February 1947):176.

2011   "International Military Tribunal for the Far East: The Judges and Prosecutors," *New Zealand Law Journal* 22 (May 21, 1946):119.

2012   Ireland, Gordon. "Uncommon Law in Martial Tokyo," *Year Book of World Affairs* 4 (1950):50–104.

2013   "Jap War Criminals Await Trial," *Life* 19 (November 12, 1945):29–33.

2014 "Joseph B. Keenan Meets the Press," *American Mercury* 70 (April 1950):456–60.

2015 Kawano, Kyōsuke. *Jimmon gōmon shokei.* Tokyo, 1970.

2016 Keenan, Joseph Berry. *Our Relations in the Far East as They Appear in the International War Crimes Trials in Tokyo.* N.p., 1946.

2017 ———, and Brenden Francis Brown. *Crimes against International Law.* Washington, D.C.: Public Affairs Press, 1950.

2018 Keita, Uematsu. *Kyokuto kokusai gunji saiban.* Tokyo: Jimbutsu oraisha, 1962.

2019 Kenwāji, S. (Lt. Col. Aubrey S. Kenworthy). "Bei Kenpeitaichō: Ichigaya no Kiroku," *Bungei Shunjū* 31, no. 1 (January 1953):128–37.

2020 Kido, Kōichi. *Kido nikki.* Tokyo, 1947.

2021 Kiyose Ichiro. *Hiroku, Tokyo saiban.* Tokyo: Yomiuri, 1967.

2022 Kojima Noboru. *Tokyo saiban.* 2 vols. Tokyo: Chuo koron, 1971.

2023 Kudryavtsev, V. "The Verdict against Japanese Militarism," *Soviet Press Translations* 4 (February 1, 1948):70–71.

2024 "Last Hope: Fate of Japan's Top War Criminals before U.S. Supreme Court," *Scholastic* 53 (December 8, 1948):14.

2025 Liu, James T. C. "The Tokyo Trial," *China Monthly* 8 (July 1947): 242–47.

2026 ———. "The Tokyo Trial: Second Look," *China Monthly* 8 (August 1947):279–80.

2027 McAfee, B. "The Tokio War Crimes Trials," *Annuaire de l'Association des Auditeurs et Anciens Auditeurs de l'Académie de Droit International de la Haye* 28 (1958):39–49.

2028 McKenzie, W. I. "The Japanese War Crimes Trials," *Michigan State Bar Journal* 26 (May 1947):16–21.

2029 Markov, M. "The Approaching Trial of Major Japanese War Criminals," *New Times* 8 (April 15, 1946):7–10.

2030 ———. "Falsification of History at the Tokyo Trial," *New Times* 17 (April 21, 1948):7–11.

2031 Meek, F. E. "War Crimes' Trials in the Pacific," *Idaho State Bar Proceedings* 21 (1947):36–42.

2032 Mignone, Frederick. "After Nuremberg, Tokyo," *Texas Law Review* 25 (May 1947):475–90.

2033 "Mills of Justice in Tokyo," *Newsweek* 32, (November 15, 1948):40.

2034 Minear, Richard H. *Victor's Justice: The Tokyo War Crimes Trials.* Princeton: Princeton University Press, 1971.

2035 Moody, Samuel B., and Maury Allen. *Reprieve from Hell.* New York: Pageant Press, 1961.

2036 Mosley, Leonard. *Hirohito, Emperor of Japan.* Englewood Cliffs, N.J.: Prentice-Hall, 1966.

2037 "Le Nuremberg d'Extrême-Orient: Le procès des criminels de guerre japonais s'est ouvert à Tokyo," *Revue de Droit International (Sottile-Geneva)* 24 (1946):142–43.

2038 "Observations on the Trial of War Criminals in Japan," *External Affairs* 1 (February 1949):12–23.

2039 Quentin-Baxter, R. Q. "Task of the International Military Tribunal at Tokyo," *New Zealand Law Journal* 25 (June 7, 1949):133–38.

2040 Raginsky, Mark, and S. Rozenblit. "What People Expected of the International Military Tribunal in Tokyo," *Soviet Press Translations* 3 (July 15, 1948):421–25.

2041 Rama Rao, J. S. "The Dissenting Judgment of Mr. Justice Pal at the Tokyo Trial," *Indian Yearbook of International Affairs* 2 (1953): 277–91.

2042 "Remember?" *New Republic* 115 (December 30, 1946):895.

2043 Riley, Walter Lee. "The International Tribunal for the Far East and the Law of the Tribunal as Revealed by the Judgment and the Concurring and Dissenting Opinions." Ph.D. dissertation, University of Washington, 1957.

2044 Riron Sha. *Kabe atsuki heya.* Tokyo, 1956.

2045 Röling, B. V. A. "The Tokyo Trial and the Development of International Law," *Indian Law Review* 7, no. 1 (1953):4–14.

2046 Russel of Liverpool, Lord. *The Knights of Bushido: A Short History of Japanese War Crimes.* London: Cassell, 1958.

2047 Satō, Kenryō. *Dai Tōa sensō kaikoroku.* Tokyo, 1966.

2048 Satō, Ryōichi. *Gyakutai no kiroku.* Tokyo, 1953.

2049 Schroeder, Paul. *The Axis Alliance and Japanese-American Relations, 1941.* Ithaca: Cornell University Press, 1958.

2050 Sebald, William J., and Russell Brines. *With MacArthur in Japan.* New York: Norton, 1965.

2051 "Sentence Japanese War Criminals," *Christian Century* 65 (November 24, 1948):1262.

2052 Shimamura Takashi. *Hiroku Tōkyō saiban.* Tokyo, 1972.

2053 Sutton, David Nelson, "The Trial of Tojo," *Virginia State Bar Association Proceedings* 60 (1949):223–46.

2054 _____. "The Trial of Tojo: The Most Important Trial in All History?" *American Bar Association Journal* 36 (January 1950):93–96, 160–65.

2055 Tajimn, Ryujūn. *Waga inochi hatera hi ni.* Tokyo, 1953.

2056 Takayanagi, Kenzo. *Kyokuto saiban to kokusaiho.* Tokyo: Yuhikaku, 1948.

2057 Takikawa Masajiro. *Tōkyō saiban o sabaku.* Tokyo: Towasha, 1952.

2058 Tanaka Masaaki. *Pa-ra hakase no Nihon muzairon.* Tokyo: Keibunsha, 1963.

2059 Tateno Nobuyuki. *Zoku Nihon senryo.* Tokyo: Kodonsha, 1964.

2060 "Tojo Tells All," *Newsweek* 31 (January 5, 1948):39.

2061 *Tōkyō Saiban: Asahi Shinbun Hotei Kisha-dan.* 9 vols. Tokyo: News-sha, 1947–1949.

2062 *Tōkyō Saiban: Asahi Shinbun Hotei Kisha-dan.* 3 vols. Tokyo: Saiban kanokai, 1962.

2063 *Tōkyō Saiban Hanketsu-kyokuto Kokusai Gunji Sai bansho Hanketsu bun.* Tokyo: Mainichi Schinbun-sha, 1949.

2064 Tōkyō saiban kenkyuki, ed. *Kyodo kenkyu Paru hanketsusho.* Tokyo: Saiban kanokai, 1966.

2065 *Tōkyō Senpan Saibansho no Kosei to Kino.* Heiwa Shobo: Kokusai Jiji Kenkyn-Jo, 1946.

2066 "Trial of Far Eastern Criminals," *Department of State Bulletin* 14 (May 19, 1946):846–48, 853.

2067 "Trial of Far Eastern War Criminals," *Department of State Bulletin* 14 (May 10, 1946):361–64.

2068 "Trial of Japanese Executioners," *Oklahoma Bar Association Journal* 17 (August 31, 1946):1269–72.

2069 "Trial of Japanese War Criminals," *Department of State Bulletin* 20 (May 1, 1949):569–71.

2070 Uematsu, Keita. *Kyokutō. Kokusai Gunji Saiban.* Tokyo, 1962.

2071 "U.S.S.R. Motives on Trying Emperor of Japan Questioned," *Department of State Bulletin* 22 (February 13, 1950):244.

2072 Vasilyev, A. N. "On Rapid Trial and Punishment of War Criminals: On the Results of the Tokio Trials," *Current Digest of the Soviet Press* 1, no. 25 (July 19, 1949):11–15.

2073 ———. "The Tokyo Trial of the Chief Japanese War Criminals," *Soviet Press Translations* 3 (April 1, 1948):195–202.

2074 Wadsworth, Lawrence W., Jr. "A Short History of the Tokyo War Crimes Trials with Special Reference to Some Aspects and Procedures." Ph.D. dissertation, American University, 1955.

2075 "Wages of Infamy: Japan's War Trials," *Newsweek* 32 (November 22, 1948):35–36.

THE DEFENDANTS: GENERAL

2076 Arima, Rainei. "Tōjō Hitori wo Semerarenu," *Seikei Shishin* 2, no. 7 (July 1955):33–34.

2077 Asahi Shimbun Hōtei Kishadan. *Tōjō Jinmon-roku.* Tokyo: Niyūsusha, 1949.

2078 Browne, Courtney. *Tojo: The Last Banzai.* New York: Holt, Rinehart and Winston, 1967.

2079 Burns, Richard Dean, and Edward M. Bennett, eds. *Diplomats in Crisis: United States-Chinese-Japanese Relations, 1919–1941.* Santa Barbara: ABC-Clio, 1974.

2080 Butow, Robert J. C. *Tojo and the Coming of the War.* Princeton: Princeton University Press, 1961.

2081 Chiang, Wen-hsien. "Dohihara Kenji and the Japanese Expansion into China 1931–1936." Ph.D. dissertation, University of Pennsylvania, 1969.

2082 "A 'Dead Man' Speaks: Japan's War Leaders," *Life* 24 (January 26, 1948):87–91.

2083 "Eager, Maybe for Death in Tokyo," *Newsweek* 32 (December 13, 1948):41.

2084 "The Guilty: Hideki Tojo," *Collier's* 113 (February 5, 1944):60.

2085 Hanayama, Shinshō. "Dai Ōjō Datta," *Daiyamondo* 40, no. 17 (May 15, 1952):146–50.

2086 _____. *Heiwa no hakken: Sugamo no Sei to Shi no Kiroku.* Tokyo: Asahi Shinbunsha, 1949.

2087 _____. "Last Days of Tojo," *Collier's* 125 (May 6, 1950):28.

2088 _____. *The Way of Deliverance: Three Years with Condemned Japanese War Criminals.* Translated by Hideo Suzuki, Eiichi Noda, James K. Sasaki. New York: Scribner's, 1950.

2089 Hirota Koki denki bankokai. *Hirota Koki.* Tokyo, 1966.

2090 "International Hangings: Japanese War Criminals," *Commonweal* 49 (November 26, 1948):165.

2091 Kodama, Yoshio. *I Was Defeated.* Translated by Fukuda Taro. Tokyo, 1959.

2092 Markov, M. "Mamoru Shigemitsu and His Patrons," *Current Digest of the Soviet Press* 3, no. 24 (July 28, 1951):11–12.

2093 Matsumoto Shigekazu. "Togo gaisho to Taiheigo senso," *Kokusai seiji* 33 (1966):52–67.

2094 Piggott, Francis S. G. *Broken Thread: An Autobiography.* Aldershot, Eng.: Gale and Polden, 1950.

2095 "Sentence Japanese War Criminals," *Christian Century* 65 (November 24, 1948):1262.

2096 "Seven Old Men: Japan's War Leaders," *Time* 53 (January 3, 1949):18–19.

2097 Shigemitsu Mamoru. *Gaiko Kaisoroku.* Tokyo, 1953.

2098 _____. *Japan and Her Destiny.* Translated by Oswald White and edited by Francis S. G. Piggott. New York: E. P. Dutton, 1958.

2099 _____. *Sugamo nikki.* Tokyo, 1953.

2100 Tojo, Hideki. "Kyokuto no Shinjōsei ni Tsuite," *Gaikō Jihō* (December 15, 1933):68–78.

2101 Usui, Katsumi. "Hirota koki ron," *Kokusai seiji* 1 (1960):40–52.

2102   Yabe, Teiji (henchosa). *Konoe Fumimaro.* 2 vols. Tokyo: Kō-bundō, 1952.

Subsidiary Proceedings, the Far East, 1945–1949

THE TRIALS OF GENERALS YAMASHITA (1945) AND HOMMA (1946), MANILA

Documents

2103   SCAP. *The Case of General Yamashita: A Memorandum by Courtney Whitney, Chief, Government Section.* Tokyo: SCAP, 1950.

2104   *United States of America vs. Tomoyuki Yamashita, before the Military Commission Convened by the Commanding General, United States Army Forces, Western Pacific* [Proceedings]. 34 vols. in 14. Manila, 1945.

General

2105   Daly, James J. A. "The Yamashita Case and Martial Courts," *Connecticut Bar Journal* 21 (April-June 1947):136–58, 210–29.

2106   Fairman, Charles. "The Supreme Court on Military Jurisdiction: Martial Rule in Hawaii and the Yamashita Case," *Harvard Law Review* 59 (July 1946):833–82.

2107   Feldhaus, J. Gordon. "The Trial of Yamashita," *South Dakota Bar Journal* 15 (October 1946):181–93.

2108   Fuqua, Ellis E. "Judicial Review of War Crimes Trials," *Journal of Criminal Law and Criminology* 37 (May-June 1946):58–64.

2109   Ganoe, James T. "The Yamashita Case and the Constitution," *Oregon Law Review* 25 (April 1946):143–58.

2110   Guy, G. F. "Defense of Yamashita," *Wyoming Law Journal* 4 (Spring 1950):153–80.

2111   Kagao, Shunin. *Montenrupa ni inoru.* Tokyo, 1953.

2112   Katona, Paul. "Japanese War Crime Trials," *Free World* 12 (November 1946):37–40.

2113   Kuhn, Arthur K. "International Law and National Legislation in the Trial of War Criminals—The Yamashita Case," *American Journal of International Law* 44 (July 1950):559–62.

2114   Lim, M. "Yamashita and Homma Trials—Highlights," *Philadelphia Law Journal* 22 (January 1947):4–12.

2115   "Manila Infamies," *Newsweek* 26 (November 19, 1945):52.

2116   Potter, John Deane. *The Life and Death of a Japanese General.* New York: New American Library, 1962.

2117   Reel, Adolf Frank. *The Case of General Yamashita.* Chicago: University of Chicago Press, 1949.

2118   ———. "Even His Enemy," *Ohio Bar Association Report* 19 (June 3, 1946):163–75.

2119   ———, and N. Levy, "Tiger of Malaya: Review of the Case of General Yamashita," *Saturday Review of Literature* 32 (October 8, 1949): 42–43.

2120   Saka, Kuniyasu. *Hitō sen to sono sensō saiban.* Tokyo, 1967.

2121   "Sober Afterglow: The Case of General Yamashita," *Time* 54 (November 7, 1949):26–27.

2122   Sullivan, James D. "Jurisdiction of Commission Established to Try War Criminals," *Notre Dame Lawyer* 21 (March 1946):237–39.

2123   "Two Japanese War Criminals," *New Republic* 114 (February 25, 1946):269.

Appeals Before the U.S. Supreme Court

2124   *Homma v. Patterson,* 327 US 759 (1946).

2125   *In re Yamashita,* 327 US 1 (1946).

The Shanghai Trial, 1946

2126   Saka, Kuniyasu, ed. *Sensō saiban, Shanhai hōtel.* 1 vol. to date. Tokyo, 1967.

2127   "Shanghai Execution," *Life* 23 (July 14, 1947):34–35.

The Yokohama Trials, 1945–1949

2128   "Insufficient Evidence," *Time* 52 (December 20, 1948):26.

2129   Lyman, A. "Yokohama War Crimes Trials—A Review," *Journal of the Bar Association of the District of Columbia* 17 (June 1950):267–80.

2130   Miller, R. W. "War Crimes Trials at Yokohama," *Brooklyn Law Review* 15 (April 1949):191–209.

2131   Saka, Kuniyasu, ed. *Sensō saiban, Yokohama hōtel.* 1 vol. to date. Tokyo, 1967.

2132   Spurlock, P. E. "Yokohama War Crimes Trials—The Truth about a Misunderstood Subject," *American Bar Association Journal* 36 (May 1950):387–89, 436–38.

THE INDONESIA TRIAL, 1946

2133 Saka Kuniyasu, ed. *Shijitsu kiroku, sensō saiban Ran-In hōtel.* 1 vol. to date. Tokyo, 1968.

THE GOZAWA TRIAL, SINGAPORE, 1946

2134 Sleeman, Colin, ed. *Trial of Gozawa Sadaichi and Nine Others.* London: William Hodge, 1948.

THE "DOUBLE TENTH" TRIAL, SINGAPORE, 1946

2135 Mallal, Bashir, ed. *The Double Tenth Trial: War Crimes Court in re Lt. Sumida Haruzo and Twenty Others.* Singapore: Malayan Law Journal Office, 1947.

2136 Sleeman, Colin, and S. C. Silkin, eds. *Trial of Sumida Haruzo and Twenty Others (The "Double Tenth" Trial).* London: William Hodge, 1951.

THE TRIAL OF OTOZO YAMADA, ET AL. (THE KHABAROVSK TRIAL), KHABAROVSK, RUSSIA, 1949

2137 "Advocate of Plague," *Current Digest of the Soviet Press* 2, no. 2 (April 15, 1950):28–29.

2138 *Documents relatifs au procès des anciens militaires de l'armée japonaise accusés d'avoir préparé et employé l'arme bactériologique.* Moscow: Éditions en langues étrangères, 1950.

2139 "Ill-starred Defenders of War Criminals," *Current Digest of the Soviet Press* 2, no. 11 (April 29, 1950):22–23.

2140 "Indictment in the Case of Former Servicemen in the Japanese Army . . . Charged with Preparing and Using Bacteriological Weapons," *Current Digest of the Soviet Press* 1, no. 52 (January 24, 1950):35–43.

2141 "Justice Demands International Trial of Japanese War Criminals," *USSR Embassy Information Bulletin* 10 (February 24, 1950):112–13.

2142 *Material on the Trial of Former Servicemen of the Japanese Army, Charged with Manufacturing and Employing Biological Weapons.* Moscow: Foreign Languages Publishing House, 1950.

2143 Mayevsky, V. "Monstrous Crimes Committed by Japanese Barbarians," *USSR Embassy Information Bulletin* 10 (February 10, 1950):93.

2144 Raginsky, M. "Monstrous Atrocities of the Japanese Imperialists, *New Times* 2 (January 8, 1950):3–7.

2145 _____, and S. Rosenblatt. "Khabarovskij process nad japonskimi vrjennimi presteysnikami," *Sovetskoe Gosudarstvo i Pravo* 3 (1950–1951): 8–25.

2146 "Trial of Former Japanese Soldiers," *Current Digest of the Soviet Press* 2, no. 1 (February 18, 1950):21–27.

2147 Vasilyev, A. N. "The Atrocities of the Aggressors Have Been Exposed," *Soviet Press Translations* 5 (July 1, 1950):411–13.

Establishment of the "Law of Nuremberg": Contemporary Review Articles, 1945–1951

2148 Alcalà-Zamora y Castillo, N. "Il processo dei criminali di guerra," *Jus* 1 (October 1950):208–31.

2149 Alexander, Eva V. "Trials of War Criminals," *Women Lawyers Journal* 32 (March 1946):28–29, 49–52.

2150 Allen, Florence E. "Nuremberg Trial Implements World Law," *Women Lawyers Journal* 34 (Winter 1948):6–8, 26–28, 30.

2151 Aschenauer, Rudolf. *Zur Frage einer Revision der Kriegsverbrecherprozesse.* Nuremberg: Selbstverlag, 1949.

2152 Bartolomeo Carlomagno, Roberto. *El castigo de los criminales de guerra.* Córdoba, Arg.: Imprementa de la Universidad, 1949.

2153 Behling, Kurt. "Nürnberger Lehren," *Juristische Rundschau* 3 (1949):502–05.

2154 Belgion, Montgomery. *Victor's Justice.* Chicago: Henry Regnery, 1949.

2155 Belloni, G. A. "Criminalita di Guerra," *Guistizia Penale* 51 (January 1946):1–8.

2156 Beyer, Stanley J. "German War Criminals," *New Republic* 123 (November 20, 1950):4.

2157 Brand, G. "War Crimes Trials and the Laws of War," *British Yearbook of International Law* 26 (1949):414–27.

2158 Briggs, Herbert W. "New Dimensions in International Law," *American Political Science Review* 46 (September 1952):677–98.

2159 British Peoples Party. *Failure at Nuremberg: An Analysis of Trial, Evidence and Verdict.* London: British Peoples Party, Research Department, 1946.

2160 Brügel, J. W. "Die allgemeine Erklärung der Menschenrechte," *Europa-Archiv* 4 (October 20, 1949):2529–34.

2161 Bull, H. A. "Nürnberg Trial—Value to Civilization," *Federal Rules Decisions* 7 (July 1947):175–82.

2162   Caloyanni, Mégalos A. "Cour pénale internationale et code répressif des nations," *Revue de Droit International (Sottile-Geneva)* 23 (1945): 219–27.

2163   ————. "La Guerre-Crime et les criminels de guerre," *Revue Internationale de Droit Pénal* 17 (1946):6–12.

2164   ————. "Memorandum on International Criminal Legislation and Peace," *Revue Internationale de Droit Pénal* 17 (1946):305–32.

2165   ————. "Le Procès de Nuremberg et l'avenir de la justice pénale internationale," *Revue de Droit International (Sottile-Geneva)* 24 (October-December 1946):174–82.

2166   Carter, Edward F. "The Nuremberg Trial: A Turning Point in the Enforcement of International Law," *Nebraska Law Review* 28 (March 1949):370–86.

2167   "Commission Formulates Nuremberg Principles," *United Nations Bulletin* 9 (August 1, 1950):108–10.

2168   Cowles, Willard B. "Trials of War Criminals (Non-Nuremberg)," *American Journal of International Law* 42 (April 1948):299–319.

2169   Daly, Edward J. "War Crime Trials," *Connecticut Bar Journal* 23 (March 1949):2–10.

2170   De La Pradelle, P. *Le procès des Grands Criminels de Guerre et le développement du droit international.* Paris: Éditions Internationales, 1947.

2171   Diéguez Lamazares, Juan. "El juicio de Nuremberg," *Annuario de la Sociedad Cubana de Derecho Internacional* 21 (1949):67–71.

2172   Donnedieu de Vabres, Henri. "La Codification du droit pénal international," *Revue Internationale de Droit Pénal* 19 (1948):21–35.

2173   ————. "De l'Organisation d'une juridiction pénale internationale," *Revue Internationale de Droit Pénal* 20 (1949):1–8.

2174   Dunn, Benjamin J. "Trial of War Criminals," *Australian Law Journal* 19 (March 15, 1946):356–61.

2175   Ečer, Bohuslav. "Hlavni materialne prevni normy norimberské ho procesu," *Pravnik* 85, nos. 1–2 (1946):1–10.

2176   ————. "Lessons of the Nuremberg Trial," *Central European Observer* 24 (1947):70–71, 103–05.

2177   Fairman, Charles. "Some New Problems of the Constitution Following the Flag," *Stanford Law Review* 1 (June 1949):587–645.

2178 Galbo, José Luís. *Crimenes y justicia de guerra (notas sobre patología del derecho penal).* Havana: J. Montero, 1950.

2179 "German Churches and the War Crimes Trials," *Christian Century* 65 (July 7, 1948):677.

2180 Glaser, S. "La Charte du Tribunal de Nuremberg et les nouveaux principes du droit international," *Schweizerische Zeitschrift für Strafrecht* 63 (1948):13–38.

2181 Graven, Jean. "De la justice internationale à la paix (Les enseignements de Nuremberg)," *Revue de Droit International (Sottile-Geneva)* 24 (October-December 1946):183–212; 25 (January-March 1947):3–17.

2182 Gray, Leslie B. "Handling the War Criminal," *Nevada State Bar Journal* 11 (January 1946):8–14.

2183 Green, L. C. "Trials of War Criminals," *Solicitor* 14 (July 1947): 160–62.

2184 Haensel, Carl. "Der Ausklang von Nürnberg," *Neue Juristische Wochenschrift* 2 (1949):367–70.

2185 Hankey, Lord. *Politics, Trials, and Errors.* Chicago: Henry Regnery, 1950.

2186 Harding-Barlow, M. "International Law and the Nuremberg Trial," *South African Law Journal* 65 (August 1948):375–86.

2187 Hartlmayr, F. "Nürnberger Kriegsverbrecherprozess und Völkerrecht," *Österreichische Monatshefte* 1 (1946):329–32.

2188 Hauxhaust, H. A.; O. Cunningham; C. F. Wennerstrum; and J. T. Brand. "Forum on War Crimes Trials," *American Bar Association Proceedings* [Section of International and Comparative Law] (1948):372–85.

2189 Hazan, Edouard Tawfik. "Étude critique du jugement de Nuremberg," *Revue de droit international pour le Moyen-Orient* 1 (May 1951): 33–42; 1 (January 1952):173–86.

2190 Hogan, Willard N. "War Criminals," *South Atlantic Quarterly* 45 (October 1946):415–24.

2191 Honig, F. "Criminal Justice in Germany Today: Crimes against Humanity before German Courts," *Year Book of World Affairs* 5 (1951): 131–52.

2192 _____. "War Crimes Trials: Lessons for the Future," *International Affairs* 26 (1950):522–32.

2193   Horsky, Charles A. "Status of Prosecutions against German and Japanese War Criminals," *Lawyers Guild Review* 6 (May-June 1946): 485–89.

2194   Hugueney, Louis. "Le procès de Nuremberg devant les principes modernes du droit pénal international," *Revue Internationale de Droit Pénal* 19 (1948):277–80.

2195   Ivrakis, S. C. "Nürnberg: Confusion and Catharsis: An Inquiry into Some of the Legal and Philosophical Issues of the Trial." M.A. thesis, Cambridge University, 1950.

2196   Jackson, Robert H. "Nürnberg in Retrospect: Legal Answer to International Lawlessness," *Canadian Bar Review* 27 (August-September 1949):761–81; *American Bar Association Journal* 35 (1949):813–16, 881–87.

2197   Jackson, William E. "Putting the Nuremberg Law to Work," *Foreign Affairs* 25 (July 1947):550–65.

2198   ———. "Simplified Primer [Review of *Final Judgment*, by Victor H. Berstein]," *Saturday Review of Literature* 30 (May 10, 1947):15, 34.

2199   ———. "Was Nuremberg Justified?" *Collier's* 119 (April 19, 1947): 15.

2200   Jaspers, Karl, "The Significance of the Nürnberg Trials for Germany and the World," *Notre Dame Lawyer* 22 (January 1947):150–60.

2201   Jescheck, H.-H. "Die Entwicklung des Völkerstrafrechts nach Nürnberg," *Schweizerische Zeitschrift für Strafrecht* 72 (1957): 217–48.

2202   Katzenberger, K. "Das Recht der politischen Säuberung: Das Verhältnis des Nürnberger Urteils zum Befreiungsgesetz (U.S. Zone) und die aus dem Nürnberger Urteil für die Praxis der Sprechkammer sich ergebenden Konsequenzen," *Süddeutsche Juristenzeitung* 3 (1948):41–49.

2203   Keenan, Joseph Berry. "Observations and Lessons from International Criminal Trials," *University of Kansas City Law Review* 17 (April-June 1949):117–28.

2204   Klefisch, Theodor. "Gedanken über Inhalt und Wirkung des Nürnberger Urteils," *Juristische Rundschau* 1 (1947):45–49.

2205   Latersner, Hans. *Verteidigung deutscher Soldaten: Plädoyers vor alliierten Gerichten.* Bonn: Girardet, 1950.

2206   Lautern, Mark. *Das Letzte Wort über Nürnberg: Fassade und Sumpf in den Kriegsverbrecher-Prozessen.* Buenos Aires: Dürer-Verlag, 1950.

2207 Lepnhardt, Hans. "The Nuremberg Trial: A Legal Analysis," *Review of Politics* 11 (October 1949):449–60.

2208 Maynard, J.-A. "Crimes et criminels de guerre, problème étudié par un groupe de juristes aux États-Unis," *Revue Internationale de Droit Pénal* 17 (1946):333–42.

2209 Meltzer, Bernard D. "A Note on Some Aspects of the Nuremberg Debate," *University of Chicago Law Review* 14 (April 1947):455–69.

2210 Morgan, John H. "Nuremberg and After," *Quarterly Review* 285 (April-October 1947):318–36, 605–25.

2211 Morgenthau, Hans J.; Erich Hula; and Moorehouse F. X. Millar. "Views on Nuremberg: A Symposium," *America* 76 (December 7, 1946): 266–68.

2212 Mosler, Hermann. "Der Einfluss der Rechtsstellung Deutschlands auf die Kriegsverbrecherprozesse," *Süddeutsche Juristenzeitung* 2 (July 1947):362–70.

2213 Munro, Hector A. "Nuremberg and Law Enforcement," *New Commonwealth Quarterly* 9 (1948):101–03.

2214 Neumann, Franz. "The War Crimes Trials," *World Politics* 2 (October 1949):135–47.

2215 "Nuremberg Jurist Returns," *America* 79 (June 5, 1948):213.

2216 Paton, G. W. "The War Trials and International Law," *Res Judicatae* 3 (October 1947):122–32.

2217 Pergler, Charles. "War Crimes and War Criminals," *Journal of the Bar Association of the District of Columbia* 13 (September 1946): 385–92.

2218 Risse, Friedrich Viktor. *So zersetzt Moskau den Westen*. Munich: Internationale Demokratische Kampfliga, 1954.

2219 Sawicki, Jerzy. "Prawo norymberskie e polskie prawo karne," *Pantswo i Prawo* 3 (1948):54–63.

2220 Simon, S. *La galerie des monstres: À Nuremberg dans les coulisses du plus grand procès de l'histoire*. Nancy: Imprimerie Vagner, 1947.

2221 Smith, H. A. "The Nuremberg Trials," *Free Europe* 13 (1946): 201–04.

2222 Snyder, Orville C. "It's Not Law—The War Guilt Trials," *Kentucky Law Journal* 38 (November 1949):81–104.

2223　Solow, Herbert. "A Rather Startling Result," *Fortune* 39 (April 1949):158–66.

2224　Sottile, Antoine. "Un peu plus de justice, S.V.P.! (À propos de certains verdicts et acquittements prononcés par les tribunaux militaires internationaux)," *Revue de Droit International (Sottile-Geneva)* 26 (October-December 1948):372–85.

2225　Spain, Ian. "Trials of War Criminals," *Australian Law Journal* 20 (September 1946):1269–72.

2226　Spiropoulos, Jean. "Formulation of the Nürnberg Principles," *Revue Hellénique de Droit International* 4 (April-June 1951):129–62.

2227　Steinbauer, Gustav. *Ich war Verteidiger in Nürnberg: Ein Dokumentenbeitrag zum Kampf um Österreich.* Klagenfurt: Kaiser, 1950.

2228　Storey, Robert G. "El impacto de Nuremberg sobre el derecho internacional," *Revista Peruana de Derecho Internacional* 8 (January-April 1948):33–43.

2229　Trainin, Aaron. "From Nuremberg to Tokyo," *New Times* 12 (March 17, 1948):11–14.

2230　Utrikespolitiska Institutet, Stockholm. *Nürnbergprocessen I–II.* Stockholm: Kooperativa förbundets bokförlag, 1946.

2231　Van Bogaert, E. *Beschouwingen over Nuremberg.* Gent: De Vlam, 1951.

2232　Wade, D. A. L. "A Survey of the Trials of War Criminals," *Journal of the Royal United Services Institution* 96 (February 1951):66–70.

2233　Walkinshaw, Robert B. "The Nuremberg and Tokyo Trials: Another Step toward International Justice," *American Bar Association Journal* 35 (April 1949):299–302, 362–63.

2234　"What's a Criminal," *Time* 51 (April 19, 1948):87.

2235　Witenberg, J. C. "De Grotius à Nuremberg: Quelques réflexions," *Revue Générale de Droit International Public* 51 (1947):89–112.

2236　Wright, Quincy. "The Law of the Nuremberg Trial," *American Journal of International Law* 41 (January 1947):38–72.

World War II Trials: Retrospective Literature, 1951–

General

2237　Baird, Jay W., comp. *From Nuremberg to My Lai.* Lexington, Mass.: Heath, 1972.

2238 Blum, Howard. *Wanted! The Search for Nazis in America.* New York: Quadrangle, 1977.

2239 D'Amato, Anthony A.; Harvey L. Gould; and Larry D. Woods. "War Crimes and Vietnam: The 'Nuremberg Defense' and the Military Register," *California Law Review* 57 (November 1969):1055–1110.

2240 Farer, Thomas J. *The Laws of War Twenty-five Years after Nuremberg.* New York: Carnegie Endowment for International Peace, 1971.

2241 Kelly, Joseph B. "A Legal Analysis of the Changes in War," *Military Law Review* 13 (1961):89–119.

2242 Rie, Robert. "War Crimes Trials," *American Journal of International Law* 48 (July 1954):470–74.

2243 Storey, Robert G. *Final Judgment? Pearl Harbor to Nuremberg.* San Antonio: Naylor, 1968.

2244 Taylor, Telford; Louis Henkin; Herbert Wechsler; Richard Falk; R. L. Smith McKeithen; and Robert MacCrate; panelists. "War Crimes, Just and Unjust Wars, and Comparisons between Nuremberg and Vietnam," *Columbia Journal of Law and Social Problems* 8, no. 1 (Fall 1971): 101–34.

EUROPE

2245 Alexandrov, G. N., and M. J. Raginsky, comps. *Internationale Konferenz zu Fragen der Verfolgung von Nazi-und Kriegsverbrechen: Moskau, 25.–28. März 1969.* Moscow: APN-Verlag, 1969.

2246 Amchan, Morris. "Nuremberg Revisited," *Federal Bar Journal* 30, no. 3 (Summer 1971):242–53.

2247 Arzinger, R. *Rehabilitierung der faschistischen Kriegsverbrecher, eine Gefahr für den Frieden in Europa.* Berlin: Kongress-Verlag, 1954.

2248 Benton, Wilbourn E., and Georg Grimm, eds. *Nuremberg: German Views of the War Crimes Trials.* Dallas: Southern Methodist University Press, 1955.

2249 Bernstein, V. H. "Reunion in Warsaw: Remembering Nuremberg, Meeting of the Former Trial Correspondents," *Nation* 204 (January 23, 1967):112–16.

2250 Birmingham, Robert L. "The War Crimes Trial: A Second Look," *University of Pittsburgh Law Review* 24 (October 1962):132–54.

2251 Cyprian, Tadeusz. *Prawo norymberskie: Bilans i perspektywy.* Warsaw: Kuthana, 1948.

2252 _____. *Przed Trybunałem świata: Refleksje w spomnienia, dokumenty.* Warsaw: Książka i Wiedza, 1962.

2253 _____. *Walka o zasady norymberskie, 1945–1955.* Warsaw: Panstwowe Wydawn. Nankowe, 1956.

2254 _____, and Jerzy Sawicki. *Ludzie i sprawy Norembergi.* Warsaw: Wydawn. Poznańskii, 1967.

2255 _____, and M. Siewvrski. *Głos ma Prokurator.* Warsaw: Iskry, 1966.

2256 D'Amato, Anthony A.; Harvey L. Gould; and Larry D. Woods. "War Crimes and Vietnam: The 'Nuremberg Defense' and the Military Register," *California Law Review* 57 (November 1969):1055–1110.

2257 Dami, Aldo. "Norimberga," *Il Politico* 21 (1956–1957):69–83.

2258 Dautricourt, J. Y. "15 jaar na nuremberg," *Rechtskundig Weekblad* 26 (1963):1465–78.

2259 Davidson, Eugene. *The Nuremberg Fallacy: Wars and War Crimes since World War II.* New York: Macmillan, 1973.

2260 Dorman, Nicholas R. "The Nuremberg Trials Revisited," *American Bar Association Journal* 47 (1961):260–64.

2261 Eitner, Lorenz. "The Criminal State and Its Servants: Reminiscences of the Nuremberg War Crime Trials," *Minnesota Review* 3, no. 2 (Winter 1963):162–78.

2262 Falk, Richard A. "Nuremberg: Past, Present and Future," *Yale Law Journal* 80 (June 1971):1501–28.

2263 _____. "The Nuremberg Defense in the Pentagon Papers Case," *Columbia Journal of Transnational Law* 13, no. 2 (1974):208–38.

2264 _____. "The Nuremberg Tradition," *Intercom* 13 (January–February 1971):29–30.

2265 Farer, Thomas J. "The Laws of War Twenty-five Years after Nuremberg," *International Conciliation* 583 (1971):1–54.

2266 Fehl, P. "Ghosts of Nuremberg: German War Criminals," *Atlantic Monthly* 229 (March 1972):70; also see R. M. W. Kempner, "Reply with Rejoinder," *Atlantic Monthly* 229 (June 1972):28.

2267 Foth, C., and G. Ender. "Twenty Years Later," *Law and Legislation in the German Democratic Republic,* no. 2 (1965):5–21.

2268 Glaser, S. "Les lois de Nuremberg et le droit international: En marge de l'ouvrage du Dr. H. H. Jescheck 'Die Verantwortlichkeit der Staatsorgane nach Völkerstrafrecht,'" *Schweizerische Zeitschrift für Strafrecht* 68 (1953):321–59.

2269 Gorski, Stephen. *German Crimes Forgotten? Reflection on the Nuremberg Trial.* London: Polish Press Agency, 1946.

2270 Granet, M. "La déportation au procès international de Nuremberg," *Revue d'Histoire de la Deuxième Guerre Mondiale* 4 (1954):99–114.

2271 Haensel, Carl. "The Nuremberg Trial Revisited," *De Paul Law Review* 13 (Spring-Summer 1964):248–59.

2272 Hahnenfeld, G. "Die Herkunft der in dem Nürnberger Urteil gegen die sogenannten Hauptkriegsverbrecher angewandten allgemeinen Lehren des Strafrechts." Doctor of Law dissertation, Frankfurt University, 1959.

2273 Haney, G. "Friedensvertrag und Nürnberger Juristenprozess," *Neue Justiz* 16 (1962):54–59.

2274 Härtle, Heinrich. *Die Kriegschuld der Sieger.* Göttingen: K. W. Schütz, 1966.

2275 Hartmann, E. "Probleme des traditionellen Völkerrechts im Urteil des Internationalen Militärgerichtshofes zu Nürnberg." Doctor of Law dissertation, Heidelberg University, 1952.

2276 Henkys, R. *Die nationalsozialistischen Gewaltverbrechen: Geschichte und Gericht.* Stuttgart: Kreuz-Verlag, 1964.

2277 Herzog, J.-B. "La giustizia penale internazionale a vent anni da Norimberga," *Democrazia and Diritto* 8 (1967):5–20.

2278 Hirschbach, Frank. "Black Milk: The Treatment of Guilt in German Post War Literature," *Minnesota Review* 3, no. 2 (Winter 1963): 247–56.

2279 Hoffmann, Ernst, ed. *Das Urteil von Nürnberg gilt.* Schriftenreihe: Der Deutsche Imperialismus und der Zweite Weltkrieg, Nr. 6. Berlin: Rütten und Loening, 1960.

2280 Huband, C. R. "Nuremberg Revisited," *Manitoba Bar News* 31, no. 3 (August 1959):53–58.

2281 Internationale Föderation der Widerstandkämpfer (FIR), comp. *Nürnberg 1946 . . . und heute? Die Ziele Hitlers und der Nazis, ihre Verurteilung durch die Welt, ihr gefährliches Wiederaufleben: Eine alarmierende Dokumentation.* Frankfurt am Main: Röderberg, 1966.

2282 Ivanova, I. M. "Njurnbergskie principy mizdunarodnum prove," *Sovetskoe Gosudarstvo i Pravo* 8 (1960):83–90.

2283 Jackson, Robert H. "Nürnberg in Retrospect: Legal Answer to International Lawlessness," *Canadian Bar Review* 27 (August-September 1949):761–81; *American Bar Association Journal* 35 (1949):813–16, 881–87.

2284 Jaworski, Leon. *After Fifteen Years.* Houston: Gulf Publishing, 1961.

2285 Klafowski, A. "The Prosecution of Nazi Criminals as a Problem of International Law," *Polish Western Affairs* 5, no. 2 (1964):266–74.

2286 Kohl, M. "Die Nürnberger Prinzipien als Bestandteil des allgemein-demokratischen Völkerrechts in ihrer Bedeutung für die Sicherung des Friedens," in *Deutschlanfrage und Völkerrecht,* edited by R. Arzinger. Berlin: Zentralverlag, 1962.

2287 Kranzbühler, Otto. "Nuremberg Eighteen Years Afterwards," *De Paul Law Review* (Spring-Summer 1965):333–47.

2288 _____. "Wert oder Unwert historischer Strafprozesseerötert am Nürnberger Beispiel," in "Möglichkeiten und Grenzen für die Bewaltigung historischer und politischer Schuld in Strafprozessen," edited by Karl Foster, *Studien und Berichte der Katholischen Akademie in Bayern,* Würzburg, 1962, vol. 19.

2289 Kraske, Erich. "Klassisches Hellas und Nürnberger Prozess," *Archiv des Völkerrechts* 4 (September 1953):183–89.

2290 Kraus, Herbert. "Nuremberg Trial of the Major War Criminals: Reflections after Seventeen Years," *De Paul Law Review* 13 (Spring-Summer 1964):233–40.

2291 _____. *Vorbemerkung zu "Das Urteil von Nürnberg 1946."* Munich, 1961.

2292 Lippert, D. I. "Codification of the Nürnberg Principles," *Los Angeles Bar Bulletin* 28 (February 1953):157–58, 166–75.

2293 Maxwell Fyfe, Sir David (1st Earl of Kilmuir). *Nuremberg in Retrospect: Being the Presidential Address of the President of the Holdsworth Club. . . .* Birmingham: Holdsworth Club of the University of Birmingham, 1956.

2294 Merle, Marcel. "Nuremberg vingt ans après," *Revue de Droit Contemporain* 14, no. 1 (1967):11–18.

2295 "Nuremberg Revisited," *Newsweek* 69 (May 29, 1967):23.

2296 "The Nuremberg Trials and Objection to Military Service in Viet-Nam," *American Society of International Law Proceedings* 63 (1969): 140–81.

2297 *Nürnberger Prozess gestern und heute.* Berlin: Staatsverlag der Deutschen Demokratischen Republik, 1966.

2298 Paolini, F. *A dieci anni dal processo di Norimberga la sua giustificazione.* Bologna: Cappelli, 1956.

2299 Polevi, Boris. *Nürnberger Tagebuch.* Translated from Russian by Harry Burck. Berlin: Verlag Volk und Welt, 1971.

2300 Poltorak, Arkadii I. *Niurnbergskii process: Osnovnye problemy.* Moscow: Izd. Nauka, 1966.

2301 _____. *Nuremberg Epilogue.* Translated by David Skirsky. Moscow: Progress Publishers, 1971.

2302 _____, and N. S. Lebedva. "25-Letie Niurnbergskogo processa," *Voprosy Istorii* 9 (1971):85–106.

2303 _____, and Y. Zaitsev. *Remember Nuremberg.* Moscow: Foreign Languages Publishing House, n.d.

2304 Quintano Ripollés, A. "Dix ans après Nuremberg," *Revue Internationale de Droit Pénal* 26 (1956):45–57.

2305 Sawicki, Jerzy. *Als sei Nürnberg nie gewesen . . . Die Abkehr von den völkerrechtlichen principien der Nürnberger Urteile.* Berlin: Zentralverlag, 1958.

2306 _____. *Jaki kdyby Norimbeck nikdy nebyl.* Prague: Nakladatelstvi politicke Literatary, 1962.

2307 _____. *From Nuremberg to the New Wehrmacht.* Warsaw: Polonia Publishing House, 1957.

2308 Smirnow, L. N. *Nürnberger Prozess gestern und heute.* Berlin, 1966.

2309 Steiniger, P. A., comp. *Der Nürnberger Prozess: Aus den Protokollen, Dokumenten und Materialien des Prozesses gegen die Hauptkriegsverbrecher vor dem Internationalen Militärgerichtshof.* 2 vols. 5th ed. Berlin: Deutscher Verlag der Wissenschaften, 1962.

2310 Steiniger, P. A., and K. Leszcyński, eds. *Der Juristenprozess.* Berlin: Deutscher Verlag der Wissenschaften, 1969.

2311   Thorpe, Gerald L. "The Nuremberg Trials: Considerations and Suggestions," *Intercom* 13 (January-February 1971):33–35.

2312   Trapp, Erwin. *Die kriegsrechtliche Bedeutung der Nürnberger Urteile.* Düsseldorf: M. Triltsch, 1957.

2313   Volkov, A. "Principy Niurnbergskogo poiogovora i mezdunarodnoe pravo," *Sovetskoe Gosudarstvo i Pravo* 1 (1957):27–37.

2314   Walsh, Moira. "Judgment at Nuremberg," *America* 106 (January 20, 1962):542–44.

2315   Wasserstrom, Richard. "The Relevance of Nuremberg," *Philosophy and Public Affairs* 1, no. 1 (Fall 1971):22–46.

2316   Wiesenthal, Simon. *The Murderers among Us.* New York: McGraw-Hill, 1967.

2317   Woetzel, Robert K. "Comments on the Nuremberg Principles and Conscientious Objection, with Special Reference to War Crimes," *Catholic Lawyer* 16 (Summer 1970):257–63.

2318   _____. *The Nuremberg Trials in International Law.* New York: Praeger, 1960.

2319   Yrigoyen, Jaime. *El proceso de Nuremberg y el derecho internacional.* Lima, 1955.

2320   Žourek, J. "Les principes de Nuremberg, étape décision dans l'évolution du droit international," *Revue de Droit Contemporain* 8, no. 2 (1961):107–28.

FAR EAST

2321   Hart, Franklin A. "Yamashito, Nuremberg and Vietnam: Command Responsibility Reappraised," *Naval War College Review* 25, no. 1 (September-October 1972):19–36.

2322   Kajima, Morinosuke. *Modern Japan's Foreign Policy.* Rutland, Vt.: Tuttle, 1969.

2323   Raginsky, M., and S. Boudkevitch. "Les crimes ne doivent pas se répéter: Vingt ans après le Procès de Tokyo," *La Vie Internationale* 8 (1968):97–103.

2324   Röling, Bernard V. A. "The Tokyo Trial in Retrospect," in *Buddhism and Culture: Dedicated to Dr. Daisetz Teitaro Suzuki in Commemoration of His Ninetieth Birthday,* edited by Yamaguchi Susumu. Kyoto: Nakano Press, 1960, pp. 247–66.

Post–World War II Era

THE VIETNAM WAR, 1946–1975

Bibliographies

2325 Blaustein, A. P. "Current Legal Bibliography: Viet Nam," *Law Library Journal* 61 (1968):20–22.

2326 Leitenberg, Milton, and Richard Dean Burns. *The Vietnam Conflict: Its Geographical Dimensions, Political Traumas and Military Developments.* Santa Barbara: ABC-Clio, 1973.

2327 "Vietnam Bibliography," *New York University Law Review* 45 (June 1970):749–59.

North Vietnamese Literature

2328 Vietnam (Democratic Republic). *Commission for Investigation of the U.S. Imperialists' War Crimes in Vietnam.* Prague: Peace and Socialism Publishers, 1967.

2329 ———. *U.S. War Crimes in Viet Nam.* Hanoi: State Commission of Social Sciences, Juridical Science Institute, 1968.

General

2330 Alford, N. H., Jr. "The Legality of American Involvement in Vietnam: A Broader Perspective," *Yale Law Journal* 75 (1966):1109–21.

2331 Andonian, J. K. "Law and Vietnam," *American Bar Association Journal* 54 (May 1968):457–59.

2332 Auchincloss, K. "Who Else Is Guilty?" *Newsweek* 77 (April 12, 1971):30–32.

2333 Bishop, J. W., Jr. "Question of War Crimes," *Commentary* 54 (December 1972):85–92.

2334 Boohar, Charles W., Jr. "Honorable Discharge: A Farewell to Responsibility for War Crimes," *William and Mary Law Quarterly* 12, no. 4 (Summer 1971):878–94.

2335 Bucholz, E. "Kampf gegen Aggression und Kriegsverbrechen des USA—Imperialismus in Vietnam," *Staat und Recht* 8 (1969):505.

2336 Citizens Commission of Inquiry. *The Dellums Committee: Hearings on War Crimes in Vietnam: An Inquiry into Command Responsibility in Southeast Asia.* New York: Vintage, 1972.

2337 D'Amato, Anthony A.; Harvey L. Gould; and Larry D. Woods. "War Crimes and Vietnam: The 'Nuremberg Defense' and the Military Register," *California Law Review* 57 (November 1969):1055–1110.

2338 "Deplorable and Repulsive," *Time* 88 (July 29, 1966):13.

2339 Deutsch, Eberhard. "Legality of the War in Vietnam," *Washburn Law Journal* 7 (1968):153–86.

2340 Falk, Richard A. "International Law and the United States Role in the Viet Nam War," *Yale Law Journal* 75 (1966):1122–60.

2341 _____. *The Six Legal Dimensions of the Vietnam War*. Princeton: Princeton University, Center for International Studies, 1968.

2342 _____. "U.S. in Vietnam: Rationale and Law," *Dissent* 13 (May–June 1966):275–84.

2343 _____, ed. *The Vietnam War and International Law*. 3 vols. Princeton: Princeton University Press, 1968–1972.

2344 _____; Gabriel Kolko; and Robert Jay Lifton; comps. *Crimes of War: A Legal, Political Documentary and Psychological Inquiry into the Responsibility of Leaders, Citizens, and Soldiers for Criminal Acts in Wars*. New York: Random House, 1971.

2345 Farer, Tom J.; R. G. Gard; and Telford Taylor. "Vietnam and the Nuremberg Principles: A Colloquy on War Crimes," *Rutgers Camden Law Journal* 5 (Fall 1973):1–78.

2346 Ferencz, B. B. "War Crimes and the Vietnam War," *American University Law Review* 17 (June 1968):403–20.

2347 Firmage, Edwin B. "Law and the Indochina War: A Retrospective View," *Utah Law Review* 1974, no. 1 (Spring 1974):1–24.

2348 Friedmann, Wolfgang. "Law and Politics in the Vietnamese War: A Commentary," *American Journal of International Law* 61 (1967):776–84.

2349 "Guilty Minority: First U.S. War Crimes Trials to Come Out of Vietnam," *Time* 91 (January 5, 1968):31–32.

2350 Hart, Franklin A. "Yamashito, Nuremberg and Vietnam: Command Responsibility Reappraised," *Naval War College Review* 25, no. 1 (September–October 1972):19–36.

2351 Havens, C. W., III. "Release and Repatriation of Vietnam Prisoners," *American Bar Association Journal* 57 (January 1971):41–44.

2352 Herman, Edward S. *Atrocities in Vietnam: Myths and Realities*. Boston: Pilgrim Press, 1970.

2353 Hoffman, Stanley. "War Crimes: Political and Legal Issues," *Dissent* 18 (December 1971):530–34.

2354 Hooker, Wade S., Jr., and David H. Savesten. "Geneva Convention of 1949: Application in the Vietnamese Conflict," *Virginia Journal of International Law* 5 (1965):243–65.

2355 Hull, Roger, and John Novogrod. *Law and Vietnam.* Dobbs Ferry, N.Y.: Oceana Publications, 1968.

2356 "If North Vietnam 'Convicts' Captured U.S. Fliers—," *U.S. News and World Report* 61 (August 1, 1966):20–21.

2357 "An Instructive Episode," *Nation* 203 (August 8, 1966):108.

2358 Knoll, Erwin, and Judith Nies McFadden, eds. *War Crimes and the American Conscience.* New York: Holt, Rinehart and Winston, 1970.

2359 Kolko, Gabriel. "War Crimes and the Nature of the Vietnam War," *Journal of Contemporary Asia* 1 (Autumn 1970):5–14.

2360 Langer, Herman P. "The Making of a Murderer," *American Journal of Psychiatry* 127 (January 1971):950–53.

2361 Lawyers Committee on American Policy towards Vietnam. *Vietnam and International Law: An Analysis of the Legality of the U.S. Military Involvement.* Flanders, N.J.: O'Hare Books, 1967.

2362 Liska, G. *War and Order: Reflections on Vietnam and History.* Baltimore: Johns Hopkins Press, 1968.

2363 *Livre noir de crimes americaines au Vietnam.* Paris: Fayard, 1970.

2364 Lobel, W. N. "Legality of the United States' Involvement in Vietnam: A Pragmatic Approach," *University of Miami Law Review* 23 (Summer 1969):792–814.

2365 Meeker, Leonard C. "The Legality of United States Participation in the Defense of Vietnam," *Department of State Bulletin* 54 (March 28, 1966):474–89.

2366 ———. "Viet-Nam and the International Law of Self-Defense," *Department of State Bulletin* 56 (January 9, 1967):54–63.

2367 Meyrowitz, Henri. "Le Droit de la guerre dans le conflict vietnamien," *Annuaire Français de Droit International* 13 (1967):153–201.

2368 Moore, John Norton. "International Law and the United States Role in Viet Nam," *Yale Law Journal* 76 (1966–1967):1051–94.

2369 ———. "Law and Politics in the Vietnamese War: A Response to Professor Friedmann," *American Journal of International Law* 61 (October 1967):1039–53.

2370 _____. *Law and the Indo-China War*. Princeton: Princeton University Press, 1972.

2371 _____. "The Lawfulness of Military Assistance to the Republic of Viet-Nam," *American Journal of International Law* 61 (January 1967): 1–34.

2372 Murphy, Charles F., Jr. "Indochina: Lingering Issues of Law and Policy," *Duquesne Law Review* 10 (Winter 1971):155.

2373 _____, and M. G. Sibley. "War in Vietnam: A Discussion," *Natural Law Forum* 13 (1967):196–209.

2374 Partan, D. G. "Legal Aspects of the Vietnam Conflict," *Boston University Law Review* 46 (1966):281–316.

2375 Possony, S. T. *Aggression and Self-Defense: The Legality of U.S. Action in South Vietnam*. Philadelphia: University of Pennsylvania, Foreign Policy Research Institute, 1966.

2376 "Punishment for War Crimes: Duty of Discretion?" *Michigan Law Review* 69 (June 1971):1312–46.

2377 Ramsey, Paul. "Is Vietnam a Just War?" *Dialogue* 6 (Winter 1967): 19–29.

2378 Robertson, D. W. "Debate among American International Lawyers about the Vietnam War," *Texas Law Review* 46 (July 1968):898–913.

2379 Russett, Bruce M. "Vietnam and Restraints on Aerial Warfare," *Ventures* 9, no. 1 (1969):55–61.

2380 Schell, Jonathan. *The Village of Ben Suc*. New York: Knopf, 1969.

2381 Schick, Franz B. "Some Reflections on the Legal Controversies Concerning America's Involvement in Vietnam," *International and Comparative Law Quarterly* 17, (1968):953–95.

2382 Sheerin, J. B. "War Crimes in High Places," *Catholic World* 213 (July 1971):163–64.

2383 Smith, Delbert D. "The Geneva Prisoner of War Convention: An Appraisal," *New York University of Law Review* 42 (November 1967): 880–914.

2384 Smylie, J. H. "American Religious Bodies, Just War, and Vietnam," *Journal of Church and State* 11, no. 3 (1969):383–408.

2385 Taylor, Telford. *Nuremberg and Vietnam: An American Tragedy*. Chicago: Quadrangle, 1970.

2386 "Two Sides of Atrocity: Americans Committing Atrocities Receive Sentence," *Time* 90 (July 14, 1967):38.

2387 Van den Haag, E. "When Is a Crime a War Crime?" *National Review* 23 (November 5, 1971):1227–32.

2388 Vietnam Veterans against the War. *The Winter Soldier Investigation: An Inquiry into American War Crimes.* N.p.: Beacon Press, 1972.

2389 "War in Southeast Asia: A Legal Position Paper," *Gonzaga Law Review* 6 (Fall 1970):79.

2390 "The War in Southeast Asia: A Legal Position Paper," *New York University Law Review* 45 (June 1970):695–726.

2391 "Whose War Crimes? Views of Telford Taylor," *Newsweek* 77 (February 22, 1971):29.

2392 Wright, Quincy. "Legal Aspects of the Viet-Nam Situation," *American Journal of International Law* 60 (1966):750–69.

2393 Wrong, Dennis H. "War Crimes and Politics," *Dissent* 18 (August 1971):327–29.

My Lai (Song My) Massacre and Trial

/General/

2394 Calmeyer, Bengt. *Massakven ved My Lai.* Oslo: Helge Erichsen, 1970.

2395 Cooper, N. G. "My Lai and Military Justice—To What Effect?" *Military Law Review* 59 (Winter 1973):93–127.

2396 "Defendant No. 5: T. K. Willingham," *Newsweek* 75 (February 23, 1970):52.

2397 Falk, Richard A. "Song My: War Crimes and Individual Responsibility: A Legal Memorandum," *Transactions of the Grotius Society* 7 (January 1970):33–40.

2398 Gerber, William. "War Atrocities and the Law," *Editorial Research Reports* 1 (January 7, 1970):3–20.

2399 Gershen, Martin. *Destroy or Die: The True Story of Mylai.* New Rochelle, N.Y.:Arlington House, 1971.

2400 Goldstein, Joseph; Burke Marshall; and Jack Schwartz; eds. *The My Lai Massacre and Its Cover-up: Beyond the Reach of Law?* New York: Free Press, 1976.

2401   Granger, W. "Pinkville Atrocity: That Was Our Orders," *New Republic* 161 (December 13, 1969):16–17.

2402   "Great Atrocity Hunt: Murder at Songmy and the American Conscience," *National Review* 21 (December 16, 1969):1252.

2403   Hammer, Richard. *One Morning in the War: The Tragedy at Song My (Pinkville).* London: Hart-Davis, 1970.

2404   Herman, Edward S. *Atrocities in Vietnam: Myths and Realities.* Boston: Pilgrim Press, 1970.

2405   Hersh, Seymour M. *My Lai Four: A Report on the Massacre and Its Aftermath.* New York: Random House, 1970.

2406   Johansen, Robert C. "U.S. War Crimes: The Guilt at the Top," *Progressive* 35 (June 1971):19–23.

2407   McWilliams, Wilson C. *Military Honor after My Lai.* New York: Council on Religious and International Affairs, 1972.

2408   "Military Law—Nuremberg Rule of Superior Orders—United States Court Martial Tribunal Admits Evidence of United States War Crimes in Vietnam in Support of Superior Orders of Defense" [by Martin Redish], *Harvard International Law Journal* 9 (Winter 1968):169–81. [See entry no. 2635.]

2409   "My Lai: A Question of Orders," *Time* 97 (January 25, 1971):24.

2410   "My Lai: Jurisdiction over the Guilty Civilians," *New England Law Review* 3 (Fall 1970):105.

2411   "My Lai Incident as a Case in Law," *U.S. News and World Report* 67 (December 22, 1969):43–46.

2312   "My Lai Massacre: The Need for an International Investigation," *California Law Review* 58 (May 1970):703.

2413   Novak, M., and W. Barthelmes. "My Lai and the National Conscience," *Commonweal* 94 (April 30, 1971):183–87.

2414   "Nürnberg and Viet Nam," *Time* 89 (May 26, 1967):20.

2415   Oberly, James. *Vietnam and the American War Crimes Dilemma: Independent Study.* N.p., 1971.

2416   Paulson, Stanley L., and John Banta. "Killings at My Lai: 'Grave Breaches' under the Geneva Conventions and the Question of Military Jurisdiction," *Harvard International Law Journal* 12 (Spring 1971): 345–55.

2417   Paust, J. J. "After My Lai: The Case for War Crime Jurisdiction over Civilians in Federal District Courts," *Texas Law Review* 50 (December 1971):6.

2418   Reston, James B. "Is Nuremberg Coming Back to Haunt Us?" *Saturday Review* 53 (July 18, 1970):14–17, 61.

2419   Rubin, A. P. "Legal Aspects of the My Lai Incident," *Oregon Law Review* 49 (April 1970):260ff.; also see J. J. Paust, "Response [to 'Legal Aspects of the My Lai Incident']," *Oregon Law Review* 50 (Winter 1971): 138ff.

2420   "Songmy Inquiry," *America* 122 (April 4, 1970):365.

2421   "Tragedy at Song My: The Case Deepens," *U.S. News and World Report* 68 (March 30, 1970):28.

2422   United States, Congress, House of Representatives. *Investigation of the My Lai Incident: Report, under the Authority of House Resolution 105, July 15, 1970.* 91st Cong., 2d sess. Washington, D.C.: GPO, 1970.

2423   "War Crimes Issue: Nagging Questions," *Newsweek* 74 (December 8, 1969):34–35.

2424   "Who Is Responsible for My Lai," *Time* 97 (March 8, 1971):18–19.

2425   Zoll, D. A. "My Lai and the State of the Army," *National Review* 23 (October 8, 1971):1112–14.

/The Trial of Lieutenant William Calley/

2426   Calley, William L., as told to John Sack. *Lieutenant Calley: His Own Story.* New York: Viking Press, 1971.

2427   "Calley Case: U.S. Army Lieutenant Charged with Slaying of South Vietnamese Civilians," *Newsweek* 74 (November 24, 1969):40.

2428   "Calley Goes on Trial," *Newsweek* 76 (November 30, 1970):16–17.

2429   "Calley's Confession: My Lai Pretrial," *Time* 96 (October 12, 1970):15.

2430   "Calley's Defense," *Newsweek* 76 (December 21, 1970):25–26.

2431   "Calley's Defense: Anger, Hate, Fear, Orders," *Newsweek* 77 (March 8, 1971):51–52.

2432   "Can Calley Get a Fair Trial?" *Time* 94 (December 26, 1969):22.

2433   "Command Influence: Pretrial Hearing," *Newsweek* 75 (February 2, 1970):28.

2434 Greenhaw, Wayne. *The Making of a Hero: The Story of Lieut. William Calley, Jr.* Louisville: Touchstone Publishing, 1971.

2435 Hammer, Richard. *The Court-Martial of Lt. Calley.* New York: Coward, McCann and Geoghegan, 1971.

2436 Kelman, Herbert C., and Lee H. Lawrence. "Assignment of Responsibility of the Case of Lt. Calley: Preliminary Report of a National Survey," *Journal of Social Issues* 28, no. 1 (1972):177–212.

2437 Merick, W. S. "Massacre Trial: A Shift in the War," *U.S. News and World Report* 67 (December 15, 1969):23–28.

2438 Quinn, Robert E., and William H. Darden. "Opinion: United States v. William L. Calley, Jr.," *International Law* 8 (July 1974):523–39.

2439 Steinfels, P. "Calley and the Public Conscience," *Commonweal* 94 (April 16, 1971):128.

2440 "The Trial Begins," *Newsweek* 69 (May 2, 1967):54.

2441 "Trial's End," *Time* 89 (May 19, 1967):37.

/The Trial of Captain Ernest Medina/

2442 McCarthy, Mary. *Medina.* New York: Harcourt Brace Jovanovich, 1972.

2443 ———. "Reflections: A Transition Figure," *New Yorker* 48 (June 10, 1972):38ff.

/The Peers Report/

2444 Goldstein, Joseph; Burke Marshall; and Jack Schwartz. *The My Lai Massacre and Its Cover-up: Beyond the Reach of Law?* New York: Free Press, 1976.

2445 Hersh, S. M. "Reporter at Large: Peers Inquiry," *New Yorker* 47 (January 22, 1972):34ff.; 47 (January 29, 1972):40ff.

2446 "Official U.S. Report on My Lai Investigation," *U.S. News and World Report* 67 (December 8, 1969):78–79.

2447 "Peers Report," *America* 126 (June 17, 1972):626.

2448 "Peers Report," *Nation* 210 (March 30, 1970):354.

The Stockholm ("Bertrand Russell") Tribunal, 1967

2449 Dansk Bertrand Russell råd. *Krigsforbrydelsesprocessen: Ansvarlig over for presseloven: Ebbe Reich.* Copenhagen: Dansk Bertrand Russell Råds Arbejdsudvalg, 1967.

2450 DeWeerd, H. A. *Lord Russell's War Crimes Tribunal.* Santa Monica: RAND Corporation, 1967.

2451   Duffet, John, ed. *Against the Crime of Silence: Proceedings of the Russell International War Crimes Tribunal, Stockholm.* New York: Bertrand Russell Foundation, 1968.

2452   Julin, Gosta. "Evidence at Stockholm: The Judges Are Everywhere," *Nation* 206 (June 5, 1967):712.

2453   Levin, Bernard. "Bertrand Russell: Prosecutor, Judge and Jury," *New York Times Magazine* (February 19, 1967):24ff.

2454   Melman, Seymour; Melvyn Baron; and Dodge Ely. *In the Name of America: The Conduct of the War in Vietnam by the Armed Forces of the United States.* New York: Clergy and Laymen Concerned about Vietnam, 1968.

2455   Messing, J. H. "American Actions in Vietnam: Justifiable in International Law?" *Stanford Law Review* 19 (June 1967):1307–36.

2456   Röling, B. V. A. "De processen von Nurenberg en Tokyo en die van Stockholm-Roskilde," *Ars Aecqui* 7 (1968):312–18.

2457   Rosenwein, Sam. "International War Crimes Tribunal: Stockholm Session," *Guild Practitioner* 27 (Winter 1968):22–29.

2458   Russell, Bertrand. *War Crimes in Vietnam.* London: George Allen and Unwin, 1967.

2459   _____, and Jean-Paul Sartre, eds. *Das Vietnam Tribunal oder Amerika vor Gericht.* Translated by S. Reisner. Hamburg: Rowohlt, 1970.

2460   Sartre, Jean-Paul. *Le Jugement final.* Paris: Gallimard, 1968.

2461   "Sartre's Séance," *Time* 89 (May 12, 1967):30.

2462   Sheer, Robert. "Lord Russell," *Ramparts* 5 (May 1967):16–23.

2463   *Tribunal Russell: Le jugement de Stockholm (collection d'idées actuelles).* Paris: Gallimard, 1967.

2464   *Tribunal Russell II: Le jugement final (collection d'idées actuelles no. 164).* Paris: Gallimard, 1968.

ALGERIAN CIVIL WAR, 1954–1962

2465   Anley, Henry. *In Order to Die.* London: Burke, 1955.

2466   Bedjaoui, Mohammed. *Law and the Algerian Revolution.* Brussels: International Association of Democratic Lawyers, 1961.

2467   Benabdallah, M.; M. Oussedik; and J. Vergès. *Nuremberg pour l'Algérie!* Paris: François Maspero, 1961.

2468   Clark, Michael K. *Algeria in Turmoil: A History of the Rebellion.* New York: Praeger, 1959.

2469   Horne, Alistair. *A Savage War of Peace: Algeria 1954–1962.* London: Macmillan, 1977.

2470   Jones, Mervyn. *Ordeal: The Trial of Djamila Bouhired: Condemned to Death in Algiers, July 15th, 1957.* London: Union of Democratic Control Publications, n.d.

2471   Jureidini, Paul A. *Case Studies in Insurgency and Revolutionary Warfare: Algeria, 1954–1962.* Washington, D.C.: American University, Special Research Office, 1963.

2472   Leulliette, Pierre. *St. Michael and the Dragon: Memoirs of a Paratrooper.* Translated by John Edwards. Boston: Houghton Mifflin, 1964.

2473   Paret, Peter. *French Revolutionary Warfare from Indochina to Algeria.* New York: Praeger, 1964.

2474   Schmitt, Gaston. *Toute la vérité sur le procès Pucheau par un des juges.* Paris: Plon, 1963.

APPREHENSION, TRIAL, AND EXECUTION OF ADOLF EICHMANN, 1961–1962

/Documents/

2475   Israel, Ministry of Foreign Affairs. *Eichmann in the World Press.* Jerusalem: Ministry of Foreign Affairs, Information Division, 1961.

2476   Israel, Police, Bureau 6. *Adolf Eichmann* [Transcript of Cross Examination by Israeli Police]. 6 vols. Jerusalem, 1961.

2477   Israel, Public Information Centre. *The Attorney-General of the Government of Israel v. Adolf, the Son of Adolf Karl Eichmann.* 3 vols. Jerusalem: Public Information Centre, Prime Minister's Office, 1961–1962.

2478   Israel, Supreme Court. *Adolf, the Son of Adolf Karl Eichmann v. the Attorney-General of the Government of Israel: Minutes of Session no. 1–7, March 22–May 29, 1962. Criminal Appeal no. 336.61.* Jerusalem, 1962.

2479   Poliakov, Leon, ed. *Le procès de Jérusalem: Jugement et documents.* Paris: Calmann-Levy, 1963.

2480   Servatius, Robert. *Strafverfahren gegen Adolf Eichmann; AZ: District-Gericht Jerusalem 40/61; AZ: Supreme Court Jerusalem 336/61.* Cologne, 1963.

/General/

2481 Alexandrov, Victor. *Six millions de morts: La Vie d'Adolf Eichmann.* Paris: Plon, 1960.

2482 American Jewish Committee. *The Eichmann Case in the American Press.* New York: Institute of Human Relations Press, 1962.

2483 Anders, Gunther. *Wir Eichmannsöhne: Offener Brief an Klaus Eichmann.* Munich: Beck, 1964.

2484 Arendt, Hannah. *Eichmann in Jerusalem: A Report on the Banality of Evil.* New York: Viking Press, 1963.

2485 Aronéanu, E. "L'Arrestation d'Eichmann et le droit international," *Revue Défense Nation* 2 (1960):1444–56.

2486 Auerbach, Ludwig, ed. *Der Eichmann-Prozess im Meinungsbild von SBZ-Flüchtlingen.* Munich: Infratest, 1961.

2487 Baade, H. W. "The Eichmann Trial: Some Legal Aspects," *Duke Law Journal* 3 (1961):400–420.

2488 Bentwich, Norman. "The Trial of Adolf Eichmann," *Solicitor Quarterly* 1 (1962):303–08.

2489 Buskes, J. J., et al. *Eichmann was niet alleen.* Amsterdam: Comite "Procès Eichmann," 1961.

2490 Cohen, Nathan. *Rechtliche: Gesichtspunkte zum Eichmann-Prozess.* Frankfurt am Main: Europäische Verlagsanstalt, 1963.

2491 Comer, J. D. "The Eichmann Trial: Historic Justice?" *Georgia Bar Journal* 23 (1961):491–511.

2492 Cutler, P. "The Eichmann Trial," *Canadian Bar Journal* 4 (1961): 352–71.

2493 Draper, G. I. A. D. "The Eichmann Trial: A Judicial Precedent," *International Affairs* 38 (1962):485–93.

2494 *Eichmann: Henker, Handlanger, Hintermänner: Eine Dokumentation.* Berlin: Ausschuss für Deutsche Einheit, 1961.

2495 Fawcett, J. E. S. "The Eichmann Case," *British Yearbook of International Law* 38 (1964):181–215.

2496 Fiszer, H. *Eichmann: Materialien und Kommentare.* Warsaw: Zachodnia Agencja Prasowa, n.d.

2497 Friedmann, Tuvyah. *The Hunter.* Edited and translated by David C. Gross. Garden City, N.Y.: Doubleday, 1961.

2498   Glock, Charles Y.; Gertrude J. Selznick; and Joe L. Spaeth. *The Apathetic Majority: A Study Based on Public Responses to the Eichmann Trial.* New York: Harper and Row, 1966.

2499   Gollancz, Victor. *The Case of Adolf Eichmann.* London: V. Gollancz, 1961.

2500   Graven, Jean. "Comment juger le jugement Eichmann? Le bilan du procès," *Revue Internationale de Criminologie et de Police Technique* 16, no. 1 (1962):19–60.

2501   Green, L. C. "Aspects juridiques du procès Eichmann," *Annuaire Français de Droit International* 9 (1964):150–90.

2502   ———. "The Eichmann Case," *Modern Law Review* 23 (1960): 507–15.

2503   ———. "Legal Issues of the Eichmann Trial," *Tulane Law Review* 37 (June 1963):641–84.

2504   ———. "The Maxim 'nullem crimen, sine lege' and the Eichmann Trial," *British Yearbook of International Law* 38 (1964):457–71.

2505   Grün, Herbert. *Proces u Jeruzalemu, 1961.* Zagreb: Naprijed, 1962.

2506   Guri, Haim. *Le Cage de verve (journal du procès Eichmann).* Translated by Raphaël Cidor. Paris: Éditions A. Michel, 1964.

2507   Handlin, Oscar. "The Ethics of the Eichmann Case," *Issues* 15 (1961):1–8.

2508   Harel, Israel. *The House on Garibaldi Street.* New York: Viking Press, 1975.

2509   Hausner, Gideon. *Justice in Jerusalem.* New York: Harper and Row, 1966.

2510   Herzberg, A. J. *Eichmann in Jerusalem.* The Hague: B. Bakker, 1962.

2511   Holthusen, H. E. "Hannah Arendt, Eichmann und die Kritiker," *Vierteljahrshefte für Zeitgeschichte* 13 (April 1965):178–90.

2512   Kastner, R. *Der Kastner-Bericht über Eichmann: Menschenhandel in Ungarn.* Munich: Kindler, 1961.

2513   Kaul, Friedrich, Karl. *Der Fall Eichmann.* 2d ed. Berlin: Verlag das Neue Berlin, 1961.

2514   Kempner, Robert M. W. *Eichmann und Komplizen.* Zurich: Europa Verlag, 1961.

2515 Kittrie, N. N. "A Post Mortem of the Eichmann Case, the Lessons for International Law," *Journal of Criminal Law and Criminology* 55 (1964):16–28.

2516 Kuehnrich, H. *Judenmörder Eichmann: Kein Fall der Vergangenheit.* Berlin: Dietz Verlag, 1961.

2517 Lasok, D. "The Eichmann Trial," *International and Comparative Law Quarterly* 11 (April 1962):355–74.

2518 Leavy, Z. "The Eichmann Trial and the Rule of Law," *American Bar Association Journal* 48 (1962):820–25.

2519 Linze, Dewey W. *The Trial of Adolf Eichmann.* Los Angeles: Holloway House Publishing, 1961.

2520 *Lov na Eichmanna: Proces nacističkom Genocidu.* Zagreb: Novinarsko izdaračko Poduzeće, 1961.

2521 Minerbi, S. *La Belva in gabbia: Eichmann.* Milan: Longanesi, 1962.

2522 Mňačko, Ladislav. *Já, Adolf Eichmann. . . .* Prague: Stání nakl. Politické Literatury, 1961.

2523 Montfort, François de. *Adolf Eichmann, levez-vous!* Paris: Presses de la Cité, 1961.

2524 Mulisch, H. *De zaak 40/61: Een reportage.* Amsterdam: de Bezige Bij, 1962.

2525 Musmanno, Michael A. *The Death Sentence in the Case of Adolf Eichmann: A Letter to His Excellency Itzhak Ben-Zvi, President of the State of Israel.* Pittsburgh, 1962.

2526 ———. "The Objections in Liminie to the Eichmann Trial," *Temple Law Quarterly* 35 (1961):1–22.

2527 Nellessen, Bernd, ed. *Der Prozess von Jerusalem: Ein Dokument.* Düsseldorf: Econ-Verlag, 1964.

2528 Oppenheimer, M. *Eichmann und die Eichmänner: Dokumentarische Hinweise auf den Personenkreis der Helfer und Helfershelfer bei der Endlösung.* Ludwigsburg: Schromm Verlag, 1961.

2529 Papadatos, Peter. *The Eichmann Trial.* New York: Praeger, 1964.

2530 Pardo, P. *Processo al Terzo Reich.* Rome: Editori Riuniti, 1962.

2531 Parsons, George R., Jr. "Israel's Right to Try Eichmann," *New Republic* 144 (March 20, 1961):13–15.

2532 ———. "Note," *Cornell Law Quarterly* 46 (1961):326–66.

2533 Pearlman, Maurice. *The Capture and Trial of Adolf Eichmann.* New York: Simon and Schuster, 1963.

2534 Pendorf, Robert. *Mörder und Ermördete: Eichmann und die Judenpolitik des Dritten Reiches.* Hamburg: Rütten und Loening, 1961.

2535 Rassinier, Paul. *Le véritable procès Eichmann: Ou, Vaingueurs incorrigibles.* Paris: Les sept couleurs, 1962.

2536 Reynolds, Quenton; Ephraim Katz; and Zwy Aldonby. *Minister of Death: The Adolf Eichmann Story.* New York: Viking Press, 1960.

2537 Robinson, Jacob. *And the Crooked Shall Be Made Straight: The Eichmann Trial, the Jewish Catastrophe, and Hannah Arendt's Narrative.* New York: Macmillan, 1965.

2538 Robinson, N. *Eichmann and the Question of Jurisdiction.* New York: World Jewish Congress, 1960.

2539 Rogat, Yosal, *The Eichmann Trial and the Rule of Law.* Santa Barbara: Center for the Study of Democratic Institutions, 1961.

2540 Rolin, H. "Le Procès Eichmann," *Journal des Tribunaux* 76 (1961): 325–26.

2541 Rosenne, Shabtai. *Six Million Accusers: Israel's Case against Eichmann.* Jerusalem: Jerusalem Post, 1961.

2542 Rousseau, C. "Affaire Eichmann: Arrestation et enlèvement en territoire argentin par des agents du gouvernement israélien d'un ressortissant allemand recherché pour crimes de guerre," *Revue Générale de Droit International Public* 64 (1960):772–86.

2543 Russell of Liverpool, Lord. *The Record: The Trial of Adolf Eichmann for His Crimes against the Jewish People and against Humanity.* New York: Knopf, 1963.

2544 Santander, Silvano. *El gran proceso: Eichmann y el ante la Justicia.* Buenos Aires: Ediciones Silva, 1961.

2545 Schmorak, Dov. B. *Der Prozess Eichmann: Dargestellt an Hand der in Nürnberg und Jerusalem vorgelegten Dokumente sowie der Gerichtsprotokolle.* Vienna: H. Deutsch, 1964.

2546 ———, ed. *Sieben Zeugen sagen aus im Eichmann-Prozess.* Berlin: Arani, 1962.

2547 Schön, Dezsö. *A Jeruzsálemi Per.* Tel Aviv: Uj Kelet-Kiadás, 1962.

2548 Schwarzenberger, G. "The Eichmann Judgment," *Current Legal Problems* 15 (1962):248–66.

2549 Servatius, Robert. *Verteidigung Adolf Eichmann: Plädoyer.* Bad Kreuznach: F. Harrach, 1961.

2550 Silving, H. "In re Eichmann: A Dilemma of Law and Morality," *American Journal of International Law* 55 (April 1961):307–58.

2551 Taylor, Telford. "Large Questions in the Eichmann Case," *Revue de Droit International (Sottile-Geneva)* 39 (1961):46–52.

2552 Wiesenthal, Simon. *Ich jagte Eichmann: Tatsachenbericht.* Gütersloh: Bartelsmann Lesering, 1961.

2553 Wighton, Charles. *Eichmann: His Career and Crimes.* London: Oldhams Press, 1961.

2554 Woetzel, Robert K. *The Nuremberg Trials in International Law: With a Postlude on the Eichmann Case.* New York: Praeger, 1962.

2555 Wucher, Albert. *Eichmanns gab es viele: Ein Dokumentarbericht über die Endlösung der Judenfrage.* Munich: Droemersche Verlagsanstalt, 1961.

2556 Zeiger, Henry A., ed. *The Case against Adolf Eichmann.* New York: New American Library, 1960.

PAKISTAN CIVIL WAR, BANGLADESH, 1972–1973

2557 Dutt, R. Palme. "India, Pakistan and Bangladesh," *New World Review* 40 (Winter 1972):10–17.

2558 Mehrish, Brijesh Narain. *War Crimes and Genocide: The Trial of Pakistani War Criminals.* Delhi: Oriental Publishers, 1972.

2559 Morris-Jones, W. H. "Pakistan Post Mortem and the Roots of Bangladesh," *Political Quarterly* 43 (April-June 1972):187–200.

MOZAMBIQUE MERCENARIES TRIAL, LUANDA, 1976

2560 Burchett, Wilfred, and Derek Roebuck. *The Whores of War: Mercenaries Today.* New York: Penguin, 1978.

IV. Subsidiary Issues

Trial Procedures

2561 Alderman, Sidney S. "Background and Highlights of the Nuremberg Trial," *I.C.C. Practitioners' Journal* 14 (November 1946):99–113.

2562 Behle, Calvin A. "War Crimes Trials," *Nevada State Bar Journal* 13 (April 1948):55–67.

2563 Cramer, Myron C. "Military Justice and Trial Procedure," *American Bar Association Journal* 29 (July 1943):368–71.

2564 Dickinson, George. "Japanese War Trials," *Australian Quarterly* 24 (June 1952):69–75.

2565 Dodd, Thomas J. "The Nuremberg Trials," *Pennsylvania Bar Association Quarterly* 18 (January 1947):138–52.

2566 Ferencz, Benjamin B. "Nürnberg Trial Procedure and the Rights of the Accused," *Journal of Criminal Law and Criminology* 39 (July-August 1948):144–51.

2567 Fratcher, William F. "American Organization for Prosecution of German War Criminals," *Missouri Law Review* 13 (January 1948):45–75.

2568 ———. "Review by Civil Courts of Judgments of Federal Military Tribunals," *Ohio State Law Journal* 10 (Summer 1949):271–300.

2569 Fuqua, Ellis E. "Judicial Review of War Crimes Trials," *Journal of Criminal Law and Criminology* 37 (May-June 1946):58–64.

2570 Gormley, W. Paul. "The Procedural Status of the Individual before Supernational Judicial Tribunals," *University of Detroit Law Journal* 41, no. 4 (April 1964):405–46.

2571 Green, Adwin Wigfall. "The Military Commission, *American Journal of International Law* 42 (October 1948):832–48.

2572 "Habeas-Corpus in Kriegsverbrecherprozessen," *Archiv des öffentlichen Rechts* 75 (1949):225–28.

2573   Hogan, Willard N. "War Criminals," *South Atlantic Quarterly* 45 (October 1946):415–24.

2574   Homu-Sho, Hosel Chosa Kyoku. *Senso hanzai saiban kankai horel shu.* Senso hanzai saiban shiryo. 3 vols. Toky: Homu-Sho, 1967.

2575   Hudson, Manley O. *International Tribunals Past and Future.* Washington, D.C.: Carnegie Endowment for International Peace and Brookings Institution, 1944.

2576   International Committee for Penal Reconstruction and Development. *Report on Rules and Procedure Relating to Punishment of Crimes Committed in the Course of and Incidental to the Present War.* London: Cambridge University Press, 1943.

2577   Jackson, Robert H. "The Nuremberg Trial: An Example of Procedural Machinery for the Development of International Substantive Law," in *David Dudley Field: Centenary Essays Celebrating One Hundred Years of Legal Reform,* edited by Alison Reppy. New York: New York University School of Law, 1949, pp. 314–24.

2578   Kippenberger, H. K. "War Criminals Trials Law Reports: A Review of 'Law Reports of Trials of War Criminals, Selected and Prepared by the United Nations War Crimes Commission,'" *New Zealand Law Journal* 23 (July 1, 1947):180–82.

2579   Kolander, Morris W. "War Crimes Trials in Germany," *Pennsylvania Bar Association Quarterly* 18 (April 1947):274–80.

2580   Kuhn, Arthur K. "International Law and National Legislation in the Trial of War Criminals—The Yamashita Case," *American Journal of International Law* 44 (July 1950):559–62.

2581   Levy, Albert G. D. "The Law and Procedure of War Crimes Trials," *American Political Science Review* 37 (December 1943):1052–81.

2582   Lund, T. G. "Legal Procedure at the Nuremberg Trials," *Fortnightly Law Journal* 16 (July 2, 1946):41–43.

2583   Mendelsohn, John. "Trial by Document: The Problem of Due Process for War Criminals at Nuernberg," *Prologue* 7, no. 4 (Winter 1975): 227–34.

2584   Monneray, Henri. *La preuve documentaires et testimonials au procès de Nuremberg.* Paris: Editions A. Pédone, 1948.

2585   ———. "La preuve documentaires et testimonials au procès de Nuremberg," *Revue Générale de Droit International Public* 52 (January-June 1948):20–49.

2586 Nobleman, Eli E. "Procedure and Evidence in American Military Government Courts in the United States Zone of Germany," *Federal Bar Journal* 8 (January 1947):212–48.

2587 Richman, Frank N. "Highlights of the Nünberg Trials," *Federal Rules Decisions* 7 (February 1948):581–84.

2588 Trainin, Aaron N. "Court Procedure at Nuremberg," *Soviet News* 1330 (December 21, 1945):2.

2589 ———. "La procédure à Nuremberg," *Revue de Droit International (Sottile-Geneva)* 24 (April-September 1946):77–81.

2590 "Trial of Axis War Criminals: The Question of Procedure" [by Hector A. Munro], *Fortnightly Law Journal* 13 (November 15, 1943): 119–22. [See entry no. 728.]

2591 "Trial of Civilians by Military Tribunals under the Uniform Code of Military Justice," *George Washington Law Revue* 21 (June 1953): 711–37.

2592 Tsai, Paul Chungtseng. "Judicial Administration of the Laws of War: Procedures in War Crimes Trials." Doctor of Law dissertation, Yale University, 1957.

2593 Underhill, L. K. "Jurisdiction of Military Tribunals in the United States over Civilians," *California Law Review* 12 (1924):75–98, 159–78.

2594 Vambery, Rustem. "The Law of the Tribunal," *Nation* 163 (October 12, 1946):400–401.

Superior Orders, Command Responsibility, and Military Necessity

2595 Arins, Alfred. "Military Leadership and the Law," *California Law Review* 47 (December 1959):828–71.

2596 Berger, Jacob. "Legal Nature of War Crimes and the Problem of Superior Command," *American Political Science Review* 38 (December 1944):1203–08.

2597 Boissier, Pierre. *Völkerrecht und Militärbefehl: Ein Beitrag zur Frage der Verhütung und Bestrafung von Kriegsverbrechen.* Translated from French by Dirk Forster. Stuttgart: K. F. Koehler Verlag, 1953.

2598 Brown, A. W. "Military Orders as a Defense in Civil Courts," *Journal of Criminal Law and Criminology* 8 (1917–1918):190–210.

2599 "Command Responsibility for War Crimes," *Yale Law Journal* 82 (May 1973):1274–1304.

2600   Cork, Lord. "Obedience to Lawful Commands," *Journal of the Royal United Services Institution* 96 (May 1951):258–62.

2601   Coste-Floret, Paul. "La répression des crimes de guerre et le fait justificatif tiré de l'ordre supérieure," *Recueil Dalloz Sirey* 1 (1945):21–22.

2602   Daniel, Aubrey M. "The Defense of Superior Orders," *University of Richmond Law Review* 7, no. 3 (Spring 1973):477–509.

2603   Daube, David. *The Defense of Superior Orders in Roman Law.* Oxford: Clarendon Press, 1956.

2604   "Defense of Superior Orders," *Law Journal* 101 (August 24, 1951): 467.

2605   De Giulio, Anthony P. "Command Control: Lawful versus Unlawful Application," *San Diego Law Review* 10 (1972):72–107.

2606   Dinstein, Y. *The Defence of "Obedience to Superior Orders" in International Law.* Leiden: Sijthoff, 1965.

2607   Downey, William Gerald, Jr. "The Law of War and Military Necessity," *American Journal of International Law* 47 (April 1953):251–62.

2608   Duke, M. L. "A Plea of Superior Orders," *Marine Corps Gazette* 55 (March 1971):34–39.

2609   Dunbar, N. C. H. "Military Necessity in War Crimes Trials," *British Yearbook of International Law* 29 (1952):442–52.

2610   ———. "Quelques aspects du problème de l'obéissance auz orders supérieurs en temps de guerre," *Le Droit au Service de la Paix* 1 (1957): 24–47.

2611   ———. "The Significance of Military Necessity in the Law of War," *Juridical Review* 67 (August 1955):201–12.

2612   ———. "Some Aspects of the Problem of Superior Orders," *Juridical Review* 63 (December 1951):234–61.

2613   E. "The Plea of 'Superior Orders' in War Crime Cases," *Law Journal* 95 (July 28, 1945):242–43.

2614   Faulkner, Stanley. "War Crimes: Responsibilities of Individual Servicemen and of Superior Officers," *Guild Practitioner* 31 (Summer-Fall 1974):131–44.

2615   Finch, George A. "Superior Orders and War Crimes," *American Journal of International Law* 15 (1921):440–45.

2616   Fuhrmann, Peter. *Der höhere Befehl als Rechtifertigung im Völkerrecht.* Munich: Beck, 1963.

2617 Glaser, Stefan. "L'ordre hiérarchique en droit pénal international," *Revue de Droit Pénal et de Criminologie* 33 (1953):283–330.

2618 ———. "Quelques remarques sur l'état de droit international," *Revue de Droit Pénal et de Criminologie* 32 (March 1952):570–603.

2619 ———. "Responsabilité pour la participation à une guerre-crime: Les soldats qui y prennent part encourent-ils une responsabilité pénale?" *Revue de Science Criminelle et de Droit Pénal Comparé* 24 (1969): 593–622.

2620 Green, L. C. "Superior Orders and the Reasonable Soldier," *Canadian Yearbook of International Law* 8 (1970):61–103.

2621 Grenfell, Russell. "The Question of Superior Orders," *Journal of the Royal United Services Institution* 96 (May 1951):263–66.

2622 Hart, Franklin A. "Yamashito, Nuremberg and Vietnam: Command Responsibility Reappraised," *Naval War College Review* 25, no. 1 (September-October 1972):19–36.

2623 Hazan, Edouard Tawfik. *L'état de nécessité en droit pénal interétatique et international.* Paris: Éditions A. Pédone, 1949.

2624 Howard, Kenneth A. "Command Responsibility for War Crimes," *Journal of Public Law* 21, no. 1 (1972):7–22.

2625 Lewy, Guenter. "Superior Orders, Nuclear Warfare, and the Dictates of Conscience: The Dilemma of Military Obedience in the Atomic Age," *American Political Science Review* 55, no. 1 (March 1961):3–23.

2626 Muller-Rappard, E. *L'ordre supérieur militaire et la responsabilité pénale du subordonné.* Paris: Éditions A. Pédone, 1965.

2627 "Obedience to Lawful Commands," *Journal of the Royal United Services Institution* 96 (February 1951):71–73.

2628 O'Brien, William V. "The Law of War, Command Responsibility, and Vietnam," *Georgetown Law Journal* 60 (February 1972):605–64.

2629 ———. "The Meaning of 'Military Necessity' in International Law," *World Polity* 1 (1957):109–76.

2630 Papadatos, P. A. *Le problème du commandement hiérarchique en droit pénal.* Athens: Éditions de l'auteur, 1961.

2631 ———. *Le problème de l'ordre reçu en droit pénal.* Travaux de droit, d'économie, de sociologie et de sc. politiques nr. 27. Geneva: Droz, 1964.

2632 Parks, William H. "Command Responsibility for War Crimes," *Military Law Review* 62 (Fall 1973):1–104.

2633   Paston, David George. *Superior Orders as Affecting Responsibility for War Crimes.* New York: H. G. Publishing, 1946.

2634   "The Plea of 'Superior Orders' in War Crimes Cases" [by E.] , *Law Journal* 95 (July 28, 1945):242–43. [See entry no. 2613.]

2635   Redish, Martin. "Military Law—Nuremberg Rule of Superior Orders—United States Court Martial Tribunal Admits Evidence of United States War Crimes in Vietnam in Support of Superior Orders of Defense," *Harvard International Law Journal* 9 (Winter 1968):169–81.

2636   Röling, B. V. A. "Oorlogsmisdrijven en het beroep op ambtelijk bevel," *Nederlands Juristenblad* 46 (1971):514–19.

2637   Sack, Alexander N. "Punishment of War Criminals and the Defense of Superior Orders," *Law Quarterly Review* 60 (January 1944): 63–68.

2638   ———. "War Crimes and the Defense of Superior Orders in International Law," *Lawyers Guild Review* 5 (January-February 1945):11–17.

2639   Siegert, Karl. *Repressalie, Requisition und höherer Befehl: Ein Beitrag zur Rechtfertigung der Kriegsverurteilten.* Göttingen: Göttingen Verlagsanstalt, 1953.

2640   Smith, H. A. "The Defence of Superior Orders," *Journal of the Royal United Services Institution* 96 (November 1951):617–19.

2641   Talerico, Anthony, Jr. "Operation Justice," *United States Naval Institute Proceedings* 73 (May 1947):509–21.

2642   Tallow, Adamin A. *Command Responsibility: Its Legal Aspect.* Quezon City, 1965.

2643   Volger, T. "Zum Zinwand des 'Handelns auf Befehl' im Völkerstrafrecht," *Revue de Droit Pénal Militaire et de Droit de la Guerre* 7 (1968):111–29.

2644   Walter, H. R. "Das Problem des Handelns auf Befehl im Licht der Nürnberger Prozess." Doctor of Law dissertation, Heidelberg University, 1950.

2645   Weber, Hellmuth von. "Die strafrechtliche Verantwortlichkeit für Handeln auf Befehl," *Monatsschrift für Deutsches Recht* 2 (1948):34–42.

2646   Wilner, Alan M. "Superior Orders as a Defense to Violations of International Law," *Maryland Law Review* 26 (Spring 1966):127–42.

2647   Würtenberger, Thomas. "Der Irrtum über die Völkerrechtsmässigkeit des höheren Befehls im Strafrecht," *Monatsschrift für Deutsches Recht* 2 (1948):271–73.

Ex Post Facto

2648 Dunbar, N. C. H. "Maxim nullem crimen sine lege in Law of War," *Juridical Review*, pts. 2, 3 (August-December 1959):176–96.

2649 Graveson, R. H. "Der Grundsatz 'nulla poena sine lege' und Kontrollratsgesetz nr. 10," *Monatsschrift für Deutsches Recht* 1 (1947):278–81.

2650 Hall, Jerome. "Nulla Poena Sine Lege," *Yale Law Journal* 47 1937):165ff.

2651 Hofmannsthal, F. von. "War Crimes Not Tried under Retroactive Law," *New York University Law Quarterly Review* 22 (January 1947): 93–99.

2652 Ireland, Gordon. "*Ex Post Facto* from Rome to Tokyo," *Temple Law Quarterly* 21 (July 1947):27–61.

2653 Karanikas, Demetre I. "Le principe de la non-rétroactivité des lois pénales après la guerre," *Revue Hellénique de Droit International* 3 (January-March 1950):136–40.

2654 Konvitz, Milton R. "*Ex Post Facto* at Nuremberg," *Commentary* 1 (July 1946):91–92.

2655 Roux, J. A. "A propos de la non-retroactivité de la loi pénale," *Revue de Droit International* (Sottile-Geneva) 25 (1947):179–86.

2656 Smead, Elmer E. "The Rule against Retroactive Legislation: A Basic Principle of Jurisprudence," *Minnesota Law Review* 20 (1936):775ff.

Organizational and Group Criminality

2657 Arens, Richard. "Nuremberg and Group Prosecution," *Washington University Law Quarterly* 1951 (June 1951):329–57.

2658 Becker, Walter. "Die Lüge Tatbestandsmerkmal bei Organisationsverbrechen," *Die Spruchgerichte* 2 (1948):257–61.

2659 Bornhörd, Jürgen. *Die Strafbarkeit der "Conspiracy" im Strafrecht der Vereinigten Staaten von Nordamerika.* Bonn: Röhrscheid, 1964.

2660 Breetzke, E. "Vom Unrecht bei dem Organisationsdelikt," *Die Spruchgerichte* 3 (1949):51–56.

2661 Busch, Richard. "Das Verbrechen gegen die Menschlichkeit als Grundlage des Organisationsverbrechens," *Die Spruchgerichte* 3 (1949): 56–60.

2662 De Touzalin, H. "Réflexions à propos du délit d'appartenance sur un essai d'unification des règles de répression en matière d'infractions aux lois et coutumes de la guerre," *Revue de Droit Pénal Militaire et de Droit de la Guerre* 4 (1965):133–58.

2663 Dreher, Eduard. "Die Entwicklung der Strafzumessungsprobleme in der Rechtsprechung zum Organisationsverbrechen," *Die Spruchgerichte* 3 (1949):7–11.

2664 Güde, K. "Zur Deutung des Organisationsverbrechens," *Deutsche Rechtszeitschrift* 3 (1948):201–02.

2665 Haensel, Carl. "Hauptprobleme des Organisationsverbrechens," *Die Spruchgerichte* 2 (1948):100–104.

2666 ———. *Das Organisationsverbrechen: Nürnberger Betrachtungen zum Kontrollratsgesetz Nr. 10.* Munich: Biederstrin, 1947.

2667 Herzog, Jacques-Bernard. "Les organisations nationales-socialistes devant le Tribunal de Nuremberg," *Revue Internationale de Droit Pénal* 17 (1946):343–59.

2668 Jackson, Robert H. "Law under Which Nazi Organizations Are Accused of Being Criminal," *Temple Law Quarterly* 19 (April 1946): 371–89.

2669 Jerusalem, Franz. "Die allgemeine Rechtslehre und die Konstruktion des Organisationsverbrechens," *Die Spruchgerichte* 2 (1948):261–62.

2670 ———. "Zum Begriff des Organisationsverbrechens," *Die Spruchgerichte* 2 (1948):129–30.

2671 Katzenberger, K. "Das Korps der politischen Leiter im Urteil von Nürnberg," *Neue Juristische Wochenschrift* 1 (July 1948):371–75.

2672 Kirchner, Carl, "Tateinheit und Tatmehrheit beim Organisationsverbrechen in der Rechtsprechung des Obersten Spruchgerichtshofes," *Die Spruchgerichte* 2 (1948):305–07.

2673 ———. "Die Urteilbarkeit des Schuldspruchs beim Organisationsverbrechen," *Die Spruchgerichte* 3 (1949):5–7.

2674 Mayer, Hellmuth. "Die materielle Gerechtigkeit der Strafen für die Mitgliedschaft in den verbrecherischen Organisationen," *Die Spruchgerichte* 1 (1947):17–19.

2675 Meyrowitz, Henri. *La Répression par les Tribunaux Allemands des Crimes contre l'Humanité et de l'Appartenance à une organisation Criminelle, en application de la loi no. 10 du Conseil de Contrôle Allié.* Paris: Librairie Générale de Droit et de Jurisprudence, 1960.

2676 Mittelbach, Hans. "Die Bestrafung der Zugehörigkeit zu verbrecherischen Organisationen," *Zentral Justizblatt für die Britische Zone* 1 (1947):33–36.

2677 ———. "Das Verfahren gegen Angehörige Verbrecherischen Organisationen," *Zentral Justizblatt für die Britische Zone* 1 (1947):71–74.

2678 Offenberg, K. "Zum Täterkreis beim Korps der politischen Leiter," *Die Spruchgerichte* 2 (1948):289–90.

2679 Rauschenbach, Gerhard. *Der Nürnberger Prozess gegen die Organisationen: Grundlagen, Probleme, Auswirkungen auf die Mitglieder und strafrechtliche Ergebnisse.* Rechtsvergleichende Untersuchungen zur gesamten Strafrechtswissenschaft. Neue Folge. Heft 13. Bonn: Röhrscheid, 1954.

2680 Sauer, Wilhelm. "Humanitäts- und Organisationsverbrechen: Zur Weiterbildung des Strafrechts," *Die Spruchgerichte* 1 (1947):6–9.

2681 Sontag, E. "Das Organisationsverbrechen des neuen deutschen Strafrechts," *Schweizerische Zeitschrift für Strafrecht* 64 (1949):65–71.

2682 Weber, H. von. "Die allgemeinen Lehren des Strafrechts in ihrer Anwendung auf das Organisationsverbrechen," *Die Spruchgerichte* 2 (1948):193–99.

2683 Werner, Wolfhart. "Der Tatbestand des Organisationsverbrechens," *Die Spruchgerichte* 1 (1947):59–61.

2684 ———. "Das Unrechtsbewusstsein des Organisationsangehorigen: Eine Erwiderung auf den Artikel Dr. H. Mittelbachs," *Die Spruchgerichte* 2 (1948):233–34.

Individual Responsibility, Collective Guilt

2685 Cohen, Marshall; Thomas Nagel; and Thomas Scanlon; comps. *War and Moral Responsibility.* Princeton: Princeton University Press, 1974.

2686 Corbett, Percy E. *The Individual and World Society.* Princeton: Princeton University Press, 1953.

2687 Cowles, Willard B. "High Government Officials as War Criminals," *American Society of International Law Proceedings* (1945):54–68.

2688 Deutsch, Harold C. "Nazi War Crimes and the German Collectivity," *Minnesota Review* 3, no. 2 (Winter 1963):154–62.

2689 Donnedieu de Vabres, Henri. "Les limites de la responsabilité des personnes morales," *Revue Internationale de Droit Pénal* 21 (1950): 339–51.

2690 Dubost, C. "Les crimes des états et la coutume pénale internationale," *Politique Étrangère* 11 (1946):553–68.

2691   Dumas, J. "Du deni de justice considéré comme condition de la responsabilité internationale des Etats en matière criminelle," *Revue de Droit International et de Législation Comparée* 10 (1929):277–307.

2692 _____. "Responsabilité internationale des Etats à raison des crimes et délits commis sur leur territoire au préjudice d'étrangers," *Recueil des Cours de l'Académie de Droit International* 36 (1931):183–261.

2693   Durand, Ch. "La responsabilité internationale des états pour déni de justice," *Revue Générale de Droit International Public* 38 (1931):694–748.

2694   Ehrenzweig, A. "Soldiers Liability for Wrongs Committed on Duty under American and International Law," *Cornell Law Quarterly* 30 (1944): 179–217.

2695   Falk, Richard A. "War Crimes and Individual Responsibility: A Legal Memorandum," *Trans-Action* 7 (January 1970):33–40.

2696   Fischlschweiger, Hagen. "Zum Problem der Kollektivhaftung," *Juristische Blätter* 73 (1951):30–34.

2697   Fraser, Lindley. *Germany between Two Wars: A Study of Propaganda and Warguilt.* London: Oxford University Press, 1945.

2698   Freeman, A. V. *The International Responsibility of States for Denial of Justice.* London: Longmans, Green, 1938.

2699 _____. "Responsibility of States for Unlawful Acts of their Armed Forces," *Recueil des Cours de l'Académie de Droit International* 88 (1955): 267–415.

2700   Garcia-Mora, M. R. *International Responsibility for Hostile Acts of Private Persons against Foreign States.* The Hague: Nijhoff, 1962.

2701   Giebultonitz, J. *Odprowiedzialnosc przesteprow wojennych w swiretle prawa narodow.* Warsaw: Apoldzielnia wydawn. "Czytelnik," 1945.

2702   Glaser, Stefan. "Culpabilité en droit international pénal," *Recueil des Cours de l'Académie de Droit International* 99 (1960):467–593.

2703 _____. "L'État en tant que personne morale est-il pénalement responsable?" *Revue de Droit Pénal et de Criminologie* 29 (1949):425–52.

2704 _____. "La responsabilité de l'individu devant le droit international," *Schweizerische Zeitschrift für Strafrecht* 64 (1949):283–314.

2705 _____. "Responsabilité pour la participation à une guerre-crime: Les soldats qui y prennent part encourent-ils une responsabilité pénale?" *Revue de Science Criminelle et de Droit Pénal Comparé* 24 (1969):593–622.

2706 Gomes Grajales, Octavio. *Los crímines de guerra y la responsabilidad de los jetes de estado.* Mexico, D.F.: Imp. en Orizaba, 1947.

2707 Herczeg, István. *Parancsra tetta?* Budapest: Gondolat, 1969.

2708 Hermes, Ferdinand A. "Collective Guilt," *Notre Dame Lawyer* 23 (May 1948):431–55.

2709 ———. "The 'War Guilt' of the German People," *American Journal of Economics and Sociology* 3 (January 1944):201–16.

2710 Hetlinger, G. *Die völkerrechtliche Verpflichtung der Staaten zur Bestrafung Einzelner und das materielle Strafrecht der Bundesrepublik Deutschland.* Munich: Schön, 1965.

2711 Hoffman, G. *Strafrechtliche Verantwortung im Völkerrecht.* Frankfurt am Main: Metzner, 1962.

2712 Hossbach, F. *Von der militärischen Verantwortlichkeit in der Zeit vor dem Zweiten Weltkriege.* Göttingen: Selbstverlag, 1948.

2713 Jaspers, Karl. *The Question of German Guilt.* Translated by E. B. Ashton. New York: Dial Press, 1947.

2714 Jescheck, Hans-Heinrich. *Die Verantwortlichkeit der Staatsorgane nach Völkerstrafrecht: Eine Studie zu den Nürnberger Prozessen* Rechtsvergleichende Untersuchungen zur gesamten Strafrechtwissenschaft n. f., Heft 6. Bonn: Röhrscheid, 1952.

2715 Kaufman, Mary. "Individual's Duty under the Law of Nuremberg: The Effect of Knowledge on Justiciability," *Guild Practitioner* 27 (Winter 1968):15ff.

2716 Kelson, Hans. "Collective and Individual Responsibility in International Law with Particular Regard to Punishment of War Criminals," *California Law Review* 31 (December 1943):530–71.

2717 Landau, A., and Cz. Wasilkowski. "The Responsibility for War Crimes in Polish Law," *Demokratyczny Przeglad Prawniczy* 2, nos. 11–12 (1946):27–37.

2718 Levy, Albert G. D. "Criminal Responsibility of Individuals and International Law," *University of Chicago Law Review* 12 (June 1945): 313–32.

2719 McKeller, Peter. "Responsibility for the Nazi Policy of Extermination," *Journal of Social Psychology* 34 (November 1951):153–63.

2720 Magnol, J. "Une expérience de mise en oeuvre de la responsabilité pénale des personnes morales," *Revue Internationale de Droit Pénal* 17 (1946):58–72.

2721   Marcin, Raymond B. "Individual Conscience under Military Compulsion," *American Bar Association Journal* 57 (December 1971):1222–24.

2722   Muller-Payer, A. *Die deutsche Sünde wider das Recht.* Stuttgart: Franz Mittelbach Verlag, 1946.

2723   Myerson, Moses H. *Germany's War Crimes and Punishment: The Problem of Individual and Collective Criminality.* Toronto: Macmillan, 1944.

2724   Norgaard, Carl Aage. *The Position of the Individual in International Law.* Copenhagen: Munksgaard, 1962.

2525   Paget, R. T. "Soldat und Recht," *Wehrwissenschaftliche Rundschau* 2, no. 2 (1952):41–50.

2726   Poljokan, I. *Les responsabilités pour les crimes et délits de guerre.* Paris: Jouve, 1923.

2727   Queneudec, J. P. *La responsabilité internationale de l'état pour les fautes personnelles de ses agents.* Paris: Libr. Gén. de droit et de jurisprud., 1966.

2728   Rochette, J. *L'individu devant le droit international.* Paris: Montchrestien, 1956.

2729   Röling, B. V. A. *The Responsibility of the Legislative, Executive and Judicial Organs of the State According to International Penal Law.* The Hague: International Commission of Jurists, 1955.

2730   Roux, J. A. "Apropos des personnes morales: La responsabilité pénale des collectivités," *Revue de Droit International* 26 (1948):38–52.

2731   Sawicki, J. "Podstawy socjologicnzo-prawne odpowiedzialnosci zbrodniarzy faszystowskich," *Demokratyczny Przeglad Prawniczy* 3 (1947):30–38.

2732   Schindler, R. *Das Wesen der Volksehre: Zugleich ein Beitrag zur Frage der Kollektivschuld.* Münster: Rechts-und Staatswissenschaftliche Diss., 1948.

2733   Schneeberger, Ernest. "The Responsibility of the Individual under International Law," *Georgetown Law Journal* 25 (May 1947):481–89.

2734   Scholz, Heinrich. "Zur deutschen Kollektiv-verantwortlichkeit," *Frankfurter Hefte* 2 (1947):357–73.

2735   Société Égyptienne de Droit International. *Le Procès de Nuremberg: La responsabilité individuelle dans la perpetration des crimes contre la paix: Aperçu des opinions juridiques actuelles.* Alexandria, Egypt: Imprimerie Al-Basir, 1946.

2736 Thorneycraft, E. *Personal Responsibility and the Law of Nations.* Leiden: Nijhoff, 1963.

2737 Trainin, Aaron. "Criminal Responsibility for Propaganda of Aggression," *Voks Bulletin* 14 (1949):13–26.

2738 ———. *Hitlerite Responsibility under Criminal Law.* Translated by Andrew Rothstein and edited by A. Y. Vishinski. London: Hutchinson, 1945.

2739 ———. "The Responsibility of Hitler Germany for the Crimes and Damage Caused by Aggression," *Voks Bulletin* 8 (1943):5–14.

2740 Veicopoulos, Nicolas. "Les responsabilités des industriels dans la préparation de la guerre," *Revue de Droit International (Sottile-Geneva)* 26 (January-March 1948):53–62.

2741 Vermeil, E. "Karl Jaspers et sa conception de la responsabilité allemande," *Revue d'Histoire de la Deuxième Guerre Mondiale* 2 (1952): 1–12.

2742 Wright, Quincy. "International Law and Guilt by Association," *American Journal of International Law* 43 (October 1949):746–56.

"Acts of State," Sovereign Immunity of Rulers

2743 Angell, Ernest. "Sovereign Immunity—The Modern Trend," *Yale Law Journal* 35 (1925):150–68.

2744 Bishop, W. W., Jr. "New United States Policy Limiting Sovereign Immunity," *American Journal of International Law* 47 (January 1953): 93–106.

2745 Dunbar, N. C. H. "Act of State and the Law of War," *Juridical Review,* pt. 3 (December 1963):246–73.

2746 Glaser, Stefan. "L'acte d'état et le problème de la responsabilité individuelle," *Revue de Droit Pénal et de Criminologie* 31 (1950):1–17.

2747 Gregory, S. S. "Criminal Responsibility of Sovereigns for Wilful Violations of the Laws of War," *Virginia Law Review* 6 (1919–1920):400–421.

2748 Heller, Maxine Jacobson. "The Treatment of Defeated War Leaders." Ph.D. dissertation, Columbia University, 1965.

2749 Ireland, Gordon. "The Trial of Ex-Rulers," *Tulane Law Review* 7 (1933):279ff.

2750 Kaminski, A. J. "Obrona polityczna prze stepcow wojennjch," *Przeglad Zachodni* 9–10 (1949):222–56.

2751   Kelson, Hans. "Collective and Individual Responsibility for Acts of State in International Law," *Jewish Yearbook of International Law* 1 (1948):226–39.

2752   Kingsbury, Howard Thayer. "The 'Act of State' Doctrine," *American Journal of International Law* 4 (1910):359–72.

2753   Moore, William Harrison. *The Act of State in English Law.* London: J. Murray, 1906.

2754   Sack, Alexander N. "War Criminals and the Defense Act of State in International Law," *Lawyers Guild Review* 5 (September-October 1945):288–300.

2755   "Should Judicial Respect Be Accorded to Nazi Acts of State?" *Columbia Law Review* 47 (1947):1061–68.

2756   Verdross, Alfred. *Die völkerrechtswidrige Kriegshandlung und der Strafenspruch der Staaten.* Berlin: Engelmann, 1920.

Psychological Aspects of War Crimes

2757   Abel, Theodore. "Is a Psychiatric Interpretation of the German Enigma Necessary?" *American Sociological Review* 10 (August 1945): 457–64.

2758   Alexander, Leo. "The Molding of Personality under Dictatorship: The Importance of the Destruction Drives in Socio-Psychological Structures of Nazism," *Journal of Criminal Law and Criminology* 40 (1949): 3–27.

2759   _____. "Sociopsychologic Structure of the SS," *Archives of Neurology and Psychiatry* 59 (May 1948):622–34.

2760   _____. "War Crimes: Their Social-Psychological Aspects," *American Journal of Psychiatry* 105 (September 1948):170–77.

2761   _____. "War Crimes and Their Motivation—The Sociopsychological Structure of the SS and the Criminalization of a Society," *Journal of Criminal Law and Criminology* 39 (September-October 1948):298–326.

2762   Bayle, François. *Psychologie et éthique du national-socialisme: Étude anthropologique des dirigeants S.S.* Paris: Presses universitaires de France, 1953.

2763   Bramsted, Ernest K. *Dictatorship and Political Police: The Technique of Control by Fear.* New York: Oxford University Press, 1945.

2764   Eliasberg, Wladimer C. "War Trials," *Journal of Criminal Law and Criminology* 36 (July-August 1945):85–86.

2765 Gilbert, G. M. *The Psychology of Dictatorship: Based on an Examination of the Leaders of Nazi Germany.* New York: Ronald Press, 1950.

2766 Hertz, Frederick. *Nationality History and Politics: A Study of the Psychology and Sociology of National Sentiment and Character.* London: Routledge and Kegan Paul, 1944.

2766a Maile, Florence R., and Michael Selzer. *The Nuremberg Mind: The Psychology of the Nazi Leaders.* New York: Quadrangle, 1975.

2767 Meerloo, A. M. *Mental Seduction and Menticide: The Psychology of Thought Control and Brainwashing.* London: Jonathan Cape, 1957.

"Just War" and "Preventive War" Concepts

2768 Bailey, Sydney Dawson. *Prohibitions and Restraints in War.* London: Oxford University Press for the Royal Institute of International Affairs, 1972.

2769 Elbe, Joachim von. "The Evolution of the Concept of Just War in International Law," *American Journal of International Law* 33 (October 1939):665–88.

2770 Graham, David E. "1974 Diplomatic Conference on the Law of War: A Victory for Political Causes and a Return to the 'Just War' Concept of the Eleventh Century," *Washington and Lee Law Review* 32 (Winter 1975):25–63.

2771 Hula, Erich. "The Revival of the Idea of Punitive War," *Thought* 82 (September 1946):405–34.

2772 Jeismann, Karl-Ernst. *Das Problem des Präventivkrieges im europäischen Staatensystem mit besonderem Blick auf die Bismarckzeit.* Freiburg: Karl Alber, 1957.

2773 Johnson, James T. *Ideology, Reason, and the Limitation of War: Religious and Secular Concepts, 1200–1740.* Princeton: Princeton University Press, 1975.

2774 "Just War," *Commonweal* 87 (December 22, 1967):5–6.

2775 Kloster, Walther. *Der deutsche Generalstab und der Präventivkriegsgedanke.* Stuttgart: W. Kohlhammer, 1932.

2776 Kopelmanas, L. "The Problem of Aggression and the Prevention of War," *American Journal of International Law* 31 (April 1937):244–57.

2777 Kunz, Josef L. *"Bellum Justum et Bellum Legale,"* American *Journal of International Law* 45 (July 1951):528–34.

2778   Lammasch, Heinrich. "Unjustifiable War and the Means to Avoid It," *American Journal of International Law* 10 (October 1916):689–705.

2779   Nussbaum, Arthur. "Just War—A Legal Concept?" *Michigan Law Review* 42 (December 1943):453–79.

2780   Potter, P. B. "Preventive War Critically Considered," *American Journal of International Law* 45 (January 1951):142–45.

2781   Ramsey, Paul. *The Just War: Force and Political Responsibility.* New York: Scribner's, 1968.

2782   _____. *War and the Christian Conscience: How Shall Modern War Be Conducted Justly?* Durham: Duke University Press, 1961.

2783   Rooney, Miriam T. "Law without Justice?—The Kelson and Hall Theories Compared," *Notre Dame Lawyer* 23 (January 1948):140–72.

2784   Russell, Frederick H. *The Just War in the Middle Ages.* Cambridge: Cambridge University Press, 1975.

2785   Smith, H. A. "The Problems of the Just War," *World Affairs* 2 (October 1948):357–65.

2786   Tooke, Joan. *The Just War in Aquinas and Grotius.* London: S.P.C.K., 1965.

2787   Tucker, Robert W. *The Just War: A Study in Contemporary American Doctrine.* Baltimore: Johns Hopkins Press, 1960.

2788   Walter, LeRoy Brandt, Jr. "Five Classic Just War Theories: A Study in the Thought of Thomas Aquinas, Vitoria, Suarez, Gentili, and Grotius." Ph.D. dissertation, Yale University, 1971.

2789   Walzer, Michael. *Just and Unjust War: A Moral Argument with Historical Illustrations.* New York: Basic Books, 1977.

Aggressive War in International Law

2790   Alfaro, Ricardo J. "La cuestión de la definición de la agresión," *Revista de Derecho Internacional* 59 (September 1951):361–80.

2791   Aronéanu, Eugène. *La définition de l'aggression: Exposé objectif.* Paris: Éditions Internationales, 1958.

2792   Berkowitz, Leonard. *Aggression: A Social Psychological Analysis.* New York: McGraw-Hill, 1962.

2793   Brownlie, Ian. *International Law and the Use of Force by States.* Oxford: Clarendon Press, 1963.

2794   Bustamante y Sirvín, A. S. de. "Unlawful Aggression and Defense," *Tulane Law Review* 17 (September 1942):60–72.

2795 Castrén, Erik. *The Present Law of War and Neutrality.* Helsinki: Annales Academiae Scientiarum Fennicae, 1954.

2796 Cecil, Viscount. "Outlaw Aggression!" *United Nations Quarterly* 1 (September 1947):16–19.

2797 Chacko, C. J. "International Law and the Concept of Aggression," *Indian Journal of International Law* 3 (1963):396–412; 4 (1964):85–116.

2798 Eagleton, Clyde. *The Attempt to Define Aggression.* Worcester, Mass.: Carnegie Endowment for International Peace, 1933.

2799 Falk, Richard A. "Quincy Wright: On Legal Tests of Aggressive War," *American Journal of International Law* 66 (July 1972):560–71.

2800 Ferencz, Benjamin B., comp. *Defining International Aggression: The Search for World Peace: A Documentary History and Analysis.* 2 vols. Dobbs Ferry, N.Y.: Oceana Publications, 1975.

2801 Fitzmaurice, Sir G. G. "Definition of Aggression," *International and Comparative Law Quarterly* 1 (January 1952):137–44.

2802 Franklin, Mitchell. *The Formulation of the Conception of Aggression.* Brussels: Association Internationale des Juristes Démocrates, 1952.

2803 Garcia-Mora, M. R. "Crime against Peace in International Law: From Nuremberg to the Present," *Kentucky Law Journal* 53, no. 1 (1964): 36–55.

2804 Glaser, Stefan. "Constituye un crimen la guerra de agresión," *Revista Española de Derecho Internacional* 6 (1953):539–62.

2805 ———. "Définition de l'aggression en droit international pénal," *Revue de Droit International et de Droit Comparé* 35 (1958):633–58.

2806 ———. "La guerre d'agression à la lumière des sources du droit international," *Revue Générale de Droit International Public* 57 (July-September 1953):398–443.

2807 Gross, Leo. "Criminality of Aggressive War," *American Political Science Review* 41 (April 1947):205–25.

2808 Harvard University Research in International Law. "Draft Covenant of Law on Rights of States in Case of Aggression," *American Journal of International Law* 33 [Supplement] (October 1939):823–909.

2809 Hazard, J. N. "Why Try Again to Define Aggression?" *American Journal of International Law* 62 (July 1968):701–10.

2810 Jessup, Philip C. "The Crime of Aggression and the Future of International Law," *Political Science Quarterly* 62, no. 1 (March 1947):1–10.

2811 _____. "Force under Modern Law of Nations," *Foreign Affairs* 25 (October 1946):90–105.

2812 Komarnicki, M. Waclaw. "La définition de l'agresseur dans le droit international moderne," *Recueil des Cours de l'Académie de Droit International de la Haye* 75 (1949):1–113.

2813 Kopelmanas, L. "The Problem of Aggression and the Prevention of War," *American Journal of International Law* 31 (April 1937):244–57.

2814 Kunz, Josef. *Kriegsrecht und Neutralitätrecht*. Vienna: Springer, 1935.

2815 Langer, Robert. *Seizure of Territory: The Stimson Doctrine and Related Principles in Legal Theory and Diplomatic Practice*. New York: Greenwood Press, 1969.

2816 Liebholz, Gerhard. "'Aggression' als Zeitgeschichtliches Problem," *Vierteljahrshefte für Zeitgeschichte* 6 (April 1958):165–71.

2817 Longobardi, A. "El concepto de agresion," *Revista Argentina de Derecho Internacional* 8 (July-September 1945):246–59.

2818 McConnell, John R. "Can Law Impede Aggressive War?" *American Bar Association Journal* 50 (February 1964):131–35.

2819 McDougal, Myers S., and Florentino P. Feliciano. *Law and Minimum World Public Order: The Legal Regulation of International Coercion*. New Haven: Yale University Press, 1961.

2820 Morwiecki, Wojciech. *Walka o definicję agresji w prawi międzynarodowym*. Warsaw: Państwowe Wydawn. Nankowe, 1956.

2821 Murty, P. N. "Aggression in International Law," *India Quarterly* 7 (1951):269–81.

2822 Osgood, Robert Endicott, and Robert W. Tucker. *Force, Order, and Justice*. Baltimore: Johns Hopkins Press, 1967.

2823 Pal, Radhabinod. "What Is Aggressive War?" *Indian Law Review* 4 (1950):99–142.

2824 Pella, V. V. "Un nouveau délit: La propagande pour la guerre d'agression," *Revue de Droit International, de Sciences Diplomatiques et Politiques* 3 (1929):174–79.

2825 Pompe, Cornelis A. *Aggressive War: An International Crime*. The Hague: Nijhoff, 1953.

2826 Röling, Bernard V. A. "On Aggression, on International Criminal Law, on Criminal Jurisdiction," *Nederlands Tijdschrift voor International Recht* 2 (April-July 1955):167–96, 279–89.

2827 ———. *De strafbaarheid van de agressieve oorlog.* Groningen: J. B. Wolters, 1950.

2828 Samsonow, Michael S. *Political Philosophy of Aggression.* Menlo Park, Calif., 1961.

2829 Sayre, Francis B. "Criminal Conspiracy," *Harvard Law Review* 35 (February 1922):393–427.

2830 Serra, Enrico. *L'aggressione internazionale.* Milan: Hoepli, 1946.

2831 Stone, Julius. *Aggression and World Order: A Critique of United Nations Theories of Aggression.* Berkeley: University of California Press, 1958.

2832 ———. *Legal Controls of International Conflict.* New York: Rinehart, 1954.

2833 Thirring, Hans. "Was ist Aggression? Das Problem der Aggressionsdefinition," *Österreichische Zeitschrift für Öffentliches Recht* 5 (1952–1953):226–42.

2834 United Nations (12th Session), Special Committee on the Question of Defining Aggression. *Report of the 1956 Special Committee on the Question of Aggression, 8 October–9 November 1956.* Supplement no. 16, Official Records. New York, 1957.

2835 Urrutía Aparicio, Carlos. "La evolución del concepto de la agresión en el derecho internacional," *Revista de al Asociación Guatemalteca de Derecho Internacional* 1 (January 1954):80–105.

2836 Vignol, Rene. *La définition de l'agresseur dans la guerre.* Paris: Libraire du Recueil Sirey, 1933.

2837 Volle, Hermann. "Definition des Angreifers und Beistandsverpflichtungen in den europäischen Verträgen der Nachkriegszeit," *Europa-Archiv* 4 (1949):1977–84.

2838 Waldmann, A. "Der Angriffskrieg als internationales Verbrechen nach den Nürnberger." Doctor of Law dissertation, Erlangen University, 1951.

2839 Waldock, Claud H. M. "The Regulation of the Use of Force by Individual States in International Law," *Recueil des Cours de l'Académie de Droit International de la Haye* 81 (1953):451–517.

2840 Wright, Quincy. "The Concept of Aggression in International Law," *American Journal of International Law* 29 (1935):373–95.

2841 ———. "The Crime of 'War Mongering,'" *American Journal of International Law* 40 (April 1946):398–406.

2842 Žourek, Jaroslav. "La définition de l'agression et le droit international: Développments récents de la question," *Recueil des Cours de l'Académie de Droit International de la Haye* 92 (1957):755–860.

The Problem of the Military

GENERAL

2843 Andrzejewski, Stanislaw. *Military Organization and Society.* London: Routledge and Kegan Paul, 1954.

2844 Brotz, Howard, and Everett Wilson. "Characteristics of Military Society," *American Journal of Sociology* 51 (March 1946):371–75.

2845 Burns, C. Delisle. "Militarism," *Encyclopedia of Social Sciences* 10 (1930):446–50.

2846 Corwin, Edward S. *Total War and the Constitution.* New York: Knopf, 1947.

2847 Ekirch, Arthur A., Jr. *The Civilian and the Military.* New York: Oxford University Press, 1956.

2848 Howard, Michael, ed. *Soldiers and Governments: Nine Studies in Civil-Military Relations.* Bloomington: Indiana University Press, 1959.

2849 Huntington, Samuel P. *The Soldier and the State: The Theory and Politics of Civil-Military Relations.* Cambridge: Harvard University Press, 1957.

2850 Kerwin, Jerome G., ed. *Civil-Military Relationships in American Life.* Chicago: University of Chicago Press, 1948.

2851 Larson, Arthur, comp. *Civil-Military Relations and Militarism: A Bibliography.* Bibliography Series, no. 9. Manhatten: Kansas State University Library, 1971.

2852 Lasswell, H. D. "Garrison State," *American Journal of Sociology* 46 (1941):455–68.

2853 Lauterbach, Albert T. "Militarism in the Western World," *Journal of the History of Ideas* 5 (1944):446–78.

2854 May, Ernest R. "The Development of Political-Military Consultation in the United States," *Political Science Quarterly* 70 (1955):161–80.

2855 Millis, Walter. *Arms of the State: Civil-Military Elements in National Policy.* New York: Twentieth Century Fund, 1958.

2856 Rogers, Lindsay. "Civilian Control of Military Policy," *Foreign Policy* 18, no. 2 (1940):280–91.

2857   Smith, Louis. *American Democracy and Military Power in the United States.* Chicago: University of Chicago Press, 1951.

2858   Social Science Research Council, Committee on Civil-Military Research *Civil-Military Relations: An Annotated Bibliography, 1940–1952.* New York: Columbia University Press, 1954.

2859   Sprout, Harold. "Trends in the Traditional Relations between Military and Civilian," *Proceedings of the American Philosophical Society* 92, no. 4, (1948):264–70.

2860   Vagts, Alfred. *Defense and Diplomacy: The Soldier and the Conduct of Foreign Policy.* New York: King's Crown Press, 1956.

2861   _____. *A History of Militarism: Civilian and Military.* Rev. ed. New York: Meridian Books, 1959.

2861a   Welch, Claude E., Jr., ed. *Civilian Control of the Military: Theory and Cases from Developing Countries.* Albany: State University of New York Press, 1976.

GERMANY

German Militarism

2862   Bebel, August, and W. Liebknecht. *Gegen den Militarismus und gegen die neue Steuren.* Berlin: Expedition des "Vorwärts," 1893.

2863   Bracher, Karl Dietrich; Wolfgang Sauer; and Gerhard Schulz. *Die nationalsozialistische Machtergreifung: Studien zur Errichtung des totalitären Herrschaftssystems in Deutschland.* Cologne: Westdeutscher Verlag, 1962.

2864   Dehio, Ludwig. "Um den deutschen Militarismus," *Historische Zeitschrift* 180 (1955):43–64.

2865   Fick, H. *Der deutsch Militarismus der Vorkriegszeit: Beitrag zur Soziologie der Militarismus.* Potsdam: Protte, 1932.

2866   Fried, Hans E. "German Militarism: Substitute for Revolution," *Political Science Quarterly* 58 (December 1943):481–513.

2867   Kulbakin, W. D. *Die Militarisierung Deutschlands, 1928 bis 1930.* Berlin: Dietz Verlag, 1956.

2868   Lauterbach, Albert. "Roots and Implications of the German Idea of Military Society," *Military Affairs* 5 (Spring 1941):1–20.

2869   Liebe, Georg. *Der Soldat in der deutschen Vergangenheit.* Leipzig: Eugen Diederichs, 1899.

2870   Liebknecht, Karl. *Militarismus und Antimilitarismus.* Leipzig: Leipziger Buchdruckerei, 1907.

2871   [Quidde, Ludwig]. *Der Militarismus im Deutschland Reiche.* Stuttgart, 1893.

2872   Ritter, Gerhard. "Das Problem des Militarismus in Deutschland," *Historische Zeitschrift* 177 (1954):21–48.

2873   _____. *The Sword and the Scepter: The Problem of Militarism in Germany.* Translated by Heinz Norden. 4 vols. Coral Gables, Fla.: University of Miami Press, 1969–.

2874   Salomon, Albert. "The Spirit of the Soldier and Nazi Militarism," *Social Research* 9 (February 1942):82–103.

2875   Stenzel, Ernst. *Die Kreigführung des deutschen Imperialismus und das Völkerrecht . . . 1900–1945.* Berlin: Militärverlag der DDR, 1973.

2876   Thiessen, Johannes. *Der preussische Militarismus.* Berlin, 1919.

German Army

2877   Absolon, Rudolf, ed. *Die Wehrmacht im Dritten Reich: Aufbau, Gliederung, Recht, Verwaltung.* 7 vols. Boppard am Rhein: Harald Boldt Verlag, 1963–1977.

2878   Bennecke, Heinrich. *Die Reichswehr und der "Röhm-Putsch."* Munich: Olzog, 1964.

2879   Boeninger, Hildegard R. "Hitler and the German Generals, 1934–1938," *Journal of Central European Affairs* 14 (April 1954):19–37.

2880   Brauweiler, Heinz. *Generäle in der Deutschen Republik: Groener, Schleicher, Seeckt.* Berlin: Tell-Verlag, 1932.

2881   Carsten, Francis L. *The Reichswehr and Politics, 1918–1933.* Oxford: Clarendon Press, 1966.

2882   _____. "The Reichswehr and the Red Army, 1920–1933." *Survey* 44/45 (October 1962):115–32.

2883   Craig, Gordon. *The Politics of the Prussian Army, 1640–1945.* Oxford: Oxford University Press, 1955.

2884   Demeter, Karl. *Das deutsch Offizierkorps in Gesellschaft und Staat, 1650–1945.* 4th rev. ed. Frankfurt am Main: Bernard und Graefe Verlag, 1965.

2885   Deuerlein, Ernst. "Hitlers Eintritt in die Politik und die Reichswehr," *Vierteljahrshefte für Zeitgeschichte* 7 (April 1959):177–227.

2886 Deutsch Harold C. *The Conspiracy against Hitler in the Twilight War.* Minneapolis: University of Minnesota Press, 1968.

2887 _____. *Hitler and His Generals: The Hidden Crises, January-June 1938.* Minneapolis: University of Minnesota Press, 1974.

2888 Ebeling, Hans. *The Caste: The Political Role of the German General Staff between 1918 and 1938.* London: New Europe Publishing, 1945.

2889 Erfurth, Waldemar. *Die Geschichte des deutschen Generalstabs von 1918 bis 1945.* Berlin: Musterschmidt-Verlag, 1957.

2890 Fried, Hans Ernst [John H. E. Fried]. *The Guilt of the German Army.* New York: Macmillan, 1942.

2891 Gessler, Otto. *Reichswehrpolitik in der Weimarer Zeit.* Stuttgart: Deutsche Verlags-Anstalt, 1958.

2892 Gordon, Harold. *The Reichswehr and the German Republic 1919-1926.* Princeton: Princeton University Press, 1957.

2893 Görlitz, Walter. *History of the German General Staff.* New York: Praeger, 1953.

2894 Greiner, Helmuth. *Die oberste Wehrmachtführung, 1939-1943.* Wiesbaden: Limes Verlag, 1951.

2895 Groener, Gen. Wilhelm. "German Military Power since Versailles," *Foreign Affairs* 11 (1933):434-46.

2896 Hallgarten, George W. F. *Hitler, Reichswehr, und Industrie.* 2d ed. Frankfurt am Main: Europäische Verlagsanstalt, 1955.

2897 Herzfeld, Hans. "Zur neuren Literatur über das Heeresproblem in der deutschen Geschichte," *Vierteljahrshefte für Zeitgeschichte* 4 (October 1956):361-86.

2898 _____. *Das Problem des deutschen Heeres 1919-1945.* Laupheim: Steiner, 1952.

2899 Heusinger, Adolf. *Befehl im Widerstreit: Schicksalsstunden der deutschen Armee, 1923-1945.* Tübingen: Wunderlich, 1950.

2900 Hossbach, Friedrich. *Die Entwicklung des Oberbefehls über das Heer in Brandenburg, Preussen und im Deutschen Reich von 1655-1945: Ein kurzer Überblick.* Würzburg: Holzner, 1964.

2901 _____. *Zwischen Wehrmacht und Hitler 1934-1938.* 2d rev. ed. Göttingen: Vandenhoeck und Ruprecht, 1965.

2902 Hubatsch, Walter, and Percy Schramm. *Die deutsche militärische Führung in der Kriegswende.* Cologne, 1964.

2903 Kitchen, Martin. *The German Officier Corps, 1890–1914.* Oxford: Clarendon Press, 1968.

2904 Liddell Hart, B. H. *The German Generals Talk.* New York: Morrow, 1948.

2905 Lossberg, Bernhard von. *Im Wehrmacht Führungstab.* Hamburg: H. H. Nölke Verlag, 1949.

2906 Müller, Klaus-Jürgen. *Das Heer und Hitler: Armee und nationalistisches Regime, 1933–1940.* Stuttgart: Deutsche Verlags-Anstalt, 1969.

2907 Müller-Hillerbrand, Burkhart. *Das Heer, 1933–1945: Entwicklung des organisatorischen Aufbaues.* 3 vols. Frankfurt am Main: Mittler, 1969.

2908 O'Neill, Robert J. *The German Army and the Nazi Party, 1933–1939.* New York: J. H. Heinemann, 1966.

2909 Rosinski, Herbert. *The German Army.* New York: Praeger, 1966.

2910 Schlabrendorff, Fabian von. *Offiziere gegen Hitler.* Frankfurt am Main: Fischer-Bücherei, 1962.

2911 Schulte Bernd F. *Die Deutsche Armee 1900–1914. Zwischen Beharren und Verändern.* Düsseldorf: Droste Verlag, 1977.

2912 Schützle, Kurt. *Reichswehr wider die Nation: Zur Rolle der Reichswehr bei der Vorbereitung und Errichtung der faschistischen Diktatur in Deutschland (1929–1933).* Berlin, 1963.

2913 Taylor, Telford. *Sword and Swastika: Generals and Nazis in the Third Reich.* New York: Simon and Schuster, 1952.

2914 Thomas, Georg. *Geschichte der deutschen Wehr- und Rüstungswirtschaft (1918-1943/45).* Boppard am Rhein: Harald Boldt Verlag, 1966.

2915 Vogelsang, Thilo. *Reichswehr, Staat und NSDAP: Beiträge zur deutschen Geschichte 1930–1932.* Stuttgart: Deutsche Verlags-Anstalt, 1962.

2916 Wheeler-Bennett, John W. *The Nemesis of Power: The German Army in Politics, 1918–1945.* London: Macmillan, 1961.

German Navy

2917 Assmann, Kurt. *Deutsche Seestrategie in zwei Weltkriegen.* Heidelberg: Vowinckel, 1957.

2918   Bensel, Rolf. *Die deutsche Flottenpolitik von 1933 bis 1939: Eine Studie über die Rolle des Flottenbaus in Hitlers Aussenpolitik.* Frankfurt am Main: Mittler, 1958.

2919   Bywater, Hector C. "The Rebirth of German Sea Power," *Nineteenth Century and After* 105 (February 1929):161–70.

2920   Gröner, Erich. *Die deutschen Kriegsschiffe, 1815–1936.* Munich: J. F. Lehmanns, 1937.

2921   _____. *Die Schiffe der deutschen Kriegsmarine und Luftwaffe, 1939–45.* Munich: J. F. Lehmanns Verlag, 1954.

2922   Herwig, Holger H. "Admirals versus Generals: The War Aims of the Imperial German Navy 1914–1918," *Central European History* 5, no. 3 (September 1972):208–33.

2923   _____. *The German Naval Officer Corps: A Social and Political History, 1890–1918.* Oxford: Clarendon Press, 1973.

2924   Hubatsch, Walter. *Der Admiralstab und die obersten Marinebehörden in Deutschland 1848–1945.* Frankfurt am Main: Bernard und Graefe Verlag, 1958.

2925   _____. *Die Ära Tirpitz: Studien zur deutschen Marinepolitik 1890–1918.* Göttingen: Musterschmidt-Verlag, 1955.

2926   Lohmann, Walter, and Hans Hildebrand, eds. *Die deutsche Kriegsmarine 1939–1945: Gliederung, Einsatz, Stellenbesetzung.* 3 vols. Bad Nauheim: Podzun-Verlag, 1956–1964.

2927   Raeder, Erich. "Gegenwartsfragen der Reichsmarine," *Die Woche Berlin* (October 29, 1932):1326–32.

2928   _____. *The Struggle for the Sea.* Translated by Edward Fitzgerald. London: Kimber, 1959.

2929   Röhr, Albert. *Handbuch der deutschen Marinegeschichte.* Oldenburg: Gerhard Stalling, 1963.

2930   Saville, Allison W. "The Development of the German U-Boat Arm 1919–1935." Ph.D. dissertation, University of Washington, 1963.

2931   Stegemann, Bernd. *Die deutsche Marinepolitik 1916–1918.* Berlin: Duncker und Humboldt, 1970.

2932   Steinberg, Jonathan. *Yesterday's Deterrent: Tirpitz and the Birth of the German Battle Fleet.* New York: Macmillan, 1965.

German Air Force

2933   Baumbach, Werner. *The Life and Death of the Luftwaffe.* Translated by Frederick Holt. New York: Ballantine Books, 1967.

2934 Homze, Edward L. *Arming the Luftwaffe: The Reich Air Ministry and the German Aircraft Industry, 1919–39.* Lincoln: University of Nebraska Press, 1976.

2935 Irving, David. *The Rise and Fall of the Luftwaffe: The Life of Field Marshall Erhard Milch.* New York: Little, Brown, 1974.

2936 Killen, John. *A History of the Luftwaffe.* Garden City, N.Y.: Doubleday, 1968.

2937 Mason, Herbert Molloy, Jr. *The Rise of the Luftwaffe: Forging the Secret German Air Weapon, 1918–1940.* New York: Dial Press, 1973.

2938 Volker, Karl-Heinz. *Die Entwicklung der militärischen Luftfahrt in Deutschland 1920–1933, Plannung und Massnahmen zur Schaffung einer Flieger-truppe in der Reichswehr.* Stuttgart: Deutsche Verlags-Anstalt, 1962.

2939 _____. "Die geheime Luftrüstung der Reichswehr und ihre Auswirkung auf den Flugzeugbestand der Luftwaffe bis zum Beginn des Zweiten Weltkrieges," *Wehrwissenschaftliche Rundschau* 12 (1962):540–50.

Civil-Military Relations

2940 Craig, Gordon A. "Reichswehr and National Socialism: The Policy of Wilhelm Groener, 1928–1932," *Political Science Quarterly* 63 (1948): 194–229.

2941 Post, Gaines, Jr. *The Civil-Military Fabric of Weimar Foreign Policy.* Princeton: Princeton University Press, 1973.

2942 Rehm, Walter. "Reichswehr und politische Parteien in der Weimarer Republik," *Wehrwissenschaftliche Rundschau* 8 (1958):692–708.

2943 Salomon, Albert. "The Spirit of the Soldier and Nazi Militarism," *Social Research* 9 (February 1942):95–103.

2944 Schramm, Wilhelm Ritter von. *Staatskunst und bewaffnete Macht.* Munich: Isar-Verlag, 1957.

2945 Schüddekopf, Otto Ernst. *Das Heer und die Republik: Quellen zur politik der Reichswehrführung 1918 bis 1933.* Hanover: Norddeutsche Verlagsanstalt O. Goedel, 1955.

2946 _____. "Wehrmacht und Politik in Deutschland," *Politische Literatur* 3 (1954):232ff.

JAPAN

Japanese Militarism

2947 Benedict, Ruth. *The Chrysanthemum and the Sword: Patterns of Japanese Culture*. Boston: Houghton Mifflin, 1946.

2948 Borg, Dorothy. *The United States and the Far Eastern Crises of 1933–1938*. Cambridge: Harvard University Press, 1964.

2949 ———, and Shumpei Okamoto, eds. *Pearl Harbor as History: Japanese-American Relations, 1931–1941*. New York: Columbia University Press, 1973.

2950 Brown, Delmer M. *Nationalism in Japan: An Introductory Historical Analysis*. Berkeley: University of California Press, 1955.

2951 Colegrove, Kenneth W. *Militarism in Japan*. Boston: World Peace Foundation, 1936.

2952 Conroy, F. Hilary. "Japanese Nationalism and Expansion," *American Historical Review* 60, no. 4 (July 1955):818–29.

2953 Falk, Edwin A. *From Perry to Pearl Harbor: The Struggle for Supremacy in the Pacific*. New York: Doubleday, Doran, 1943.

2954 Feis, Herbert. *The Road to Pearl Harbor: The Coming of the War between the United States and Japan*. Princeton: Princeton University Press, 1950.

2955 Heinrichs, Waldo H. *American Ambassador: Joseph C. Grew and the Development of the United States Diplomatic Tradition*. Boston: Little, Brown, 1966.

2956 Ikeda, Sumihisa. "Tōshei-ha to Kōdō-ha," *Bungei Shunjū* 34, no. 11 (November 1956):92–108.

2957 Itō, Masanori. *Gunbatsu Koboshi*. 3 vols. Tokyo: Bungei Shunjū Shinsha, 1957–1958.

2958 Iwabuchi Tatsuo. *Gunbatsu no Keifu*. Tokyo, 1948.

2959 Jones, F. C. *Japan's New Order in East Asia: Its Rise and Fall, 1937–45*. New York: Institute of Pacific Relations, 1954.

2960 Kennedy, M. D. *The Military Side of Japanese Life*. Boston: Houghton Mifflin, c. 1923.

2961 ———. *Some Aspects of Japan and Her Defense Force*. London: Kegan Paul, 1928.

2962 Lockwood, William W. *The Economic Development of Japan: Growth and Structural Change, 1868–1938.* Princeton: Princeton University Press, 1954.

2963 Maki, John M. *Japanese Militarism: Its Causes and Cure.* New York: Knopf, 1945.

2964 Morley, James William. *Japan's Foreign Policy, 1869–1941.* New York: Columbia University Press, 1974.

2965 Smethurst, Richard J. *A Social Basis for Prewar Japanese Militarism: The Army and the Rural Community.* Berkeley: University of California Press, 1974.

2966 Stimson, Henry L. *The Far Eastern Crises.* New York: Harper, 1936.

2967 Storry, Richard. *The Double Patriots: A Study of Japanese Nationalism.* Boston: Houghton Mifflin, 1957.

2968 Tanaka Ryukichi. *Nihon Gunbatsu Anto-shi.* Tokyo, 1947.

2969 _____. *Hai-in wo Tsuku-Gunbatsu Sen-ō no Jissō.* Tokyo: Sansuisha, 1946.

2970 Tanin, O., and E. Yohan. *Militarism and Fascism in Japan.* New York: International Publications, 1934.

2971 Vespa, A. *Secret Agent of Japan: A Handbook to Japanese Imperialism.* London: Little, 1938.

2972 Yoshihashi, Takehiko. *Conspiracy at Mukden: The Rise of the Japanese Military.* New Haven: Yale University Press, 1963.

2973 Young, A. Morgan. *Imperial Japan, 1926–1938.* London: George Allen and Unwin, 1938.

Japanese Army

2974 Clyde, Paul. H. *Japan's Pacific Mandate.* New York: Macmillan, 1935.

2975 Crowley, James B. "Japanese Army Factionalism in the 1930's," *Journal of Asian Studies* 21, no. 3 (May 1962):309–26.

2976 Deverall, Richard. *The Imperial Japanese Army: Hideki Tojo's Military Socialism.* Bangalore: Deccan Herlad Press, 1951.

2977 Hayashi, Saburo. *Kōgun: The Japanese Army in the Pacific War.* Quantico, Va.: Marine Corps Association, 1959.

2978 Hsü, Shu-hsi. *A Digest of Japanese War Conduct*. Shanghai: Kelly and Walsh, 1939.

2979 ———. *The War Conduct of the Japanese*. Shanghai: Kelly and Walsh, 1938.

2980 Nakano Tomio. *Tosuiken no Dokuritsu*. Tokyo, 1934.

2981 Norman, E. Herbert. *Soldier and Peasant in Japan: The Origins of Conscription*. New York: Institute of Pacific Relations, 1943.

2982 Ozaki Yoshiharu. *Rikugun o Ugokashita Hitobito*. Odawara, 1960.

2983 Puleston, W. D. *The Armed Forces of the Pacific: A Comparison of the Military and Naval Power of the United States and Japan*. New Haven: Yale University Press, 1941.

2984 Wilds, Thomas. "How Japan Forfeited the Mandated Islands," *United States Naval Institute Proceedings* 81 (April 1955):401–07.

2985 Williams, Edward T. "Japan's Mandate in the Pacific," *American Journal of International Law* 27 (July 1933):428–29.

Japanese Navy

2986 Bywater, Hector C. *Sea-Power in the Pacific: A Study of the American-Japanese Naval Problem*. Boston: Houghton Mifflin, 1921.

2987 Hashimoto, Mochitsura. *Sunk: The Story of the Japanese Submarine Fleet, 1941–1945*. New York: H. Holt, 1954.

2988 Ikeda, Kiyoshi. *Nihon no kaigun*. 2 vols. Tokyo, 1967.

2989 Itō, Masanori. *Daikaigun o omou*. Tokyo, 1956.

2990 Morison, Samuel Eliot. *The Rising Sun in the Pacific, 1931–April, 1942*. History of United States Naval Operations in World War II, vol. 3. Boston: Little, Brown, 1948.

2991 Watts, A. G., and B. G. Gordon. *The Imperial Japanese Navy*. New York: Doubleday, 1972.

Civil-Military Relations

2992 Byas, Hugh. *Government by Assassination*. New York: Knopf, 1942.

2993 Causton, E. E. N. *Militarism and Foreign Policy in Japan*. London: George Allen and Unwin, 1936.

2994 Conroy, Hilary. "Government vs. 'Patriot': The Background of Japan's Asiatic Expansion," *Pacific Historical Review* 20 (1951):31–42.

2995   Crowley, James B. *Japan's Quest for Autonomy: National Security and Foreign Policy, 1930–1938.* Princeton: Princeton University Press, 1966.

2996   Hattori, Shiso. *Tōjō Seiken no Rekishiteki Kōkei.* Tokyo: Hakuyōsha, 1949.

2997   Kinoshita Hanji. *Nihon no Uyoku.* Tokyo, 1953.

2998   Libal, Michael. *Japans Weg in den Krieg: Die Aussenpolitik der Kabinette Konoye 1940–41.* Düsseldorf: Droste Verlag, 1971.

2999   Lory, Hillis. *Japan's Military Masters: The Army in Japanese Life.* New York: Viking Press, 1943.

3000   Maxon, Yale Candee. *Control of Japan's Foreign Policy: A Study of Civil-Military Rivalry.* Berkeley: University of California Press, 1957.

3001   Morishima Morito. *Inbo, Ansatsu, Gunto.* Tokyo, 1950.

3002   Morris, Evan I. *Nationalism and the Right Wing in Japan.* New York: Oxford University Press, 1960.

3003   Norman, E. Herbert. *Japan's Emergence as a Modern State.* New York: Institute of Pacific Relations, 1940.

3004   Scalapino, Robert A. *Democracy and the Party Movement in Prewar Japan.* Berkeley: University of California Press, 1953.

3005   Tanaka Sogoro. *Nihon Fashizumu no Genryn.* Tokyo, 1949.

3006   Takeuchi, Tatsuji. *War and Diplomacy in the Japanese Empire.* Chicago: University of Chicago Press, 1935.

3007   Yanaga, Chitoshi. "The Military and the Government in Japan," *American Political Science Review* 35 (1941):528–39.

Treatment of Prisoners of War, Noncombatants, and Irregulars

Prisoners of War

3008   Baptiste, Joseph C. "The Enemy among Us: World War II Prisoners of War." Ph.D. dissertation, Texas Christian University, 1975.

3009   Datner, Szyman. *Crimes against POW's: Responsibility of the Wehrmacht.* Warsaw: Zachodnia Agencja Prasowa, 1964.

3010   Deschaumes, Guy. *Derrière les barbelés de Nuremberg.* Paris: E. Flammarion, 1942.

3011   "Employment of Prisoners of War in Germany," *International Labour Review* 48 (September 1943):316–23.

3012 Feilchenfeld, Ernst H. *Prisoners of War*. Washington, D.C.: Georgetown University, School of Foreign Service, Institute of World Policy, 1948.

3013 FitzGibbon, Louis. *Katyn*. New York: Scribner's, 1971.

3014 Flory, William E. *Prisoners of War: A Study in the Development of International Law*. Washington, D.C.: American Council of Public Affairs, 1942.

3015 Fooks, Herbert C. *Prisoners of War*. Federalsburg, Md.: J. W. Stowell, 1924.

3016 Glaser, Stefan. "La protection internationale des prisonniers de guerre et la responsabilité pour les crimes de guerre," *Revue de Droit Pénal et de Criminologie* 31 (May 1951):897–927.

3017 Hyde, Charles Cheney. "Concerning Prisoners of War," *American Journal of International Law* 10 (1916):600–602.

3018 _____. "Japanese Executions of American Aviators," *American Journal of International Law* 37 (July 1943):480–82.

3019 Jaworski, Leon. "Military Trials of Prisoners of War," *Texas Bar Journal* 7 (October 1944):310–11.

3020 Kim, Myong Whai. "Prisoners of War as a Major Problem of the Korean Armistice, 1953." Ph.D. dissertation, New York University, 1960.

3021 Kunz, Josef L. "Treatment of Prisoners of War," *American Society of International Law Proceedings* (1953):99–111.

3022 Kurtha, Aziz Noomi. *Prisoners of War and War Crimes*. Karachi: Pakistan Herald Press, 1973.

3023 Levie, Howard S. "Penal Sanctions for Maltreatment of Prisoners of War," *American Journal of International Law* 56 (April 1962):433–68.

3024 Lewis, George G., and John Mewha. *History of Prisoners of War Utilization by the United States Army, 1776–1945*. Washington, D.C.: GPO, 1956.

3025 Maschke, Erich, ed. *Zur Geschichte der deutschen Kriegsgefangenen des Zweiten Weltkrieges*. 22 vols. Munich: Verlag Ernst und Werner Gieseking, Bielefeld, 1962–1974.

3026 Mason, J. B. "German Prisoners of War in the United States," *American Journal of International Law* 39 (1945):198–215.

3027 Mason, W. Wynne. *Prisoners of War*. London: Oxford University Press, 1954.

3028 "Prisoners of War, Criminal Responsibility." *Canadian Bar Review* 23 (1945):451, 524.

3029 *Prisoners of War in the European War* Miscellaneous Reading List, no. 22. Washington, D.C.: Carnegie Endowment for International Peace, Library, 1922.

3030 Probst, H. *Die Kriegsgefangenen nach modernem Völkerrecht.* Munich: Wild, 1911.

3031 Reitlinger, Gerald. "The Truth about Hitler's 'Commisar Order,'" *Commentary* 28 (July 1959):7–18.

3032 Stone, R. "The American-German Conference on Prisoners of War," *American Journal of International Law* 13 (1919):406–49.

3033 Trainin, Ilia A. "Questions of Guerilla Warfare in the Law of War," *American Journal of International Law* 40 (July 1946):534–62.

3034 Waldock, C. H. M. "Release of the Altmark's Prisoners," *British Yearbook of International Law* 24 (1947):216–38.

3035 Werner, G. "Les prisonniers de guerre," *Recueil des Cours de l'Académie de Droit International* 21 (1928):1–107.

3036 Wyss, G. *Die Rechtsstellung des entwichenen Kriegsgefangenen in neutrallen Staat.* Bern: P. Haupt, 1945.

3037 Zawodny, J. K. *Death in the Forest.* Notre Dame: University of Notre Dame Press, 1962.

3038 ———. "Katyn Forest Massacre: Morals in American Foreign Policy," *Minnesota Review* 3, no. 2 (Winter 1963):228–36.

Hostages

3039 Bentwich, Norman. "The Killing of Hostages," *Law Journal* 91 (November 8, 1941):405.

3040 Brungs, Bernard Joseph. "Hostages, Prisoner Reprisals, and Collective Penalties: The Development of International Law of War with Respect to Collective and Vicarious Punishment." 3 vols. Ph.D. dissertation, Georgetown University, 1968.

3041 Ginsburgs, G. "Laws of War and War Crimes on the Russian Front during World War II: The Soviet View," *Soviet Studies* 11, no. 3 (January 1960):253–85.

3042 Hammer, Ellen, and Marina Salvin. "The Taking of Hostages in Theory and Practice," *American Journal of International Law* 38 (February 1944):20–33.

3043   Kuhn, Arthur K. "The Execution of Hostages," *American Journal of International Law* 36 (April 1942):271–74.

3044   Melen, Alexander C. "La question des otages à la lumière du droit," *Revue de Droit International (Sottile-Geneva)* 24 (January-March 1946): 17–25.

3045   Pilloud, Claude. "The Question of Hostages and the Geneva Conventions," *Revue Internationale de la Croix-Rouge* [English Supplement] 4 (October 1951):187–201.

3046   Salvin, Marina. "The Taking of Hostages in Theory and Practice," *American Journal of International Law* 38 (1944):20–33.

3047   United Nations Information Organization. *The Axis System of Hostages.* London: HMSO, 1942.

3048   United States, Library of Congress, Legislative Reference Service. *Treatment of War Hostages and International Law.* Washington, D.C.: Library of Congress, 1942.

3049   Van Nispen Tot Sevenear, C. M. O. "Ik mageen onschuldige doden! Over verzetalieden en gijzelaars," *Nederlands Juristenblad* 23 (1948): 301–11.

3050   _____. *La prise d'otages: Examen de la licite des pratiques modernes d'après le droit objectif et le droit des gens positifs.* The Hague: Nijhoff, 1949.

3051   Wright, Lord. "The Killing of Hostages as a War Crime," *British Yearbook of International Law* 25 (1948):296–310.

3052   Yang, Lieu-sheng. "Hostages in Chinese History," *Harvard Journal of Asiatic Studies* 15 (December 1952):507–09.

Reprisals

3053   Albrecht, A. R. "War Reprisals in the War Crimes Trials and in the Geneva Conventions of 1949," *American Journal of International Law* 47 (October 1953):590–614.

3054   Bower, Sir Graham J. "The Law of War: Prisoners and Reprisals," *Transactions of the Grotius Society* 1 (1916):23–37.

3055   Jentsch, Hans-Joachim. *Die Beurteilung summarischer Exekutionen durch das Völkerrecht.* Marburg, 1966.

3056   Kalshoven, F. *Belligerent Reprisals.* Leiden: Sijthoff, 1971.

3057   _____. "Droits de l'homme, droit des conflits armés et représailles," *Revue Internationale de la Croix-Rouge* 53 (1971):205–15.

3058 Mason, R. Hughes. "'Trial' By Nazi Court-Martial," *South African Law Journal* 62 (November 1945):427–31.

3059 Pfenniger, H. F. "Sind persönliche Kriegsrepressalien erlaubt?" *Schweizerische Juristen-Zeitung* 60 (1964):245–51.

3060 Schuetz, Heinrich Albrecht. *Die Repressalie unter besonderer Berücksichtigung der Kriegsverbrecherprozesse.* Bonn: Röhrscheid, 1950.

3061 Stowell, Ellery C. "Military Reprisals and the Sanctions of the Laws of War," *American Journal of International Law* 36 (1942):643–50.

Partisans, Guerrillas, Irregulars

3062 Armstrong, John A., ed. *Soviet Partisans in World War II.* Madison: University of Wisconsin Press, 1964.

3063 Barrett, Roger W. [and Lester Nurick]. "Legality of Guerrilla Forces under the Laws of War," *American Journal of International Law* 40 (July 1946):563–83. [See entry no. 3079.]

3064 Baxter, Richard R. "So-Called 'Unprivileged Belligerency': Spies, Guerrillas, and Saboteurs," *British Yearbook of International Law* 28 (1951):232–345.

3065 Crozier, Brian. *The Rebels: A Study of Post-War Insurrections.* London: Chatto and Windus, 1960.

3066 Delzell, Charles F. *Mussolini's Enemies: The Italian Anti-Fascist Resistance.* Princeton: Princeton University Press, 1961.

3067 Foot, M. R. D. *Resistance: European Resistance to Nazism, 1940–1945.* New York: McGraw-Hill, 1977.

3068 Ford, W. J. "Resistance Movements in Occupied Territory," *Nederlands Tijdschrift voor International Recht* 3 (October 1956):355–84.

3069 Galula, D. *Counterinsurgency Warfare.* New York: Praeger, 1964.

3070 Gann, Lewis. *Guerillas in History.* Stanford: Hoover Institution Press, 1971.

3071 Heilbrunn, O. *Partisan Warfare.* New York: Praeger, 1962.

3072 Howell, Edgar M. *The Soviet Partisan Movement.* Department of the Army Pamphlet no. 20–244. Washington, D.C.: Department of the Army, 1956.

3073 Kennedy, Robert M. *German Anti-Guerrilla Operations in the Balkans (1941–1944).* Department of the Army Pamphlet no. 20–243. Washington, D.C.: Department of the Army, 1954.

3074 Koessler, Maximilian. "The International Law on the Punishment of Belligerent Spies: A Legal Paradox," *Criminal Law Review* 5 (1958): 21–35.

3075 Kuhnrich, Heinz. *Der Partisanenkrieg in Europa 1939–1945.* Berlin, 1965.

3076 Laqueur, Walter. *Guerilla: A Historical and Critical Study.* Boston: Little, Brown, 1976.

3077 Michel, Henri. *Les mouvements clandestins en Europe (1938–1945).* Paris: Éditions des Presses universitaires de France, 1961.

3078 Molnar, Andrew, et al. *Undergrounds in Insurgent, Revolutionary, and Resistance Warfare.* Washington, D.C.: American University, Special Operations Research Office, 1963.

3079 Nurick, Lester, and Roger W. Barrett. "Legality of Guerrilla Forces under the Laws of War," *American Journal of International Law* 40 (July 1946):563–83.

3080 Röling, B. V. A. "The Legal Status of Rebels and Rebellion," *Journal of Peace Research* 13, no. 2 (1976):149–63.

3081 Schmid, J. H. *Die völkerrechtliche Stellung der Partisanen im Krieg.* Zurich: Polygraphischer Verlag, 1956.

3082 Thienel, Philip M., et al. *The Legal Status of Participants in Unconventional Warfare.* Washington, D.C.: American University, Special Operations Research Office, 1961.

3083 Trainin, Ilia A. "Questions of Guerilla Warfare in the Law of War," *American Journal of International Law* 40 (July 1946):534–62.

3084 Trinquier, Roger. *Modern Warfare: A French View of Counterinsurgency.* New York: Praeger, 1964.

3085 Vincent, Howard. *The Juridical Basis of the Distinction between Lawful Combatant and Unprivileged Belligerent.* Charlottesville, Va.: Judge Advocate General's School, 1959.

3086 Wilson, G. G. "The Guerilla and the Lawful Combatant," *American Journal of International Law* 37 (July 1943):494–95.

3087 Woetzel, Robert K. "War Crimes by Irregular and Nongovernmental Forces," *International Relations* 3 (November 1971):995–1002, 1013.

Noncombatants

3088 Fried, John H. E. "Transfer of Civilian Manpower from Occupied Territory," *American Journal of International Law* 40 (April 1946):303–31.

3089 Hartigan, John. "Noncombatant Immunity: An Analysis of Its Philosophical and Historical Origins." Ph.D. dissertation, Georgetown University, 1964.

3090 ———. "Noncombatant Immunity: Reflections on Its Origins and Present Status," *Review of Politics* 29 (1967):204–20.

3091 Nurick, Lester. "The Distinction between Combatant and Noncombatant in the Law of War," *American Journal of International Law* 39 (October 1945):680–97.

Forced and Slave Labor

3092 Belina, Josef. *Czech Labor under Nazi Rule.* London: Lincolns-Praeger Publishers, 1943.

3093 "Compulsory Labor in France," *International Labour Review* 47 (May 1943):645–46.

3094 "Control of Employment and Mobilisation of Labour in Belgium," *International Labour Review* 47 (March 1943):272–74.

3095 Fried, John H. E., comp. *The Exploitation of Foreign Labour by Germany.* International Labour Office, Series C, no. 25. Montreal: International Labour Office, 1945.

3096 Gross, Feliks. *The Polish Worker: A Study of Social Stratum.* New York: Roy Publishers, 1945.

3097 Homze, Edward L. *Foreign Labor in Nazi Germany.* Princeton: Princeton University Press, 1967,

3098 "Killing of Russian Slave Laborers by German Soldiers in 1945—Murder under Penal Code—No Defense under International Law—No Defense of Superior Orders—Section 47, I, No. 2, Military Penal Code [Decision of the West German Federal Supreme Court, September 30, 1960, 4 St. R. 242/60, *Juristenzeitung 1962,* p. 28ff.]," *American Journal of International Law* 57 (January 1963):139–40.

3099 "Labor Conditions in Occupied Norway," *International Labour Review* 43 (June 1941):687–700.

3100 Milward, Alan S. *The Fascist Economy in Norway.* Oxford: Clarendon Press, 1972.

3101 ———. *The New Order and the French Economy.* Oxford: Clarendon Press, 1970.

3102 "Mobilisation of Foreign Labour in Germany," *International Labour Review* 50 (October 1944):469–80.

3103 Mojonny, Gerardo Luigi. *The Labor of Prisoners of War in Modern Times: An Appreciation on the Cause and the Effect of the German Conventions.* Locarno, 1955.

3104 "Organization of Labor in the Netherlands," *International Labour Review* 48 (December 1943):761–63.

3105 Schoenfeld, Margaret H. *Labor Conditions in the Netherlands.* Washington, D.C.: GPO, 1944.

3106 "Soviet-Workers in Germany," *International Labour Review* 47 (May 1943):576–90.

3107 Speek, Peter. *Foreign Workers in German War Efforts.* Washington, D.C.: GPO, 1942.

3108 United Nations Information Organization. *Slave Labour and Deportation.* London: HMSO, 1944.

Collaboration

GENERAL

3109 Basso, A. "Criminali di guerra e collaborazionisti," *Stato Moderno* 3 (October 5, 1946):435–37.

3110 Battaglini, E., and G. Vasalli, eds. *La nuova legislazione penale.* Milan: A. Guiffre, 1946.

3111 Boissaire, André. "Les Bases de la répression," *Cahiers Politiques* 8 (March 1945):12–20.

3112 Boselli, Aldo. *I reati di collaborazione col tedesco invasore.* Geneva: Società Editrice Universale, 1946.

3113 Boveri, Margaret. *Treason in the Twentieth Century.* Translated by Jonathan Steinberg. London: Macdonald, 1956.

3114 Cathala, Pierre. *Face aux Réalities.* Paris: Éditions du Triolet, 1948.

3115 Novick, Peter. *The Resistance versus Vichy: The Purge of Collaborators in Liberated France.* New York: Columbia University Press, 1968.

3116 *Les Procès de collaboration.* Paris: Éditions Albin Michel, 1948.

3117 Saltelli, Carlo. "In tempo di collaborazione presunta," *Rivista Penale* 71 (May-June 1946):484–86.

3118 Vermeylen, Pierre. "The Punishment of Collaborators," *Annals of the American Academy of Political and Social Science* 247 (September, 1946):73–77.

3119 "Wartime Collaborators: A Comparative Study of the Effect of Their Trials on the Treason Law of Great Britain, Switzerland and France," *Yale Law Journal* 56 (August 1947):1210–33.

PRINCIPAL TRIALS

The Trial of Marshal Graziani (Italy)

3120 Canevari, Emilio. *Graziani mi ha detto*. Rome: Magi-Spinetti, 1947.

3121 Pisapia, G. Domenico. "Profili giurdici del processo Graziani: Incompetenza per materia o difetto di giurisdizione," *Rivista Italiana di Diretto Penale* 2 (1949):309–19.

3122 "Il proceso Graziani," *Rivista Italiana di Diritto Penale* 2 (1949): 167–68.

3123 Repaci, A. *Il processo Graziani*. Milan: Instituto Nazionali per la Storia del Movimento di Liberazio in Italia, 1952.

The Trial of Pierre Laval (France)

3124 Cole, Hubert. *Laval: A Biography*. New York: Putnam, 1963.

3125 Laval, Pierre. *The Diary of Pierre Laval*. New York: Scribner's, 1948.

3126 Naud, Albert. *Pourquoi je n'ai pas défendu Pierre Laval*. Paris: Fayard, 1948.

3127 *Le Procès Laval, avec 19 croquis d'audience de Jean Auscher*. Lyon: R. Bounefon, 1946.

3128 *Le Procès Laval: Compte rendu sténographique*. Paris: Éditions Albin Michel, 1946.

3129 Thomson, David. *Two Frenchmen: Pierre Laval and Charles de Gaulle*. London: Cresset Press, 1951.

3130 Warner, Geoffrey. *Pierre Laval and the Eclipse of France*. New York: Macmillan, 1968.

The Trial of Henri Philippe Pétain (France)

3131 Bourget, Pierre. *Un certain Philippe Pétain*. Paris: Casterman, 1966.

3132 D'Orr, Paul Barksdale. "The Trial of Marshal Pétain," *Federal Rules Decisions* 8 (1949):377–407.

3133 Fabre-Luce, Alfred. *Le Mystère du maréchal: Le procès Pétain*. Geneva: C. Bourquin, 1946.

3134 Giardini, Casare. *Il Processo Pétain*. Milan: Rizzoli, 1947.

3135 Griffiths, Richard. *Pétain: A Biography of Marshal Philippe Pétain of Vichy.* Garden City, N.Y.: Doubleday, 1972.

3136 Jeantet, Gabriel. *Pétain contre Hitler.* Paris: Éditions de la Table Rond, 1966.

3137 Michel, Paul Louis. *Le Procès Pétain.* Paris: Éditions Médicis, 1945.

3138 Noguères, Louis. *Le véritable procès du Maréchal Pétain.* Paris: Fayard, 1955.

3139 *Procès du Maréchal Pétain.* Paris: Imprimerie des Journaux officiels, 1945.

3140 *Le Procès Pétain, avec 44 croquis d'Audience de Jean Auscher.* Lyon: R. Bonneton, 1946.

3141 Roy, Jules. *The Trial of Marshal Pétain.* Translated by Robert Baldicle. New York: Harper and Row, 1966.

The Trial of Vidkun Quisling (Norway)

3142 Hayes, Paul M. *Quisling: The Career and Political Ideas of Vidkun Quisling, 1887–1945.* Bloomington: Indiana University Press, 1972.

3143 Hemming-Sjoberg, A. *Domen over Quisling.* Stockholm: Natur och Kultur, 1946.

3144 Loock, Hans-Dietrich. *Quisling, Rosenberg, und Terboven.* Stuttgart: Deutsche Verlags-Anstalt, 1970.

3145 *Quisling-Sakan: Samlet rettsreferat med forord av . . . Trgve de Lange.* Oslo: a-s Bokkomisjon, 1945.

3146 *Straffesak mot Vidkun Abraham Lauritz Jonsson Quisling.* Oslo: Utgitt pa offentlig bekostning av Eidsvating lagstols landsvikaveling, 1946.

Extradition of War Criminals

3147 "Attitudes of Neutral Governments Regarding Asylum to War Criminals," *Department of State Bulletin* 12 (February 11, 1945):190–92.

3148 Baer, Marcel de. "The Attitudes of Neutral Countries towards War Criminals," *Message, Belgian Review* 25 (1943):7–11.

3149 Dumon, I. "Rapport sur l'extradition des personnes recherchées ou condamnées pour crime de guerre ou crime de collaboration avec l'ennemi," *Revue de Droit Pénal et de Criminologie* 27 (1947):239–61.

3150 Durdenevsky, V. "The Question of Surrender of War Criminals by Italy," *USSR Embassy Information Bulletin* 6 (May 25, 1946):427.

3151 "Extradition: An Unsolved Problem in War Crimes," *American Perspective* 1 (May 1947):112–16.

3152 "Extradition of War Criminals," *Law Journal* 95 (1945):459.

3153 Garcia-Mora, M. R. "Crimes against Humanity and the Principle of Nonextradition of Political Offenders," *Michigan Law Review* 62 (April 1964):927–60.

3154 _____. "War Crimes and the Principle of Non-Extradition of Political Offenders," *Wayne Law Review* 9 (Winter 1963):269–93.

3155 Green, L. C. "Political Offences, War Crimes and Extradition," *International and Comparative Law Quarterly* 11 (April 1962):329–54.

3156 International Society of Military Law and the Laws of War. *Quatrième Congrès international: Madrid, 9–12 mai 1967.* 2 vols. Brussels: Société internationale de droit pénal militaire et de droit de la guerre, 1969.

3157 Lachs, Manfred. "Crimes de guerre—Délites politiques," *Revue de Droit International (Sottile-Geneva)* 23 (January-June 1945):10–20.

3158 Morgenstern, Felice. "Asylum for War Criminals, Quislings, and Traitors," *British Yearbook of International Law* 25 (1948):382–86.

3159 Munro, Hector A. "War Criminals and the Neutrals," *Fortnightly Law Journal* 14 (June 15, 1944):24–27.

3160 Muszkat, Marian, and Ignacy Chamczyk. "Zagadnicnie ekstradycji przestępców wojenych," *Wojskowy Przeglad Prawniczy* 2–3 (1947): 246–63.

3161 Neumann, Robert G. "Neutral States and the Extradition of War Criminals," *American Journal of International Law* 45 (July 1951):495–508.

3162 "Policy on Surrender of War Criminals Reaffirmed," *United Nations Bulletin* 3 (November 11, 1947):624–26.

3163 Schepers, J. D. "Een volkenrechtelijk bezwaar tegen de wet over-levering inzake oologsmisdrijven," *Militair-rechterlijk Tijdschrift* 53 (1960):675–78.

3164 "Surrender and Trial of War Criminals: Committee Passes United Kingdom Resolution," *United Nations Bulletin* 3 (October 28, 1947): 567–70.

3165 "An Unsolved Problem in War Crimes," *American Perspective* 1 (May 1947):112–16. [See entry no. 3151.]

The United Nations and War Crimes

UNITED NATIONS WAR CRIMES COMMISSION, 1942–1947

3166 Barcikowski, Waclaw. "Les Nations Unies et l'organisation de la répression des crimes de guerre," *Revue Internationale de Droit Pénal* 17 (1946):297–304.

3167 Bathurst, M. E. "The United Nations War Crimes Commission," *American Journal of International Law* 39 (July 1945):565–70.

3168 Eagleton, Clyde. "Punishment of War Criminals by the United Nations," *American Journal of International Law* 37 (July 1943):495–99.

3169 Russell, Ruth B. *A History of the United Nations Charter: The Role of the United States.* Washington, D.C.: Brookings Institution, 1958.

3170 Schick, Franz B. "War Criminals and the Law of the United Nations," *University of Toronto Law Journal* 7 (Lent term 1947):27–67.

3171 Schwelb, Egon. "The United Nations War Crimes Commission," *British Yearbook of International Law* 23 (1946):363–76.

3172 United Nations, Committee on Human Rights. *Question of the Punishment of War Criminals and of Persons Who Have Committed Crimes against Humanity.* Doc. no. 1969. E/CN.4/1010. November 24, 1969. New York, 1969.

3173 United Nations, War Crimes Commission. *History of the United Nations War Crimes Commission and the Development of the Laws of War.* London: HMSO, 1948.

3174 "The United Nations War Crimes Commission," *International Law Quarterly* 1 (Spring 1947):42–44.

UNITED NATIONS AND WAR CRIMES ISSUES

Documents

3175 United Nations, Committee for the Progressive Development of International Law and Its Codification. *Disposition of Agenda Items and Check List of Documents.* Doc. A/AC.10/57, 25 July 1947; *Draft Proposal to Define the Principles Recognized in the Charter of the Nuremberg Tribunal and in the Judgment of the Tribunal and Draft Proposal for the Establishment of an International Court of Criminal Jurisdiction: Memorandum Submitted by the Delegate for France.* Doc. A/AC.10/21, 15 May 1947; *Memorandum of the Subject of Genocide and Crimes against Humanity: Submitted by the Representative of France.* Doc. A/AC.10/29, 19 May 1947; *Draft Texts Relating to the Principles of the Charter and Judgment of the Nuremberg Tribunal: Memorandum by the Delegate for France.* Doc. A/AC.10/34, 27 May 1947; *Proposals of the Delegation of Poland.* Doc. A/AC.10/38, 2 June 1947; *Draft Convention for the Prevention and Punishment of Genocide: Prepared by the Secretariat.* Doc. A/AC.10/42, 6 June 1947; *Draft Resolution on the Draft Convention on Genocide: Presented by the Delegation of the U.K.* Doc. A/AC.10/44, 6 June 1947; *Report of the Committee on the Plans for the Formulation of the principles of the Nuremberg Charter and Judgment.* Doc. A/AC.10/52, 17 June 1947; *Letter from the Chairman of the Committee to the Secretary-General on the Draft Convention on Genocide.* Doc. A/AC.10/55, 18 June 1947. Lake Success, N.Y.: United Nations, 1947.

3176   United Nations, General Assembly. *The Extradition and Punishment of War Criminals: Adopted at the 32nd Plenary Meeting, February 13, 1946: Resolutions Adopted by the General Assembly during the First Part of Its First Session from 10 January to 14 February 1946.* Res. 3(1). London, 1946.

3177   _____. *The Formulation of the Principles Recognized in the Charter of the Nuremberg Tribunal and in the Judgment of the Tribunal: Adopted at the 123rd Plenary Meeting, November 21, 1947: Official Records of the Second Session of the General Assembly, Resolutions, 16 September–29 November 1947.* Res. 177 (2). Lake Success, N.Y., 1948.

3178   _____. *The Prevention and Punishment of the Crime of Genocide: (A) Adoption of the Convention on the Prevention and Punishment of the Crime of Genocide, and Text of the Convention: (B) Study by the International Law Commission of the Question of an International Criminal Jurisdiction: (C) Application with Respect to Dependent Territories, of the Convention on the Prevention and Punishment of the Crime of Genocide, Adopted at the 179th Plenary Meeting, December 9, 1948: Official Records of the Third Session of the General Assembly, Part I, 21 September–12 December 1948, Resolutions.* Res. 260 (3). Paris, 1948.

3179   _____. *Universal Declaration on Human Rights: Adopted at the 183rd Plenary Meeting, December 10, 1948: Official Records of the Third Session of the General Assembly, Part I, 21 September–12 December 1948, Resolutions.* Res 217A (3). Paris, 1948.

3180   United Nations, International Law Commission. *Historical Survey of the Question of International Criminal Jurisdiction: Memorandum submitted by the Secretary-General.* Doc. A/CN.4/7/Rev.1. Lake Success, N.Y., 1949.

3181   United Nations, International Law Commission (1st Session). *List of Documents.* Doc. A/CN.4/10, 11 April 1949. Lake Success, N.Y., 1949.

3182   _____. *Report of the International Law Commission Covering Its First Session 12 April–9 June 1949: General Assembly, Official Records: Fourth Session. Supplement No. 10* Doc. A/925. Lake Success, N.Y., 1949.

3183   _____. *Summary Records of Meetings.* Docs. A/CN.4/SR.1–37, 12 April–9 June 1949. Lake Success, N.Y., 1949.

3184   United Nations, International Law Commission (2d Session). *Draft Code of Offenses against the Peace and Security of Mankind: Report by J. Spiropoulos.* Doc. A/CN.4/25, 26 April 1950. Lake Success, N.Y., 1950.

3185   _____. *Formulation of the Nürnberg Principles: Report by J. Spiropoulos.* Doc. A/CN.4/22, 12 April 1950. Lake Success, N.Y., 1950.

3186 _____. *Report of the International Law Commission, Covering Its Second Session 5 June–29 July 1950: General Assembly, Official Records: Fifth Session, Supplement No. 12.* Doc. A/1316. Lake Success, N.Y., 1950.

3187 _____. *Report on the Question of International Criminal Jurisdiction, by Emil Sandström.* Doc. A/CN.4/20, 30 March 1950. Lake Success, N.Y., 1950.

3188 _____. *Report on the Question of International Criminal Jurisdiction, by Ricardo Alfaro.* Doc. A/CN.4/15, 3 March 1950. Lake Success, N.Y., 1950.

3189 United Nations Information Organization. *"War Crimes and the Punishment of War Criminals,"Information Paper No. 1.* London: United Nations Information Organization, Reference Division, 1945.

General

3190 Aronéanu, Eugène. "Les Nations Unies et le crime contre l'humanité," *Revue de Droit International (Sottile-Geneva)* 26 (July-September 1948):285–87.

3191 Jackson, Robert H. "The United Nations Organization and War Crimes," *American Society of International Law Proceedings* 46 (1952): 196–204.

3192 Kelson, Hans. "Sanctions in International Law under the Charter of the United Nations," *Iowa Law Review* 31 (May 1946):499–543.

3193 Koo, Wellington. "Some Aspects of the Work of the Legal Committee of the General Assembly during the Second Part of the First Session," *American Journal of International Law* 41 (July 1947):635–50.

3194 Maugham, Viscount Frederick Herbert. *U.N.O. and War Crimes.* London: J. Murray, 1951.

3195 Mosheim, Berthold. "Die Arbeiten der Vereinten Nationen zur Frage der Rechte des Individuums und des Verbrechens der Genocide," *Archiv des Völkerrechts* 2 (1949–1950):180–93.

3196 Moussa, Amre. "The Question of War Crimes in the United Nations," *Revue Egyptienne de Droit International* 30 (1974):91–97.

3197 Schick, Franz B. "Law of Politics for the Maintenance of Peace," *Juridical Review* 59 (April 1947):50–63.

3198 "Surrender and Trial of War Criminals: Committee Passes United Kingdom Resolution," *United Nations Bulletin* 3 (October 28, 1947): 567–70.

Occupation Government

General

3199   Allen, Dan C. "Franklin D. Roosevelt and the Development of Our American Occupation Policy in Europe." Ph.D. dissertation, Ohio State University, 1975.

3200   Birkhimer, William E. *Military Government and Military Law.* 2d rev. ed. Kansas City, Mo.: Franklin Hudson Publishing, 1904.

3201   Bray, Joseph. *De l'Occupation militaire en temps de guerre: Ses effets sur les personnes et sur l'administration de la justice.* Paris: L. Larose, 1894.

3202   Chorley, R. S. T. "Military Occupation and the Rule of Law," *Modern Law Review* 8 (July 1945):119–30.

3203   Connor, Sydney, and Carl J. Friedrich, eds. *Military Government.* Annals no. 267. Philadelphia: American Academy of Political Science, 1950.

3204   Deutsch, E. P. "Military Government: Administration of Occupied Territory," *American Bar Association Journal* 33 (February 1947):133–36, 208.

3205   Fairman, Charles. "Military Occupation and the Development of International Law," *American Society of International Law Proceedings* (1947):131–41.

3206   ———. "Observations on Military Occupation," *Minnesota Law Review* 32 (March 1948):319–48.

3207   Feilchenfeld, Ernst H. *The International Economic Law of Belligerent Occupation.* Washington, D.C.: Carnegie Endowment for International Peace, 1942.

3208   Friedrich, Carl J., et al. *American Experiences in Military Government in World War II.* New York: Rinehart, 1948.

3209   Glahn, Gerhard von. *The Occupation of Enemy Territory . . . A Commentary on the Law and Practice of Belligerent Occupation.* Minneapolis: University of Minnesota Press, 1957.

3210   Graber, Doris Appel. *The Development of the Law of Belligerent Occupation, 1863–1914: A Historical Survey.* New York: Columbia University Press, 1949.

3211 Graml, Hermann. "Zwischen Jalta und Potsdam: Zur amerikanischen Deutschlandsplanning in Frühjahr 1945," *Vierteljahrshefte für Zeitgeschichte* 24 (July 1976):308–25.

3212 Gutteridge, Joyce A. C. "The Rights and Obligations of an Occupying Power," *Year Book of World Affairs* 6 (1952):149–69.

3213 Jamieson, H. M. "Some Aspects of the Law of Belligerent Occupation," *Juridical Review* 57 (April 1945):6–17.

3214 Kern, Ernst. "Die Entwicklung des Besatzungsrechts," *Deutsches Verwaltungsblatt* 65 (1950):604–08, 638–40; 66 (1951):46–48, 111–13.

3215 Kuklick, Bruce. *American Policy and the Division of Germany: The Clash with Russia over Reparations.* Ithaca: Cornell University Press, 1972.

3216 Latour, Conrad F., and Thilo Vogelsang. *Okkupation und Wiederaufbau: Die Tätigkeit der Militärregierung in der americanischen Besatzungzone Deutschlands 1944–1947.* Stuttgart: Deutsche Verlags-Anstalt, 1962.

3217 Levinthal, Louis E. "Some Problems of Military Law and Government," *Pennsylvania Bar Association Quarterly* 19 (April 1948):246–57.

3218 Lubrano-Lavadera, Capitaine. *Les Lois de la guerre et de l'occupation militaire.* Paris: Charles-Lavauzelle, 1956.

3219 Nobleman, Eli E. "Quadripartite Military Government Organization and Operations in Germany," *American Journal of International Law* 41 (July 1947):650–59.

3220 Potter, Pittman B. "Legal Basis and Character of Military Occupation in Germany and Japan," *American Journal of International Law* 43 (April 1949):323–25.

3221 Schwarzenberger, Georg. "The Extraterritorial Effects of Belligerent Occupation," *Indian Yearbook of International Affairs* 12 (1963): 56–67.

3222 Schwenk, E. H. "Legislative Powers of the Military Occupant under Article 43, Hague Regulations," *Yale Law Journal* 54 (1945):393–416.

3223 Sharp, Tony. *The Wartime Alliance and the Zonal Division of Germany.* Oxford: Clarendon Press, 1975.

3224 Smith, Herbert A. "Government of Occupied Territory," *British Yearbook of International Law* 21 (1944):151–58.

3225 _____. *Military Government.* Ft. Leavenworth: General Service Schools Press, 1920.

3226 United States, Department of State, and the Department of the Navy. *Manual of Civil Affairs Military Government.* FM 27-5, OPNAV P22-1115. Washington, D.C., 1947.

Germany

3227 Balfour, M. *Vier-Mächte-Kontrolle in Deutschland 1945-1946.* Düsseldorf: Droste Verlag, 1959.

3228 Carolus. "Out Damned Spot!" *Nation* 168 (April 16, 1949):444-45.

3229 Clay, Lucius D. *Decision in Germany.* Cambridge: Harvard University Press, 1950.

3230 Davidson, Eugene. *The Death and Life of Germany: An Account of the American Occupation.* New York: Knopf, 1959.

3231 Donnison, F. S. V. *Civil Affairs and Military Government: North-West Europe, 1944-1946.* London:HMSO, 1961.

3232 Dorn, Walter L. "The Debate over American Occupation Policy in Germany in 1944-1945," *Political Science Quarterly* 72 (1957):481-501.

3233 Dorpalen, Andreas. "Split Occupation of Germany," *Virginia Quarterly Review* 22, no. 4 (October 1946):581-97.

3234 Frederiksen, Oliver J. *The American Military Occupation of Germany, 1945-1953.* N.p.: U.S. Army, Europe, Headquarters, Historical Division, 1953.

3235 Friedmann, W. "Legal and Constitutional Position of Germany under Allied Military Government," *Res Judicatae* 3 (October 1947):133-43.

3236 Gimbel, John. *The American Occupation of Germany: Politics and the Military, 1945-1949.* Stanford: Stanford University Press, 1968.

3237 Grewe, W. *Ein Besatzungsstatut für Deutschland: Die Rechtsform der Besatzung.* Stuttgart: Koehler, 1948.

3238 Heneman, Harlow J. "American Control Organization in Germany," *Public Administration Review* 6 (Winter 1946):1-9.

3239 Holborn, Hajo. *American Military Government: Its Organization and Politics.* Washington, D.C.: Infantry Journal Press, 1947.

3240 Kaufman, E. *Deutschlands Rechtslage unter der Besatzung.* Stuttgart: Koehler, 1948.

3240 Kelson, Hans. "The Legal Status of Germany According to the Declaration of Berlin," *American Journal of International Law* 39 (1945):518–26.

3242 Pollock, James K., and James H. Meisel. *Germany under Occupation: Illustrative Materials and Documents.* Ann Arbor: George Wahr Publishing, 1947.

3243 Rheinstein, M. "Legal Status of Occupied Germany," *Michigan Law Review* 47 (November 1948):23–40.

3244 Ruhm von Oppen, Beate, comp. *Documents on Germany under Occupation, 1945–1954.* London: Oxford University Press, 1955.

3245 Smith, Jean Edward, ed. *The Papers of General Lucius D. Clay: Germany, 1945–1949.* 2 vols. Bloomington: Indiana University Press, 1974.

3246 United States, Congress, Senate. *Documents on Germany, 1944–1970.* 92d Congress. 1st sess. Washington, D.C.: GPO, 1971.

3247 United States, Department of State. *Occupation of Germany: Policy and Progress, 1945–46.* State Department Pub. no. 2783. Washington, D.C.: GPO, 1947.

3248 Van Nispen Tot Sevenear, C. M. O. *L'Occupation Allemande pendant la guerre mondiale.* The Hague: Nijhoff, 1946.

3249 Willis, F. Ray. *The French in Germany, 1945–1949.* Stanford: Stanford University Press, 1962.

3250 Wright, Quincy. "The Status of Germany and the Peace Proclamations," *American Journal of International Law* 46 (1952):299–308.

3251 Zink, Harold. *American Military Government in Germany.* New York: Macmillan, 1947.

3252 _____. *The United States in Germany, 1944–1955.* Princeton: Van Nostrand, 1957.

Japan

3253 Borton, H. "United States Occupation Policies in Japan since Surrender," *Political Science Quarterly* 62 (June 1947):250–57.

3254 Fearey, Robert A. *The Occupation of Japan, Second Phase: 1948–50.* New York: Macmillan, 1950.

3255 Fishel, Wesley R. "Japan under MacArthur: Retrospect and Prospect," *Western Political Quarterly* 4 (1951):210–25.

3256 Martin, Edwin M. *The Allied Occupation of Japan.* New York: Institute of Pacific Relations, 1948.

3257 United States, Department of State. *Occupation of Japan: Policy and Progress.* State Department Pub. no. 2671. Washington, D.C.: GPO, 1946.

3258 Ward, Robert E., and Frank J. Shulman, et al. *The Allied Occupation of Japan, 1945–1952: An Annotated Bibliography of Western Language Materials.* Chicago: American Library Association, 1974.

Allied Administration of Justice

General

3259 Donihi, Robert. "Occupation Justice," *South Texas Law Journal* 1 (Spring 1955):333–58.

3260 Fairman, Charles. *The Law of Martial Rule.* 2d ed. Chicago: Callaghan, 1943.

3261 Freeman, Allwyn V. "War Crimes by Enemy Nations Administering Justice in Occupied Territory," *American Journal of International Law* 41 (July 1947):579–610.

3262 Goodman, Leo M., comp. *Digest of Current Decisions of: 1. United States Military Government Court of Appeals. 2. District Courts, Land Bavaria. 3. British Control Commission Court of Appeals. 4. OMGUS Legal Division. 5. German Courts.* Munich, 1949.

3263 Gorman, Robert N. "Military Courts and Military Government in Occupied Areas," *Ohio Bar Association Report* 17 (1944):479–86.

3264 Inglis, L. M. "The Occupation Courts in Germany," *New Zealand Law Journal* 27 (1951):172–75.

3265 Loewenstein, K. "Law and Legislative Process in Occupied Germany," *Yale Law Journal* 57 (March-April 1948):724–60, 994–1022.

3266 Nartatez, M. C. "Right of Military Occupant to Establish Courts in Occupied Territory," *Philadelphia Law Journal* 24 (June 1949):182–85.

3267 Weiden, Paul L. "The Impact of Occupation on German Law," *Wisconsin Law Review* no. 1947 (May 1947):332–56.

Germany: U.S. Zone

3268 Davis, Franklin M., Jr. *Come as a Conqueror: The United States Army's Occupation of Germany, 1945–49.* New York: Macmillan, 1967.

3269 Fahy, Charles. "American Lawyer with the United States Military Government in Germany," *Alabama State Bar Association Proceedings* (1946):86–95.

3270 ———. "The Lawyer in Military Government (Germany)," *American Bar Association Proceedings* [Section of International and Comparative Law] (1946):29–37.

3271 Koessler, Maximilian. "American War Crimes Trials in Europe," *Georgetown Law Journal* 39 (November 1950):18–112.

3272 Loewenstein, K. "Reconstruction of the Administration of Justice in American-Occupied Germany," *Harvard Law Review* 61 (February 1948):419–67.

3273 McCauley, Worth B. "American Courts in Germany: 600,000 Cases Later," *American Bar Association Journal* 40 (December 1954):1041–45.

3274 Maier, Hedwig. "Gerichtsbarkeit über Angehörige der Alliierten Streitkräfte in der U.S.-Zone (Neuregelung durch U.S.-H.K.G. Nr. 38 und 39)," *Juristenzeitung* 9 (1954):72–73, 185–86.

3275 Maynard, J.-A. "Crimes et criminels de guerre: Problème étudié par une groupe de juristes aux États-Unis," *Revue Internationale de Droit Pénal* 17 (1946):333–42.

3276 Nobelman, Eli E. "The Administration of Justice in the United States Zone of Germany," *Federal Bar Journal* 8 (October 1946):70–97.

3277 ———. "American Military Government Courts in Germany," *American Journal of International Law* 40 (October 1946):803–11.

3278 ———. *American Military Government Courts in Germany: Their Role in the Democratization of the German People.* Washington, D.C.: Provost Marshal General's School, Military Government Department, 1953.

3279 ———. "Military Government Courts: Law and Justice in the American Zone of Germany," *American Bar Association Journal* 33 (August 1947):777–80, 851–52.

3280 Plischke, Elmer. "Denazification Law and Procedure," *American Journal of International Law* 41 (October 1947):807–27.

3281 "Travesty of Justice in the A.M.G. Tribunals," *Nation* 166 (February 21, 1948):223–24.

3282 United States, Army, Third Army Headquarters, Germany. *United States v. Albert [Alfred] Bury and Wilhelm Hafner: Review of Proceedings in the First Trial of Germans before a Military Commission for Killing an American Aviator in Violation of the Laws of War.* N.p., 1945.

Germany: British Zone

3283 "The British Court for War Criminals," *Law Journal* 95 (September 15, 1945):300.

3284 Honig, Frederick. "Kriegsverbrecher vor englischen Militärgerichten," *Schweizerische Zeitschrift für Strafrecht* 62 (1947):20–33.

3285 Jagusch, Heinrich. "Das Verbrechen gegen die Menschlichkeit in der Rechtsprechung des Obersten Gerichtshof für die britische Zone," *Süddeutsche Juristenzeitung* 4 (September 1949):620–24.

3286 Krawinkel, H. "Law in the British Zone of Germany," *Current Legal Problems* 2 (1949):245–57.

3287 Lange, R. "Die Rechtsprechung des Obersten Gerichtshofes für die britische Zone zum Verbrechen gegen die Menschlichkeit," *Süddeutsche Juristenzeitung* 3 (1948):655–60.

3288 "Legal Administration of Germany (British Zone)," *Law Journal* 97 (June 6, 1947):285.

3289 Lietzmann, Heinrich. "Die Strafgerichtsbarkeit der Kontrollkommission in der britischen Zone Deutschlands," *Monatsschrift für Deutsches Recht* 1 (September 1947):183–86.

3290 Sontag, Ernst. "Die deutschen Spruchgerichte in der britischen Zone," *Friedens-Warte* 50 (1950):51–64.

3291 "Übersicht der Rechtsprechung des Obersten Gerichtshof für die britische Zone: Zum Verbrechen gegen die Menschlichkeit," *Zentral Justizblatt für die Britische Zone* 2 (November 1948):243–46.

Germany: French Zone

3292 Degand, Henri. "Les juridictions Françaises du gouvernement militaire en Allemagne occupée," *Revue Juridique d'Alsace et de Lorraine* 28 (November 1947):237–53.

3293 Hofstetter, Albert. *Les tribunaux du gouvernement militaire en zone Française d'occupation en Allemagne.* Fribourg, 1947.

3294 Maunoir, Jean-Pierre. *La répression des crimes de guerre devant les tribunaux français et alliés.* Geneva: Éditions Médecine et Hygiène, 1956.

3295 Schwinge, Erich. "Angehörige der ehemaligen deutschen Wehrmacht und der SS vor französichen Militärgerichten," *Monatsschrift für Deutsches Recht* 3 (1949):650–54.

Austria

3296 Schuster, Lord. "Military Government in Austria with Special Reference to the Administration of Justice in Occupied Territory," *Journal of the Society of Public Teachers of Law* (1947):80–104.

Italy

3297 Campbell, Ian. "Some Legal Problems Arising Out of the Establishment of the Allied Military Courts in Italy," *International Law Review* 1 (Summer 1947):192–206.

3298 Dallari, G. "Sentenze dei tribunali militari alleati in Italia," *Giurisprudenza Completa della Corte Supreme di Cassazione-Sezione Civili* 1 (1950):676ff.

3299 Harris, C. R. S. *Allied Military Administration of Italy, 1943–1945.* London: HMSO, 1957.

3300 Podaliri, G. "Sulle sentenze dei Tribunali militari alleati in Italia," *Il foro padano* 1 (1951):949ff.

3301 "Urteil des italienischen Militärgerichts für den Bezirk Rom vom 20. Juli 1948 in Sachen Kappler," *Archiv des Völkerrechts* 3 (1951–1952): 357–66.

Japan

3302 Oppler, Alfred C. *Legal Reform in Occupied Japan: A Participant Looks Back.* Princeton: Princeton University Press, 1977.

Clemency Issues

General

3303 "Parole and Clemency Board for War Criminals Appointed," *Department of State Bulletin* 29 (November 2, 1953):599.

3304 "Procedures for Clemency and Parole for War Criminals," *Department of State Bulletin* 29 (September 21, 1953):391.

Europe

3305 "Amnesty Storm," *Newsweek* 37 (February 12, 1951):36.

3306 "Church Leaders Help Halt German Executions," *Christian Century* 65 (November 10, 1948):1195.

3307 "Execution of Death Sentences of German War Criminals Withheld," *Department of State Bulletin* 24 (March 12, 1951):412.

3308 "For Good Behavior," *Time* 55 (January 2, 1950):18.

3309 "Make an End to the War Hangings," *Christian Century* 66 (January 5, 1949):5.

3310 "Mercy," *Time* 49 (April 28, 1947):27.

3311 "Release and Rehabilitation of Nazi War Criminals," *Nation* 172 (January 27, 1951):69–70.

3312 "Shape of Things," *Nation* 172 (February 10, 1951):117–18.

3313 "Stay of Executions of German War Criminals Lifted," *Department of State Bulletin* 24 (June 4, 1951):907.

Far East

3314 "Answer to Soviet Protest on MacArthur Clemency Circular: Text of U.S. and Russian Notes," *Department of State Bulletin* 23 (July 10, 1950):60–61.

3315 "Board of Clemency for Japanese War Criminals," *Department of State Bulletin* 27 (September 15, 1952):408–09.

3316 "Japanese War Criminals Board," *Department of State Bulletin* 27 (October 27, 1952):659.

3317 "Note of Soviet Government to U.S. Government," *Current Digest of the Soviet Press* 2, no. 20 (July 1, 1950):33.

3318 "Note of the Soviet Government to the Government of USA," *USSR Embassy Information Bulletin* 11 (March 8, 1951):153.

3319 "Soviet Government's Note to U.S. Government," *Current Digest of the Soviet Press* 2, no. 35 (October 14, 1950):20.

Statutory Limitations on War Crimes

3320 "As You Were: German Reactions to Proposal to Extend Statute of Limitations," *Newsweek* 73 (May 19, 1969):48.

3321 Baumann, J. *Der Aufstand des schlechten Gewissens: Ein Diskussionsbeitrag zur Verjährung des NS-Gewaltsverbrechen*. Bielefeld: Verlag Ernst und Gieseking, 1965.

3322 Benjamin, H. "Uber die Nichtverjährung von Nazi-und Kriegsverbrechen," *Neue Justiz* 18 (1964):545–49.

3323 *Die Bestrafung der Nazi-und Kriegsverbrecher: Gebot der Menschlichkeit und Sicherung des Friedens: Dokuments und Materialien zur Verabschiedung des Gesetzes über die Nichterjährung von Nazi-und Kriegsverbrechen in d. 7. Sitzung d. Volkskammer der DDR von 1. 9. 1964.* Berlin: Staatsverlag der DDR, 1964.

3324 "Bonn May Extend Statute on War Criminals," *Christian Century* 82 (March 10, 1965):292–93.

3325 Cyprian, T. "Zur Nichtverjährbarkeit von Verbrechen gegen das Völkerrecht," *Staat und Recht* 18 (1969):25–28.

3326 Ermacora, F. "Die Verjährung von Kriegsverbrechen und Verbrechen gegen die Menschlichkeit vor Organen der Vereinten Nationen," *Österreichische Zeitschrift für Öffentliches Recht* 17 (1967):27–44.

3327 Fawcett, J. E. S. "Time Limit for Punishment of War Crimes?" *International and Comparative Law Quarterly* 14 (April 1965):627–31.

3328 Geilke, G. "Keine Verjährung für Kriegsverbrechen," *WGO* 6 (1964):164–65.

3329 Glaser, Stefan. "Quelques observations sur la prescription en matière de criminalité de guerre," *Revue de Droit Pénal et de Criminologie* 45 (1965):5–8.

3330 Jaszai, D. "On the Proscription of War Crimes and Certain Punishments Inflicted for Them," *Hungarian Law Review* 1 (1964):5–10.

3331 Kaul, F. K. "Und Wiederum: Verjährung nazistischer Kriegsverbrechen," *Neue Justiz* 20 (1966):340–41.

3332 Lekschas, J. "Zum Problem der Verjährung von Kriegs-und Naziverbrechen," *Staat und Recht* 13 (1964):1187–1203.

3333 Lerner, Nathan. "Convention on the Non-Applicability of Statutory Limitations to War Crimes," *Israel Law Review* 4, no. 4 (October 1969):512–33.

3334 Levasseur, G. "Les crimes contre l'humanité et le problème de leur prescription," *Journal de Droit International* 93 (April-May-June 1966): 259–84.

3335 Lipowscek, A. "Dekret über die Unanwendbarkeit der Verjährung aus Straftaten gegen den Frieden und die Menschlichkeit sowie auf Kriegsverbrechen V. 22. 3. 1965," *WGO* 7 (1965):89–91.

3336 Lorenz, M. "Strafrechtliche Verjährung und Rückwirkungsverbot," *Golddammers Archiv für Strafrecht* (1968):300–302.

3337 Markees, F. "O hobories is nepellinos buntetettek eleriilesenek kerdese es a nemzetkozi Jog," *Jogtudomonyi Kozlong* 20 (1965):1.

3338 Mertens, P. "L'Imprescriptibilité des crimes de guerre et des crimes contre l'humanité," *Revue de Droit Pénal et de Criminologie* 51 (1970): 204–16.

3339 _____. "La prescription des crimes de guerre en Allemagne fédérale à la lumière des évenements récents," *L'Année Politique et Economique* (1967):197–98.

3340 Paley, J. "Nazi Crimes and the Statute of Limitations," *New Republic* 152 (March 6, 1965):6–7.

3341 "Les peines prononcées pour crimes de guerre doivent-elles être imprescriptibles?" *Journal des Tribunaux* 79 (1964):530–31.

3342 Pritt, D. N. "Nazi War Crimes: Prosecution or Statutory Limitation," *New World Review* 37 (1969):46–51.

3343 Przybylski, P. "Bonn's Concealed Amnesty for Nazi and War Criminals: Menace to European Security," *German Foreign Policy* 8 (1969):243–56.

3344 Roland, M. "La prescription de crimes contre l'humanité," *Revue de Droit Contemporain* 11 (1964):115–17.

3345 Rombach, J. "De vervolgingsverjaring van misdrijven Waarop meer dan 12 jaar staat," *Nederlands Juristenblad* 40 (1965):561–63.

3346 Reuter, C. F. "Oologsmisdrijven, misdrijven tegen de menselijkheid en hun verjaring," *Tijdschrift voor Strafrecht* 79 (1970):109–69.

3347 Schoenbaum, D. L. "Time Runs Out on Germany's War-Crimes Trials," *Reporter* 32 (March 11, 1965):30–32.

3348 "Shifting the Guilt," *Time* 93 (May 2, 1969):24–25.

3349 Stoop, B. "Unfinished War? Nazi Criminals and West Germany's Twenty Year Statute of Limitations," *Christian Century* 82 (February 10, 1965):166.

3350 "Verbrechen gegen den Frieden, Kriegsverbrechen und Verbrechen gegen die Menschlichkeit verjähren nicht," *Staat und Recht* 18 (1969):4–25.

3351 Vogel, R., ed. *Ein Weg aus der Vergangenheit: Eine Dokumentation zur Verjährungsfrage und zu den NS-Prozessen*. Frankfurt-am-Main: Ullstein, 1969.

3352 Wiesenthal, Simon, ed. *Verjährung?* Frankfurt am Main: Europäische Verlagsanstalt, 1965.

Author Index

Listings are by entry number.

A

Abel, Theodore, 2757
Absolon, Rudolf, 2877
Adams, William, 276
Adcock, Sir F. E., 532
Agus, Jacob B., 439
Akita, George, 1968
Albertini, Luigi, 249
Albrecht, A. R., 414, 3053
Albrecht, R. G., 896
Albrecht-Carrié, Rene, 277
Alcalà-Zamora y Castillo, N., 2148
Alderman, Sidney S., 793, 2561
Aldonby, Zwy, 2536
Alexander, Charles W., 897
Alexander, Eva V., 2149
Alexander, Leo, 2758–61
Alexandov, G. N., 898, 899, 2245
Alexandrov, Victor, 2481
Alfaro, Ricardo J., 2790
Alfoldi, Laszlo M., 31
Alford, N. H., Jr., 2330
Allen, Dan C., 3199
Allen, Florence E., 2150
Allen, Lafe Franklin, 1980, 1981
Allen, Maury, 2035
Amaudruz, G. A., 900
Ambruster, H. W., 1572, 1573
Amchan, Morris, 2246
American Historical Association, 674
American Jewish Committee, 2482
Amos, Sheldon, 89
Anders, Gunther, 2483
Anders, Karl, 901
Anderson, A. Arnold, 675

Anderson, J. K., 533
Andler, Charles, 625
Andonian, J. K., 2331
Andrus, Burton C., 902
Andrzejewski, Stanislaw, 2843
Angell, Ernest, 2743
Anley, Henry, 2465
Appleman, John Alan, 903
April, Nathan, 904
Ardenne, R., 1809
Arendt, Hannah, 2484
Arens, Richard, 551, 2657
Argúas, M., 90
Arima, Rainei, 2076
Arins, Alfred, 2595
Armout, W. S., 534
Armstrong, John A., 3062
Arndt, Adolf, 1458, 1724, 1725
Arndt, Karl, 1439
Arnold-Forster, William, 368
Aronéanu, Eugène, 440–44, 1423, 2485, 2791, 3190
Aronson, Shlomo, 1530
Arzinger, R., 2247
Asahi, Shimbun Hōtei Kishadan, 1983, 1984, 2077
Aschenauer, Rudolf, 1702, 1703, 1721, 2151
Assmann, Kurt, 1232, 1240, 1264, 2917
Associazione nazionale partigiani d'Italia, 1870
Auchincloss, K., 2332
Audric, John, 905
Auerbach, Ludwig, 2486
Aujol, J. L., 1838
Australia
    Delegation to the Naval Conference, 361
    Department of External Affairs, 1985

Ed. Note: In place of a Subject Index, an extensive Contents has been supplied.

E

H